TO KILL A COCKROACH

An LGBTQ+Memoir

OSVALDO C. AMADOR

TO KILL A COCKROACH

For information: tokillacockroach@gmail.com

Designed by Coverkitchen
ISBN: 9780615675794

We are finely veiled with nature's attire.
The gift is honoring the blessings, no matter the vestments.
All blossoms carry uniqueness.
We are that seed in nature shrouded in mystery.

—**Osvaldo Calixto Amador**

INTRODUCTION

A universal story is timeless and should be introduced as such. It has been the ultimate journey to discover that everything universal belongs to me, as I belong to it. What follows is a collection of vignettes, hues of colorings of our humanity. We have lived many ages and many lifetimes. We are all united in the seeming fragmentation of our worlds. The universal reveals the sanctity of our human contradictions and our immortal harmony.

Above and beyond this story lies an observer, an immutable spectator who stands as the culmination of it all. This is the undefinable first cause, the essence of the whole, the spirit that encompasses all that is, has been, and shall forever be, the God incarnate in a transitory moment of time and space, experiencing itself in human form. The voices of this lore are a stream of consciousness, a dialectic within the human experience.

The longer I live, the more universal all stories become, and all the same, they remain unique at their core. Like all of life, it's all a riddle for us to discover, or not. Nothing needs to be added or subtracted, for all has been written before. This is a reminder that loneliness is a mask, as are all feelings belonging to the human creature.

Like the season's sceneries, masks sway with the winds of eternity. We are not of one season. We are as skilled as nature, versatile and unique. The intention of the spirit that has navigated these pages is to create light from darkness, to unite all the hues of broken pieces in a tapestry of unconditional love.

It is in the shrouded spirit of the unknown that I dance barren under the light of a full moon, unashamed and grateful for it all. Time has ceased, and it has lost its immediate relevance, remaining the most ephemeral of luxuries. God's voice has been found in the solitude that sat down in my silence.

At the very heart of this writing are two books, *To Kill a Mockingbird* and *Black Beauty*. It is not my intention to summarize either one. I have done the totally unacceptable by assuming the reader is acquainted with both works. If you have not had the privilege of making their acquaintance, I humbly suggest you give yourself this reward.

Harper Lee and Anna Sewell wrote about two completely different places, times, and subjects, each exposing what her eyes and heart compelled her to put into words. These women held a mirror of our social conscience before the face of our humanity. It is in the universal principle of a story that spirit rises, dancing in joyous rapture and congregating in solidarity.

It is the immutable spirit that gives rise to creation, propelling the soul to manifest in the murky waters of the unknown. To stand at the precipice, to be willing to free-fall for the birth of a hymn that reaches into the heart of our desolation, that is the quest of all creation, of all inspiration, hope, and of love itself. Loneliness is the lie that believes itself separate from its very nature. Once we discover that integration of it all is who we are, we remove the misery and the predatory instincts that corrupt our world and our lives.

Through all art, like love itself, we share our frailties and our vulnerabilities. In doing so, we are most human, divine, and courageous. Art restores the love rooted from time immemorial. At the core of all forms of expression lies that unique individual desire to be valued and loved. Not unlike love, art unites us and helps heal the individual and collective pain that is inherent in our human existence. Each unique voice is a piece of the restoration of our true humanity.

Restoration is echoed in *To Kill a Mockingbird* and *Black Beauty*. It is a theme that profoundly proclaims the salvation of the subjugated, the abducted through no fault of their own. These themes are as relevant today as they were at the times they were inspired and written. Anna Sewell's *Black Beauty* gives us a view through the eyes of the majestic horse. Harper Lee's story of a fictional town, Maycomb, Alabama, captures the racist and prejudicial attitudes predominant in the predators of the innocent. *To Kill a Cockroach* entered the sphere of my mind's eye more than twenty years ago while I was watching the film based on the book *To Kill a Mockingbird*, which I had read as a young man.

Having read the book many times over in my youth, I had forgotten the subtleties in Lee's writing. Decades later, I was taken aback at that moment on the big screen when Gregory Peck's character, Atticus Finch, says it is OK to kill a blue jay but not a mockingbird. These words uttered by Atticus were immediately shocking to my mind's eye. Did I hear him say you can kill blue jays, if you can hit them, but not a mockingbird? I asked this question to myself out loud, looking around and hoping no one could hear me.

I had been a fan of Ms. Lee's work since my early childhood, and it took me several trips into my memory to reinstate her magical symbolism. It is readily there in the book, and in the film, mockingbirds don't hurt anything. They just sing; they are innocent. The question that occurred to me, and I predict will always leave a mark on my soul, is *why kill at all?* I will never understand why Ms. Lee chose those words. I am a bird lover, and those words made my skin crawl. It wasn't until I had to kill a roach that I began to question everything, including Harper Lee's classic book.

I know that all of God's creatures serve a purpose, whether I like them or not. To kill or not to kill was only part of my question, how to kill became as relevant as killing itself. Trying to reconcile Ms. Lee's words and having to kill a cockroach was like a big bang explosion in my then black head of hair that would revolutionize my world and catapult me into self-love. I believe a man's conscience is a sacred gift. There is an intricate design between a man's conscience, his heart, his soul, and his creator that will forever remain a mystery. It is in the inexplicable interconnection within these realms that our flesh is glorified into that sacrosanct spirit that transcends all explanations, yet I believe it is this mystery that propels a man's spirit to create or destroy. It is in this realm that we find heaven or hell.

What is written here may be considered fiction. It comes from my interior, that boundless imaginative territory made up of my explorative creative spirit. It is the questions of a six-year-old boy who colored way outside the lines, using colors and curiosity to escape the cruelty encasing his world. It is the artifacts of a teenager who learns he is gay and tries desperately to fit into a world that despises who he is. His world exposes him to the kind of hatred depicted in Harper Lee's book. It is the life gifted to a simple man whose only complexity is having been born all too human indeed. This is the story of the square peg, the misfit, the forgotten. It is a story of restoration, consciousness, and how I learned to kill a cockroach. Finally, it is a story of how I found that universal unconditional love I had been searching for since the beginning of time.

Living with contradictions is the only answer to living in harmony with winter and spring. To learn to love ourselves exactly as created is the greatest gift we will ever give ourselves. We are all children in new and old attire, and we all deserve to be loved regardless of who we love or what we look like. We are the divine experiencing itself through our own uniqueness, inviting us to join that universal ancient hymn called love. Whether you believe in any principle that binds us together or not, you are uniquely intertwined in the tapestry of our humanity. You are never alone because we are nature itself.

There is pleasure in the pathless woods,
There is rapture in the lonely shore,
There is society where none intrudes,
By the deep sea, and music in its roar;
I love not Man the less, but Nature more [...]

—Lord Byron, "Childe Harold's Pilgrimage

CHAPTER 1

All things bright and beautiful,
All creatures great and small,
All things wise and wonderful,
The Lord God made them all.
Each little flower that opens,
Each little bird that sings,
He made their glowing colors,
He made their tiny wings.

—Cecil Frances Alexander,
"All Things Bright and Beautiful"

In the film *To Kill a Mockingbird*, Gregory Peck's character, Atticus Finch, remarks that you can kill all kinds of birds, including blue jays, but not mockingbirds. The film is based on Harper Lee's Pulitzer Prize–winning book *To Kill a Mockingbird*. The writer chooses words that target blue jays while differentiating the mockingbird from all others. The human species differentiates characteristics such as skin color, gender, ethnicity, and religion, just to name a few. I have often wondered if hatred is innate to humanity. Has my own prejudice stemmed from my species' constitution, or did my environment dictate my inclinations? Whichever the case may be, hatred is an ancient folk tale told from the beginning of time.

From the time I was born, so much had been decided for me. My birth determined my species, sex, parents, ethnicity, country, and economic milieu and the social, political, and historical climate of this incarnation. Some are fortunate and are adorned with the vestments of beauty and are born peacocks. Others are born with crystal-like wings that provoke repulsion in the best of us—roaches. The gods throw the dice, and we are given a life to live. If beauty is in the eye of the beholder, repulsion is in the hands of the subjugator.

This story commences somewhere in the middle. It's random and eccentric, at times seemingly without reason or rhyme. The middle substantiates the crucial material. I have learned that there are no end and no beginning, no tragedy and no joy; there are just seasons in a lifetime, lessons to be learned, a reason for it all. This story starts with the middle way. From dusk to dawn, sunrise to sunset, light to dark, from one birth to another, we carry the markings of all stretches, like a pendulum always returning to its center as it sways rhythmically with the winds of time. For as long as I can remember, I have always felt the need to express myself. This is not unique; rather, I believe it to be an inherent trait of our humanity to search for meaning and assent. There is a desire to be valued, as well as a desire to be loved. Some of us are heard, valued, and, above all, loved. Some of us are exiled to the arts of expression by brute force.

It has been a lifelong endeavor to reconcile my longing for expression with my yearning for solitude. The internal battle of the need for expression has been a relentless struggle within my soul, clashing with the unbearable downward spiral of the desire for complete abnegation. Within these pages, I have learned that the need to be supersedes the need not to be. Hemingway wrote that good writing is true writing. This is my truth: I am a blue jay, and I am an executioner. To my dismay, I am all too human indeed. Silence was my oppressor; my authentic truth is my liberator.

In the middle of my life, I lived in an isolated natural paradise that stood at the core of it all. I lived purposefully remotely, with access to civilization if the desire for it should arise. I had my own cardboard box, hut, and castle—and my very own concrete shelter. I have been gifted with the ability to create something out of nothing. I can produce a home from an empty shell and create a full life out of emptiness. I have overturned hatred into love, resentments into forgiveness, and vileness into a spiritual resurrection.

I had lived the life of an infant, a youth, a young man, and now I was living the life of the man that courage had granted me. On this particular day, I had greeted the morning as usual, joyfully reluctant. The morning started with a fresh smell. The sun was shining, and my heart was wide open. I was clear and luminous, and I had a bourgeois belief that truth was near. From what I know today, truth is never still; it can oscillate like a pendulum and life itself. Shrouding myself in the falsehood of my indoctrination gave me a temporary feeling of false security.

The weather was in the seventies under a vast, crisp, wide-open, baby-blue sky. I smelled new beginnings and victories. I had windmills to conquer and dreams to meet. It was not winter, spring, summer, or fall; it was a perfect symphony of the elements, conspiring to create the ideal moment. I was young again, as if by magic, and all my worries and yesteryears seemed distant, tucked away in a faraway land. Mountains of possibilities surrounded my very essence, the very air I breathed. The intoxication of sweet evolution mixed with the gardenias in my garden filled me with gratitude. On days like this, I could fly like an eagle, see like a hawk, and be the king of my destiny. The world was fluid, and I was enmeshed in its luminosity.

"*Dios te ama, y nunca estamos solos*," my dear mother would say to me: "God loves you, and we are never alone." I trusted these words from a woman who had learned more about good and bad days than anyone I had ever met. I was at a point in my life where my mother's words had entered that sacred space in my heart and taken up permanent residence. I now had the armor of all the wisdom accrued from every age. The past, the present, and the future were condensed in each sacred breath, and I was intertwined with the spirit of the universe. My moral compass was carved in stone. I could hear her voice on the good days and on the bad days. This morning, I saw my mother's smile among the clouds, and like a madman, I winked and smiled back.

My home was a dream, a make-believe cardboard box in my mind's eye that had come to life. I had only dreamed of having a home because the possibility of a real one was too risky. I had relegated the idea of home to the realm of impossibilities and my imagination. The actual manifestation of it was a miracle. I was now in my own Garden of Eden, and I purposefully surrounded myself with the garments of nature. The substance of the earth's raw elements has always been my place of solace. I love the majesty of trees—their roots and their texture—and if I am still enough, I am cordially invited into their secret world where their sacred language is gently revealed. As a child, I watched my mother talk to her plants. She would speak to them in the most ordinary communion. These were her best friends. Mami was forever grateful for their beauty. She was born on an island called Cuba, in the countryside near a large river, and she had made an intimate acquaintance with Mother Earth. I am my mother's son, and I too have an ordinary dialect with the diverse ecosystem that circumvallates my life.

CHAPTER 1

I speak to nature, and I hear the whispers of the leaves and the groans of the earth's pain: a gift and a curse I have often called this. Not unlike the color of my brown eyes, I inherited this without consent. I feel a closeness in the wilderness of God's majestic creation as if it were my very own blood kinship. Every tree, weed, and blade of grass conveys its essence as plainly as a spiritual hymn. The swaying palm fronds, the moon, the sun, the stars, and the chirpings of all universes, near and far, echo their messages of a world long past and the one yet to come.

I willingly give myself to the world beneath the surface of appearances; it is in the subtleties of nature that I find my very own God, my own nature. In doing so, I receive the sacred trust of the universe, and its mystery is revealed. Enthusiastically, I relinquish the visible to see what human eyes can't see, hear what our ears can't hear, and feel what few dare to feel. I set out to create the life of a dream I never before dared to dream.

In my little corner of the world, I planted like a madman, encapsulating myself within Mother Earth. I toiled with the soil, knowing it felt my embrace. All of nature responds to love; it thrives on it. Not by bread alone, but in love, for without it, we wither in a slow, decaying, empty existence. We, like nature, respond to love's healing and its majestical powers. There is no better cure for our human malady than love. I believe that we come to this dimension to learn all about love, for love is all that truly matters in the end. For me, this is the only true meaning of life. Love is the greatest force in the universe, and I keep choosing it no matter the stubbornness of its opposite. Even one of the most gifted minds the world has ever known, Albert Einstein, believed that love is the greatest force in the universe.

I had long ago ceased to have the desire to belong to the civilization that surrounded me. By my early thirties, I felt I had seen too much and knew too much. It was my paradise, not the outside landscape, that gave me solace. It seems to me that some people are naturally born to fit in, but I have never been one of those people. What one calls "normal," I perceive as abnormal. I had become accustomed to being considered odd, and my kinship was with untapped nature, and it alone sufficed. God knew my heart, and no matter how I tried, no man would ever know it as well. I was a new kind of monk who had created his own cave, and my cloister was my home, my cardboard box that, like magic, had sprouted into a bricks-and-mortar edifice.

If I needed a why or a what to live for, I found that purpose in love. The obligatory assignment for my spiritual recess had been to learn to love myself, and this took a lifetime. Meanwhile, I had my herd of domestic and wild fauna. I had been entrusted with a piece of earth that, like an infant, required the tender love of its caretaker. I had seven precious furry mutts who had rescued me, and God had rescued us all by joining our paths. They were my angels, my gurus, and if ever there were creatures who were loved, it was the assorted pack of dogs who became my reason for living.

I forget how many birds I ended up naming, a note to the reader: Nothing I write about herein was ever truly mine; it is a colloquial absurdity to call anything "mine." Nothing truly meaningful can be owned. My words are mere pointers to my imaginary reality. I trust the spirit that unites us. When I write that I had dozens of parakeets, six cockatiels, and dozens of lovebirds, I am alluding to a shared experience of space and time; I never "had" any of them because nature can't be possessed. At best, I was graced with the awareness of others' spirits within the sphere of my own realm.

Every morning, like clockwork, all the little animals came into the secluded tropical paradise I had cocreated with Mother Nature. They came to be fed, admired, and loved and to fulfill their curiosity about the odd creature called "man." Unlike the man who provided for them, they exhibited curiosity and awe toward humanity. I desperately hid my rapture of joy, which never ceased in witnessing their trust and presence.

My favorites were always the spring baby birds with their wide-open beaks, fluttering their tiny wings fiercely and avoiding being forgotten. I adored the stare of the squirrels and envied their ability to be intertwined with the strong, whirling, solid branches of the old oak trees. Then there was royalty, the ever-awaited visit from the magical hummingbird who gave seconds and minutes a new meaning. I loved them all, the blue jays, cardinals, mockingbirds, sparrows, and even the temporary snowbirds that decided the trip north was not worth the energy. These colorful sojourners endured the hot and humid Florida summers with the rest of us. Not unlike the regular plebeians for whom the luxury of a second home was not possible, they remained.

I fed them religiously, and if I was ever delayed, they would come knocking on my windows adamantly with their beaks. One day, I was surprised by the visit of a fox. I write "surprised" because although I lived in a densely natural alcove, it was still within the city of Coral Gables, and foxes are rare in city settings. I was a Cuban-born Dr. Doolittle. I was born an islander, and the island remains in my genes. The animals naturally spoke to me, and we had our sanctified relationships.

If I was lucky, a raccoon family would peek through my glass bedroom door at night. As I lay in my dimly lit room, cuddled with my favorite blanket and teacup, reading, they appeared as a group of kids whose curiosity couldn't be restrained. No painting could ever capture their shiny eyes and acrobatic maneuvers as they scrunched together to get a good look at the inside landscape. I felt blessed to be surrounded by these visitors in the middle of a metropolis. Gently, I would put my book down so as not to alert the gang of my awareness of their visit. I was as curious about them as they were about me.

Nothing could have prepared me for the abundance of trust and love these big and small sentient beings emanated on their daily visits. I was learning about love, nature, and God herself with the wisest and most delicate of masters in all of creation.

My physical home was a small cottage, and it was charming, cozy, and whimsically peaceful. Strangely, this South Florida home came with its own working fireplace. If you have ever lived in or even visited South Florida amid our winters, you would know that we could do well without a fireplace. The fireplace added a particular charm that only fireplaces can. The small, sturdy cottage was a Garden of Eden for all who entered. Few visitors ever gained the pack's trust enough to be welcomed into our private oasis, but those who did felt God's very own breath.

The furry children were loving and welcoming. Each unique and peculiar, they made each visitor feel loved with their jovial wagging tails. Little Man, a tiny Maltese weighing five pounds, of which three pounds most surely was fur, made it known that he was loving but fiercely ferocious. Briefly, he gave you an air of pride, there were two things he detested: the camera and any would-be intruder. But once you understood he was the alpha male and you were on his turf, it was not long before you got his unconditional devotion. I can't help but smile when I remember so much courage packed into a furry little five-pound body. He was one of the most adorable, loving, and intelligent canines I have ever met. He had the uncanny ability to love without shedding his strength or fearlessness. I respected and admired him so, and I told him this constantly, for he had no unbalanced ego to contend with.

A Florida home built in the past century and remaining proud and robust to date had earned itself the privilege of being a cozy nest for all of God's creatures. Withstanding many Florida storms, including massive hurricanes, this bungalow was a fortress against Mother

Nature's trimming; her tools were severe, gusting winds and heavy thunderstorms. This unobtrusive little quarter was situated in a place called Coral Gables. The city got its name upon its groundbreaking to build structures for the human populace. The digging found layers of coral rocks as part of the area's foundation. Gables are arched entryways reminiscent of Mediterranean architecture, for which the city's founder had some fondness and wished to emulate.

I made my casita on Campina, a private oasis with a wall of vegetation that made it an impenetrable fortress. If you were an unannounced visitor, you certainly would have your work cut out to gain entrance. Keeping the wall of vegetation company were two solid iron gates that kept any would-be curious stranger from being able to capture the richness inside. To know God requires a meditative solitude, and solitude was had. In this sanctuary, I found inspiration to paint and write. Later, I learned I could not paint in a so-called art studio or any place outside my abode. The muse to paint and write visited only when I was surrounded by my children and the artifacts of my lifetime. With and in that love, I found my communion with my creator and the muse to create.

I lived some of my most joyous moments in that home—and some very sorrowful and trying times. I suppose that's how life is; I get a taste of the sweetness by tasting the tang of bitterness. When I first saw that little house, it was an abandoned shack. It had been left empty with its musty odor, dust, and cobwebs. It was an orphan, a loveless child amid a wild, thriving civilization. I knew an orphan when I saw one, for this was a journey I had traveled. The eyes to its interior, the windows, were clasped shut, keeping out any ray of light from ever hinting at hope. The silence between the stark, decaying walls was death itself. Left unwanted for centuries, none dared imagine it as a home, a haven, one's very own secret hideaway. I myself hesitated, for it seemed like an insurmountable amount of work to bring it back to life. It required the patience of saints, unshakable dedication, and that ever-elusive unconditional love.

All the hesitant thoughts ended the day I was able to walk in the gardens alone. Until then, I had missed its soul. I had visited a couple of times with the inconvenience of a sales agent. The agent's chatter obscured what I was to discover on my own. I believe places have energy and perhaps even a life of their own. Walking its gardens on my own, the house spoke its language of longing to be loved. I heard and understood its prose. The decision was made. I was to purchase the abandoned little shack with cracked windows and decaying facade and make it my first real home. The pie-shaped corner lot that would become my venerated cloister is on the street called Campina.

"*Campina*" is a Spanish word for the countryside, and how perfectly, divinely, that name would fit my place of refuge. If ever I had the audacity to dream of a home, it had come in the vision of a country cottage. God has an incredible sense of humor. I have long given up on the idea of coincidences; instead, I choose to believe in a divine plan. If I could explain to you the miracles that I have witnessed in my life, well, they simply wouldn't be called "miracles." Campina was a miracle. Although shabby and abandoned, with its profound longing to be loved, it became a sanctuary for the many little animals that, like me, found refuge in its shade. As I gave this shabby abandoned home love, it retuned me to my own nature, it was the beginning of my own self-love.

This newfound Eden was a return to a journey that was well overdue. The longing I felt in its gardens was a calling to return to my nature, to God, to love. Campina was my world, filled with joy, love, and purpose. I was to live in a home on a street called "the countryside," and it was to be within a beautiful city that allowed me to come in and out of civilization at will. I was to have the best of both worlds with a solid foundation made of coral. Trust in God's infinte wisdom, for it knows best, always.

When I first moved to Campina, I had only one dog, Toto. Toto was unique, as were all my furry and feathery children who arrived after. All animals have souls, as do all living things. All have energy, and how we choose to perceive that energy determines much of who we are. Every creature is unique, regardless of breed or appearance. At birth, I was given the name Osvaldo Calixto Amador, but in the third grade, I was nicknamed Ozzie by Mrs. Brush. No matter how much Mrs. Brush tried to pronounce Osvaldo, she couldn't. Toto and Ozzie were on the way to see the Wizard, following an uncharted brick road that would reveal lessons for all eternity. As the story goes, Oz never really had anything to add to me, but I had to travel the road my soul was commanding.

Ozzie gave Toto all the best he could with the little he had. She came to him as a tiny teacup full of fleas and mistreatment. Ozzie could barely take care of himself, but when he looked into her eyes for the first time, he made a promise, not knowing how he would keep it. He promised to love and care for her for the rest of her life. Simultaneously, Ozzie prayed to God to help him with this soul he had placed on his path, for he knew he lacked the tools to navigate through his own life, much less an innocent soul who was to depend on him for her own existence. Ozzie kept his promise, and Toto gave him everything: She gave him her heart. The love of a dog is incomparable, like none other I have ever felt.

Toto was a white and tan cocker spaniel that God gave me in my early twenties to teach me about unconditional love, commitment, and responsibility as well as loss. She was my angel, and I loved and love her, for she remains a big part of me. Toto passed away not long after we moved into Campina. I can still remember her lounging in the shade of the old oak tree with its swaying moss by the wooden shed, taking in the afternoon's gentle breeze with its filtered Florida sun. Snug and complacent, she watched joyfully as her daddy toiled with the land; this sacred moment belonged to us, and we belonged to each other. Once a moment is lived, it remains embedded in our souls. Nothing, and no energy truly dies, we choose death or love; I choose love.

These were my early days in Campina. My days were filled with work and love. There was so much to do in the gardens, in the house, and in my life. But Toto made it all worthwhile—she had a garden, and Ozzie rejoiced to see her convalesce in the little cottage in the countryside by the shade of the willow trees. A goodbye to Toto was inevitable, as was a goodbye to my twenties. But I am getting way ahead of my story…to everything, its own time.

Campina needed a lot of love, and I had a lot of love to give. The windows were cracked and unfunctional, and the floors were piled one on top of the other, from ceramic tile to dusty old rugs. Underneath the layers of years of dust and wear, I discovered the most beautiful Florida pine floors. I was a lumber jack on an archeological exploration with no destination but resurrection itself. Doors were unhinged and closed permanently, requiring intricate rehabilitation. Everywhere in the countryside, abandonment was evident. I knew abandonment well and reversing its effect had been a lifetime endeavor.

The early days at Campina went by too slowly, for I wanted things done, and the more I did, the more needed to be done. Looking at life through a backward lens, those days and years went by as fast as the blink of an eye. If I could turn back the hands of time, I would stop the clock and beg it to be still here and now. Nothing ever seems to compare with the present moment when looking backward. Regardless of its pain and tragedy, yesterday's always seem to gain brightness as the years pass on.

The little corner cottage that no one cared for started to come to life. The love, care, and time I so freely offered were swallowed up by the hunger left from years of neglect. The sunlight began to slowly peek in and gently introduce a new warmth to the dark and damp abandoned little bungalow in the countryside. Campina's resurrection had begun.

As Campina was coming to life, Toto was losing hers. I cried as I sat and gave her my heart. I knew she would be gone soon, and I would miss her so. My mother, who was still living at the time, had become my best friend and consoled me much. There is no doubt in my heart that Toto knew how much I loved her, as there is no doubt of her love for me. Mami and I spoke on the phone daily, often many times a day, because I enjoyed her spirit and her optimistic way of singing through life's troubles.

Toto was the first dog my mother ever got to know and love. They had a special relationship in which the only thing apparent to me was their love; everything else was a mystery, a secret between the two of them. Toto would not be the last special furry baby for my mother, for she developed a habit of forming a hidden relationship with each one of my furry kids. She was their *abuelita*, their granny, and grannies always come with special, delectable secret treats. Toto loved her abuelita and recognized the sound of her infamous six-inch heels making their way to our doorway. My mother wore heels until she could not walk anymore; she was a brunette Dolly Parton with a couple of major exceptions.

At this time in my life, I had the best job I have ever had. I was underpaid and overworked, but I loved my mission. I was an elementary school teacher at a private Christian school. I loved my students with all my heart and soul, and I know they loved Mr. Amador. This Christian school was a private school for students from insolvent backgrounds. The teachers made very little, for the school had limited funding. I met the only financial contributor to this building, which was attached to an old chapel with stained glass windows that allowed the only affordable light in. He was a handsome young man who apparently had a lot of money and a lot of heart as well. *What a great way to have a lot,* I thought, *to contribute to a school for underprivileged students.* Too often, great wealth is equated with vulgarity. To learn of a handsome young man giving quietly from his heart to such a worthy cause is inspirational and divine at the minimum. He had no tabloids or newspaper articles and desired no recognition; he walked among us as Christ walked among the undesirables.

My students were children of different colors and shapes from all over our impoverished lands. They were all incredibly precious and unique, but I can tell you of two who marked my life forever. I will call one of them "Keena," a skinny, raggedy, wide-eyed little girl born with an overdose of enthusiasm and the energy to go with it. Keena kept Mr. Amador busy, and she was as lively as a gifted farm in the midst of springtime. Her long, skinny legs were hardly ever still. She was the queen bee of the already rambunctious student body. Her effervescent social life matched her personality. Keena loved freedom, and the four old walls of our classroom were a prison that tormented her soul. She gave the whole school a run for its money. As for me, she allowed me to discover a new meaning to my ever-evolving patience and unconditional love.

It was hard to remain upset at Keena for long. No matter what she did, I knew she never meant any harm. Keena was always just being Keena. She was authenticity personified, as all children are. She was born with a big personality and a skinny little body. She did what she knew how to do best: She could revive the dead with joy and felt an insatiable need to spread her gospel to anyone who would lend her an ear. Hallelujah! Her voice would shout during our daily Mass, the only voice distinguishable from valleys and mountains miles away. It did not matter how many springs, waterfalls, or oceans roared; her voice surpassed every obstacle of the jungle. Her calling was an "Ode to Joy," and it was recognized by the fluttering butterflies in our Lord's Garden. Everyone heard Keena; she had a voice, a God-given, purposeful voice.

Keena was at home anywhere and everywhere an audience for her gospel was found. She did not seek recognition or accolades. She spread the good news gratuitously as the mockingbird, and it was in her nature to sing for the sake of singing. It did not matter much to Keena that she did not look the part of a queen bee. Her absence of self-awareness made Keena more endearing to me, and I suspect all others. What few knew was that Keena was born HIV-positive because her mother had injected herself with crack and heroin all through her pregnancy. Keena's mom contracted the virus and passed it on to the new life in her womb. Keena's mom was in and out of rehabs and prison cells, leaving little Ms. Preacher in the care of her uncle, who did not hesitate to use the whooping belt ferociously on her skinny legs. In her short years in this world, her little body endured the kind of pain to shame our entire human race.

Keena's story was sad, but you would never know it if you saw her in Mr. Amador's class. She was jovial and optimistic about her daily world. She came and went, not giving attention to the abuse she suffered in her daily living. Her purpose was to shine her big white teeth, laughing out loud—even if she was dying inside. She was made of magic, of that spirit given to the few who can carry its weight. She was the singing cotton picker of her ancestors; she was courage and strength incarnate. She was a pharaoh from the Nile, a shaman, a prodigy, and I had the blessing of crossing paths with her soul. I did my best to improve those kids' lives, at least while in my class, but I knew it was never enough. They were born on the wrong side of the tracks, the gods throw the dice, and there is a life to be endured. She remains Keena wherever she may find herself today. I am certain her light continues to shine, for once a magician, always a magician. Keena was a fairy from above, an angel in a puny body made of fairy dust.

To put it mildly, I had a trying childhood, which was part of why I wanted to be a teacher. I had the desire to make a difference in a child's life. As a gay man, I knew that the possibility of having my own children was zero to none. At the height of my youth, homophobia was as rambunctious as the student body at the overcrowded Christian schoolhouse. The thought of gay marriage was not even on the periphery of possibilities. A gay man adopting a child was considered, as I am afraid may still be so, an abomination of the greatest kind. I rejoice in seeing my younger gay brothers and sisters making a full life for themselves with equalities I never dared to dream of. We have a long way to go, but let us rejoice in how far we have come—and the beat goes on for the souls of all colors of the rainbow.

I love kids, and I love teaching. Teaching was a calling from my heart. I believe there are teachers from the heart and teachers from the university. Both can make a difference, and a combination of the two is the best blend. But if I had to pick one over the other, I would choose teachers from the heart any ol' time. Teachers from the heart are likely born to teach. They are the ones who don't complain and who use their own money to buy supplies for those students who can barely buy lunch. The best teachers teach with love and from love, not from academia alone. They never resent their students—OK, maybe momentarily, but not long enough for the students to feel it. I was fortunate to have had a few teachers from the heart, and they made all the difference in my life. Making a difference in a child's life, is the reason real teachers continue the endless battle of teaching with little if any resources.

Another precious bloom sprouting in the old schoolhouse was Muhammad. Muhammad was the child who loved spending time alone in the dilapidated old chapel that adjoined our classroom. He, unlike Keena, was a loner like Mr. Amador. He preached no gospel, and silence was his best friend. If you did not know him, you would think him solemn. On the other hand, if you knew him like Mr. Amador got to know him, you understood he was at peace with himself. His voice was as subtle as the breeze that occasionally made it through the cathedral cracks.

Muhammad was a little Brown boy in my colorful classroom who admired his teacher's ties as, I learned, he did his character. Muhammad was always aware of any new ties I wore, which usually came from a nearby thrift store. He came to class in uniform, as was expected of all the students, but unlike all the other students, he always maintained the appearance of a dignified gentleman. No matter what time of day it was, even after having time outside in the playground, he always had his hair immaculately combed and his shirt tucked in. His tie was never loose, unlike Mr. Amador's, whose tie was typically loose at the collar by around lunchtime. Muhammad's white shirts were always crisp and starched—and never untucked.

He was not Christian; he was Muslim. I suspect he was at this Christian school because the alternative was bleak in his hood. I don't think there could be a better-groomed elementary student in the world. He was the opposite of Keena in that he seldom spoke or spread any gospel. His communion was a tête-à-tête with God in the hot, humid, dimly lit chapel. His presence was huge, regardless of his silence, because his spirit was bigger than any voice he could mutter. A benevolent spirit is powerful when the power of benevolence is known, and Muhammad knew without a doubt that he was a child of God.

As Toto's health was deteriorating, my mother learned of a litter of mutts that had recently been born. Without my knowing, she surprised me with a wiry, blondish terrier mix. Having seen the puppy, whom I would later call Teresita, or Teddy for short, I couldn't keep her out of my mind, but I had not decided to raise her. As much as I love dogs, I was not sure I wanted another dog at the time. Losing Toto had taken a heavy emotional toll, and I did not know if I had it in me to lose another dog if I outlived it, which was, given all logic, what the future held. This is where the spirit came in through a little Brown boy called Muhammad.

One day, I was sitting at my desk, thinking about Teresita and Toto. Losing Toto was not a sadness my eyes could hide. As a child, I had learned to pretend everything was well in my world, mostly because doing otherwise could have cost me my life. But my eyes are the windows to my soul, and when I'm sad, there is a certain upside-down smile that takes over where my lids are meant to be. I am not easy to read, even if you are the best at reading souls. As a child, I had to learn to keep my emotions to myself, and I learned to endure the most severe pain without showing a clue. My eyes, of course, well, that is a crystal ball for the magician who knows how to read crystal balls. Muhammad taught me he was the best of soul readers.

As I was working away at my desk, pretending the world was a bowl of cherries with a few inevitable nuts, Muhammad approached my desk with the quietness of an ant. He asked me what was wrong with me. I was surprised and mumbled something that I can't remember. His question was as loud as the big bang must have been, an atomic bomb explosion, or the clash of the Titans. I was rushed back to the present by his sincere question. This was the child who barely spoke in class to the other students—much less would I have predicted he would ask Mr. Amador a personal question. What this precious child told me next, I felt coming from the divine power of the universe, and he used a voice I barely heard to break the doubtful spell I had allowed myself to be engulfed in.

"You are stronger than you think, you should never be afraid of anything."

CHAPTER 1

How did he know? As those words slipped quietly out of his mouth, like a sacred secret shared between master and initiate, he turned around and walked away as silently as he had walked toward me. Instantly, I was awakened. Something in me heard his soft but strong voice, and all at once, I came back from the drifting sea of doubts. Instantly, I knew that I should embrace Teresita and not be afraid of tomorrow's pain, for I had to learn that to love is to risk pain and that this risk is not an option in life—it is life itself. I had wanted to stop loving because loving was attached to pain. What a silly endeavor I was proposing for myself, as if not loving would be a painless option. To love is to risk pain, but not to love is to not live. I chose to live and love, and the messenger was a little Brown boy with a soft voice that was barely heard.

Hearing Muhammad's words stopped me from closing my heart. I understood that if I stopped loving, I would stop life itself. Love is the very essence of life; it is like the very air we breathe. The next day, I welcomed love and pain into my life by opening to Teresita the iron gates that I had helped construct. The construction of the walls I was building around my heart came to a halt. I knew Muhammad was unique, but after that day, I wanted to bow whenever I saw him. Allah, Allah, God bless Muhammad. To love takes courage; not to love is to die in flesh and spirit.

Keena and Muhammad showed lessons of love and spirit to Mr. Amador, and I became a better man for being open to the big messages in small apparel. Keena spread her loving gospel despite her pain; somehow, she was able to love without fear. Her pain was transmuted into joy, and her hallelujah is heard to this day by those who got to know her true essence. Muhammad carried the message silently and with impeccable poise. He taught me that it's not how loud one's voice is but that what matters is to be certain to have a voice, no matter the medium one chooses. To have a voice, even when one is silenced, is a God-given right worth any stumbles in our journey. Regardless of how we choose to carry our own unique message, we are worthy.

These were the days of my life in my early thirties. Days full of to-dos and not-to-dos. I was working on my graduate degree, building a home for myself, learning revelations, and letting go of loved ones whose mission on this earth was coming to an end. My days and nights were as ordinary as life can be, keeping in mind how extraordinary what we call the "ordinary" can often be. I had lived the life of an infant, a youth, and now I was living the life of a man, officially indoctrinated into the dogmas of Western adulthood. I had been and had become so very often before. What I knew for certainty were only uncertainties. Everything was a lesson, I had not arrived anywhere, and I was in a hurry on the road to Oz with only destination on my mind. If I could find the answers, if I could hold onto one certainty, something, anything, then I would have arrived somewhere. But I could not. I could not hold onto anything. I was trying to hold air in my hands, water, and everything slipped away, leaving nothing but the moment.

To breathe and exhale is a full life in one breath. In every breath, we live a life full of hope, dreams, and uncertainties. Our lives are in this present moment; all else is illusion, maya, delusions, and emptiness to be filled or not. Every breath is sacred, filling us up with unknowns until our very last one, when perhaps all will be known. The lesson I was learning was that to not let love in was like not breathing, like stopping life itself. Regardless of all the uncertainties, love and breathing are life itself in its purest form. Silence should never keep us from expressing ourselves; we are love in its purest form, and we should never allow fear, resentments, or bitterness to block our light. These were but some of the lessons Mr. Amador learned in an impoverished Christian school for the forgotten children born on the wrong side of the tracks. Grasp onto nothing, sing your song, and let go of everything like water through your hands.

As this night approached, it was silent, with the exception of the night creatures' hymns. All around me, the world grew pitch-black, and no one was wandering about but the neighborhood stray cats. I was sitting in an old rocking chair on my front porch, and on time, as usual, the crickets chirped, and the stars revealed themselves. With Toto on my lap, the breeze was unusually cool, and the full moon shone its magic upon the grateful earth. As usual, the predictable routine brought with it another closure. I was glad, for I had become tired, and a rest was needed. Soon I was to sleep, and that was the only freedom I had ever known. The night's closure would acquiesce to nature as it folded away, content in bliss. All under the heavenly gaze was in divine order with uncanny predictability. All the worries of the world would become the memories of a day gone by. I was learning to grasp every moment, and tonight, Ozzie had Toto, the moon, and the stars. I was momentarily at peace with my humble place among Mother Nature's infinity.

As I watched the day depart, part of me yearned for the freshness of the morning, the newness of youth, hope, and a glimpse of the promised land. I wondered about God or the lack thereof. I waited for eternal sleep to arrive, but it was delayed. As usual, the ghost of loneliness arrived on time without delay. The ghost sat in and/or around my solar plexus, exactly where Toto's body lay in comfortable oblivion. I felt severely separated from humanity: I was in an empty shell I had learned to call myself. This self, this "I" that I had too often misunderstood, dissolved under the grandeur of the heavenly deities. God's voice played hide-and-seek: It hid, and I forever sought. I had an endless journey toward finding God, to feel God, to find myself, and like air and water, I could never hold onto either one for more than an ephemeral moment.

I dragged out the farewell, the goodbye to the illusory day, night, and the genuine moment of discernment I had been granted when Muhammad's silence spoke. What I was really hoping for was that love would never die. I wished that Toto would remain forever; I wished for eternity. I had been in search of love, incessantly, since the beginning of time. To live, to love, to be loved: I aspired to this more than the richness of all the ages. This need to reunite, this quest, was hardly new to me. My life had been full of goodbyes, and I detested them so. As a young gay man, I had said goodbye to a generation of friends ravaged by the HIV virus. I had only an ephemeral God. Not unlike the God I forever sought, I had missed my mother all my life, this night I missed her and the security of her womb.

As usual, I allowed myself to forget that I was alone in all my thoughts and that I would never, in all my striving, understand the vast universe of which I was an unwilling hostage. I remembered all the lives of my beautiful, young, vibrant friends who had crossed the stretch between life and death, and I knew they could hear my yearnings, my cries for salvation, and my need to reunite. Their faces were etched on my soul. My body was tired, and my mind was exhausted. Spending time with the spirits, dead or alive, takes its toll.

I gently stood, holding Toto in my arms, feeling her soft fur, and trying not to break her sleeping spell. Her trust was undeniable; she looked up at me with her sleepy eyes and immediately understood we were venturing into la-la land. With the pace of a man who has lived a million lives, the old soul in me walked the few steps it took to get to the door of my newfound land on an isolated street called Campina. It was good to be home. Patiently and unaware of itself, a colossal Florida cockroach was confidently poised between me and the entrance to my desired refuge: the door to the resurrecting cabin in the woods. I cringed and felt an immediate revulsion, for I had not anticipated this visitor. To be or not to be the subjugator, this was the beginning of one of the most important questions on my quest.

CHAPTER 2

I never let my schooling interfere with my education.

—Mark Twain

During my most severe depression, my therapist, Angelina—a Marlo Thomas look-alike and my Jewish mom—encouraged me to write. "I write to save my life." I found this in an old, dusty pile of my writings. My life had been difficult; this I knew. There was a time in my life that depression sucked all my energy, and doing the most menial task was a massive effort. The idea of writing was a task tantamount to running a marathon for someone unable to crawl. I trusted Angelina's advice, and I wrote ramblings, delusions, poetry, and my emotions. My writings became splattered ink on coffee-stained paper, scattered around my decaying self. My grammar, my foundational education, was minimal. Reading, painting, and disjointed, discursive writing were not cultivated within the walls of the established educational culture.

CHAPTER 2

As a child, I taught myself how to read. I went to eighteen schools from kindergarten to the seventh grade, and that was the last grade I attended. From the time I learned the alphabet, I decided I would read—and I knew I would need to do this mostly on my own. I understand now why as a child I was called "*el viejito*," the old man. The adults who called me él viejito were referring to an old soul in a child's body. They perceived a soul that knew too much for his few years on this earth. What I knew I had learned early on, and that was that pain was real and that injustice existed. I learned cruelty before ever entering the hallways of education.

It has been reading and painting that have allowed me temporary distractions from my deep-seated loneliness, felt from my crib. I never believed I could be heard, seen, or felt. My silence was self-preservation. In my world, silence was truly golden—even under dire pain. The words I heard early on were razor-sharp, meant to dismember its listener.

It has been in the books I've read that I have found true companionship. The authors are my mentors, teachers, friends, and loved ones. A good film, a piece of artwork, and a good book momentarily allow me the feeling of belonging. I have always loved colors, words, and the sublime symphony they can create. Exposing one's inner world is the courage of any true artist; it is shared altruistically, and by doing so, it gives life to the lifeless. I have never been interested in one subject matter: it all matters. What attracts me are the lessons, the feelings that surface from an expression that finds a semblance of equanimity in another's perspective. I witnessed so much chaos during my childhood that I became uncompromising in proclaiming equilibrium no matter how seemingly chaotic the expression. To find balance in a Jackson Pollock painting is sublime to the likes of me. I yearned to be united by the art forms presented in my journey, and art was the medium God used to break the darkness that enveloped me.

Books have consistently revealed secrets that my soul has felt from all eternity. Words have been pointers in my long journey back home. My voice was silenced early; my soundless journey commanded that I find my own language. I painted images that were never seen and wrote words that were never read. I learned hymns in the songs of the birds, the swaying of the leaves, and the crash of the ocean's waves. I mimicked the parrot that mimicked the people, and I sang the songs that no one could hear. My inner world was chosen for me from a place with no memory. My childhood was silence, the silence of el viejito.

I remember when I resolved to speak little, if at all. At the age of six, a teacher molested me. It was at a private school in that sunny state called Florida. While the other students played in the field, enjoying their childhood innocence, the man who taught physical education sat me on his lap and placed my little hands on his private parts. The feeling was terror, a terror I carried with me most of my life. I did not speak for the rest of that day. I became physically ill, and when I arrived at my abuela's home, my stomach was clenched, as was my entire body. I did not understand what had happened or why, but I knew from that day on how terror and shame felt. I consciously decided never to speak again. I did not want to be seen, I wanted to be Casper the ghost from that day on.

When I wrote that I was silenced early on, I meant that shame and terror paralyzed my voice. This incident did more than that; it took my innocence away, my childhood, my free spirit, and my freedom to believe in a safe world. I remained ashamed for most of my life. I felt dirty, less than, and something inside of me had died forever. Osvaldito, mini me, carried the venomous poison bravely while daily tummy aches clenched him from inside, twisting at him with unbearable brute force, causing a heavy soreness that would remain indefinitely.

CHAPTER 2

From that day, he wanted never to be seen or heard. The little boy my mother called Osvaldito remained sick throughout the school year, and most of his adult life due to a predator, who I later learned had a wife and children of his own. I saw his family in a school event one late fall afternoon, and the children had the saddest faces after my very own.

The molestation went on; this I can feel. I have very little access to these memories, but the traumatic experience has always been felt by my body. I became distracted in all things, for the pain in my tummy took all my energy to comfort. I feared teachers, I feared men, and I feared being seen. I wanted to be invisible, and I washed my hands incessantly. Water became sacred, and I bathed longer than anyone thought I should. I knew that the terror I felt was mine and should not be shared. Shame has a way to envelop its victim, like a spider envelops its prey. I drew, I scribbled, and I escaped into my imagination. The adults thought me lazy and defective. As the labels kept piling up, my silence kept growing. The world outside me was hostile and reprimanded who I was. I was a little boy who understood nothing but terror, shame, and severe tummy aches, God was out to lunch.

Art removed my isolation and enabled me to enter a shared dimension where I could feel human. The written word became my god because I did not have to listen, I did not have to speak, and most importantly, I did not have to be seen. I could read, paint, and remain invisible. I desired this with all my heart and soul regardless of the loneliness that trapped me. My mother gifted me a poem that went like this:

"From that instance of happiness, that sublime veil had slipped, the artist, possessed of that universal spirit, reincorporates me to life. The life I had on so many occasions detested. It was necessary, all the suffering, it was necessary in order to discover the home that corresponds to the soul and that brings light to the artist inspiration in which the pen rests and is able to sing to the same life."

My mother was a poet, an uneducated poet, if there can be such a thing. An artist is much like a teacher, some are born, and some are created, both can be good, but if I had to choose? Like me, she wrote to ease her pain. As a child, I saw in films that people who read books were smart and valued, and perhaps there began my love for the books that carried words. I knew as a child that I could use Crayola crayons to make pretty pictures, albeit pretty for my eyes only. No one knew my love for these two mediums that God used to guide and save my life—not even myself. Truth be told, no one has been more surprised at God's revelation than me; for all I knew, he hid.

All anyone knew was that I did not want to go to school. The solution for this was to move Osvaldito from school to school. Osvaldito was shy, inhibited, ashamed, and terrorized. Wherever he went, he was the new kid in the school, making him a sure target for predators of all size and shapes, the bullies who hide their fears by terrorizing others. The layers of discrimination created a profoundly timid disposition that would remain with me all my life.

I learned little in any of these schools except to keep quieter and remain as invisible as possible. Visibility meant being bullied by the children as well as the adults. I was labeled "disabled" not because I was a miscreant or ill-behaved, but because I could not focus or did not desire to do so. The truth is, I did not understand the education in front of me. Being a recluse in my inner sanctum removed me from the outer traumas and from the outer learning as well. I had no energy for the outside world; my energy went to fight that monster I later called "the ghost of loneliness" that made its home in my stomach. Moving from school to school cut me off from all the lessons being taught. This was a no-win situation for Osvaldito. Then entered grace, a book called *Black Beauty*. The reader, writer, painter, and the whole of the man I would become owes much to the day *Black Beauty* came into my life.

CHAPTER 2

As a child, I lived with my paternal grandmother, Josepha. Josepha was in her second marriage, and the man I called Tata was my step-grandfather. With us lived, a first cousin from my father's side. We lived in a small, two-bedroom, two-bath apartment that had a vast wild field surrounding it. In this field, I spent much time with my imaginary friends. My otherworldly friends have been more natural, loyal, dependable, and loving throughout my life than any living companion. Josepha was a maid at a hotel directly behind the building we lived in. All we had to do was cross a wide, empty field of wild vegetation, and there it was: the Okeechobee Resort.

Abuela cleaned a lot of rooms at that hotel, and I was often brought along because I suppose there was no one to take care of me. Some days, if my abuela was in a good mood and I begged enough, she would let me go into the hotel's pool. I loved that. I love water, it provokes in me that clarity of a spiritual baptism sheltered in a natural womb. I had a desire to cleanse the sin I was paying for, which I had never committed, and water was the cleanser that loosened the dirt off my body and spirit. But shame and terror remained, and water kept passing through my hand, washing only the surface, never deep enough to wipe out the generational curse I had been catapulted into.

The hotel was not fancy at all, the lobby where I spent some of my Saturdays and Sundays, playing with my imaginary friends as Abuela cleaned the rooms, had a stench of pipe smoke. It seemed to me that everything in the lobby had been in its spot since the beginning of time. The dust collected around the brochures with the Florida beaches and splashing fake tourist models on it. No one ever bothered to pick up the dusty old catalogs, perhaps because they were not interested in tourism at all. People came and went, but none looked like the faded caricatures on the dusty brochures. I watched, I smelled, and I learned. The hotel was a forgotten carnival full of clandestine clowns parading suspiciously their immense guilt.

In that pipe-smelling, dust-filled lobby sat two men who were my grandmother's bosses. They had a television, which was always on; it was loud, to blur out any unnecessary and unwelcome interruptions from the imitation tourists. These men were brothers and happily content with just each other. Everything they needed was in this smoke-filled hotel lobby with plastic plants and flowers piercing from all angles. Some plastic leaves hung from the cork ceiling, which was stained yellow from the pipe smoke. On a good fall day, when the sunlight was able to penetrate through the buried dust on the vacancy sign hanging in the window, you could see Charlotte, the spider from *Charlotte's Web*, trapping the big Florida flies. This was strange, as were all the worlds that Osvaldito observed and inhabited. Sometimes, I watched with a sad curiosity how the flies tried to escape their prison made of the thinnest thread without any victory. They were trapped in silence. Like me, they went unheard—even if in silence they were screaming the only language allowed while in the hands of a predator.

My grandmother was a hefty woman, physically strong and intimidating. Few people, if any, dared to mess with her. She was a combination of Satan and Mother Teresa. I have learned to try to give everyone the benefit of the doubt. I have also learned that most people do their best with what they have. Unfortunately, some people's best can be the worst for others. Josepha, my paternal grandmother, was the worst for many people. It took many years to learn and understand what real forgiveness is. She was one of my earliest and most crucial female caregivers, and I never felt safe around her. A man touched my body and hurt my stomach, and Josepha hurt my spirit with her words, which I tried desperately to bury in my silent world.

Tata, the only grandfather I ever knew, was a tall man, and not unlike everyone else, he was an-enigma to me. I will never forget that he owned and treasured his guns. Before I was six years old, he waved a gun in front of me and my dog, Blackie, as a menace. Blackie and I were terrified, and I ran away from him, carrying little Blackie with me into the bathroom to hide, but he came in, and as we both trembled in fear and crouched inside the bathtub, he pointed the gun at us for being cowards. I will never forget the fear I felt that day, and I will never forget Blackie's trembling. I will never know what it is like to be a roach, but I do feel a high degree of empathy for them, for I have often felt like less than a roach, and this was one of those times.

What does this have to do with writing, books, or painting? This was the world I lived in as a child—being molested at school, being transferred from one school to another, being bullied at school, and fearing my caretakers. But in these conditions, I found refuge in books and crayons. My mother was nowhere to be found, she was surviving as best she could, and my father was left behind in Cuba. I had been separated from him since I was nine months old. More about the woman I called Mami and my father later. For now, suffice it to say that I met my father in my teens, and I have always felt a profound need for more time with Mami.

I will tell you the story of the day hope came into my life. It was customary for my grandmother to wake up around four thirty in the morning to prepare Tata's lunch and help him on his journey to work. My grandmother would sit me on a vinyl dining room chair with a couple of huge Cuban crackers with butter from "*El Refugio*." Sometimes it was butter, others it was mayonnaise; a toss-up like throwing dices. El Refugio was a government food bank that Cubans who had immigrated to Miami to escape Communism could access. I can tell you that the best butter I have ever had in my life came from El Refugio.

I watched the ritual every morning, Tata's movements were synchronized with his stoic philosophical inclination from the moment he woke up. There was a serene, austere dance to his morning routine. Putting on his socks was a well-orchestrated endeavor of the utmost importance. Tata and Abuela hardly spoke, but their coming and going was a language all of their own. Abuela would lay out his police uniform as *Abuelo* went into the bathroom; Abuelo would reappear, and he would be ready to put on a spanking-clean, bright-white, ironed undershirt to rival any Chinese deluxe dry cleaner.

Abuela would come in from the kitchen to mumble something I could never really hear because the fans in the hot and humid apartment were already spinning. The words were difficult to decipher in my half-sleepy head. Perhaps I was born with a hearing loss. No one would have noticed if I had, but I did grow up to be a man with hearing loss. In many ways, silence has endured. I waited, watching the play as I did every morning, and no matter how many times I had seen it before, I was always mesmerized. Mozart himself could have never conducted a more beautiful symphony between two human beings.

The play always seemed to have a grand finale that culminated with the feeling of forlorn love. It had been much earlier in my life when a farewell to my homeland and my father would change my destiny. But this feeling of forlorn love seems to have always grasped me, even as a five-year-old. Something inside of me understood the profound, sacred, silent dance between two lovers. I think it's like poetry; each poem carries the unique essence of the poet. And, honestly, who can explain poetry? Intellectualism and art are like politics; they make strange bedfellows. To define poetry, you might as well try to define love. Impossible.

The final act was Tata putting on the belt that would carry his revolver. Tata's revolver was his crown. I often watched the ritual of Abuelo cleaning his gun. It all happened at the dining room table. He would bring out the shoebox that carried the mystery. Many types of cloth and small tools with tentacles, like a roach's legs attached to its thorax, were spread on the dining table. I would sit quietly across from Tata and watch the cleansing. The table, not unlike every piece of furniture in Abuela's apartment, had a clear vinyl cover to save the cloth underneath for a forever life. Every Cuban household I can remember as a child had furniture covered with vinyl, flowers that were mostly plastic, and a cheap calendar with the Cuban flag hung somewhere on the premises.

I would watch in total silence as Tata maneuvered this riddle I did not yet understand: guns. There was always the patting of the gun in the holster. Three pats to his side companion signaled he was ready to face the world with a trusted friend. This was the final clue that the play was coming to an end. And for all intents and purposes, no more dramatic ending was needed.

Their love was a Cuban Romeo and Juliet story based in Hialeah, Florida, without the unnecessary dramatics. I never witnessed any affection between Abuela and Tata other than the fleeting kiss as he walked out the door. So subtle was this kiss that, had I been taking a bite out of one of the humongous Cuban crackers, I would have missed the only physical intimacy I would ever witness between the two. Love and intimacy were scarce and were not given at El Refugio. Without exception, love takes on many forms, and theirs was based on pragmatism and not theatrics.

That morning, Abuela and I were going to the Grand Union. I loved going places, a temporary reprieve from the similar four walls that tormented Keena. For most children, everything is seen for the very first time. I was going on an exploration, a grand journey filled with so much territory to discover. Abuela never learned to drive a car, and I don't think she ever cared to. It did not bother her that we would always have to walk or take a bus wherever the journey was to be. Abuela needed to go to the Grand Union, which was a huge supermarket, and I was all in for the walk. Abuela and I crossed the massive field of vegetation behind our building and headed to the left. Soon, we arrived at an old wooden bridge that made crackling wooden sounds as I sauntered over the Okeechobee Waterway. Underneath this old bridge was a deep mystery that called to me. I wanted to jump over and join the shaded narrow highway of water that led to worlds that my insides already knew.

There was a full forest between the river and me, different from the one behind Abuela's. This long, narrow, dark ocean of water was full of life with intertwining leaves and logs of all shapes and sizes floating freely down the highway of never-never land. Logs rolled in harmony with the river's flow, swaying gently in kinship with the early-morning breeze. So many life-forms and spiritual fairies were whirling over the surface of this painting.

Huge roots sprouted from the side of the riverbank with mastery, like wooden sculptures made by Michelangelo himself. It was an exalted invitation to join the traveling light. An abandoned canoe drifted back and forth like the great Florida ocean waves playing catch-me-if-you-can. I fancied it a houseboat where I could escape the miseries of intrusive reality. I often regret not running away and joining the river, but Abuela would have been furious, and I knew that terror too well to risk the flight.

Abuela's hand was holding mine as we walked, but I did not mind it. I felt protected, and being chained together by the palms of our hands was a small price to pay for the momentary security of my world. It seems odd to feel protection and terror from the same person, but I had no choice: These were the options available. To feel respect for a caregiver is one thing, but to feel terror felt alien, and I could not rationalize it, but as usual, I felt it.

The air was hope itself. It was a tickling adventure playing with my young, pale skin. The whirling butterflies in spring swooshed by me, jovially tempting me to jump, skip, and run to catch up to them and play. The sun smiled down benevolently, reminding me of the warmth of my childhood and the crusade ahead. I had the perfect walk through a rainforest, the Amazon, and I heard the roar of Niagara Falls simultaneously.

There was never a better walk than this one. I was the luckiest boy alive. Osvaldito learned to smile inside himself as all children do, regardless of the outer reality. Perhaps, this is part of the reason why later in life I understood Keena so well. I built so many worlds during our walks that I could hardly hear Abuela if she startled me to demand that I pay attention and hold tighter to her hand as we encountered civilization. I hated to be interrupted; it was a total infringement of my imaginary inner smile. But I had no choice. If I did not listen, a bullhorn called Abuela's loud voice would pull me into her world sooner rather than later.

The Grand Union had its own merits. Oh, no, not like the bridge or its underworld: It was another jungle, a cornucopia of colors, smells, and sweet-flavored edibles perfectly fit for the belly of this hungry explorer. I have always loved sweets, but there is a special sweet that I would like to be buried with—it's called a doughnut. I simply know I could live on plain glazed doughnuts for the rest of my life. As a man with pockets full of coins, I have to watch out for this craving; it has never left me.

We arrived, and the doors opened, sliding by themselves with that spiritual electricity gifted from the heavens. I was transported into a psychedelic visual. Here were the most beautiful, brightly lit colors my eyes had ever seen. Here I found my destiny. Among this profusion, this explosion of orgasmic hues, began the history of what you are reading. Hope is always around the corner, let it reign.

Every aisle was full of intrigue, making my brain explode with inspiration. Every aisle had its character, its unique aroma. I was transfixed by all the eruptions of smells, temperatures, and possibilities, which my salivary glands screamed to grasp. There were cash registers ringing, cartwheels rolling, aromas of bakers from foreign lands intermingling their language, and smells with roses and peppermint all captivating my inner child's imagination. There were aisles and aisles of possibilities and dreams to conquer.

My favorite aisle was the one where they kept the neatly stacked boxes of sweetly colored and often reachable cereal boxes. I had been around the aisles a few times, and I knew the best of the best. I even knew the worst of the worst: the meat section. The "*carniceria*," as Abuela would call it, was always my least favorite. This remains my least favorite part of any grocery store to this day.

I started the journey into vegetarianism when I was twenty-one years old in a New York steak house in Madison Square Garden. I remember precisely when they brought out the bloody steak and placed it in front of me, that this would not digest well with my eyes or my alimentary canal. The decision was made there and then to never eat meat again. If you have ever looked into a cow's peaceful and noble eyes, if you have touched soul to soul as I have, you could never eat their flesh, much less slaughter them.

Seeing dead meat wrapped in Styrofoam and see-through plastic makes me want to look far away, in order to forget that there but for the grace of God go I. To this day, I cannot stand to see lobsters alive in a tank with their claws tied, waiting to be bought and boiled, all for a few minutes of desire. Too often, on another side of town, we'd go to a condensed form of the Grand Union called "*La Bodega*," where whole pieces of cows were hung with metal hooks from above, and I could see the insides of one of my favorite friends. If the notion of reincarnation turns out to be true, as a wise investment for any future potential lives, I eat as low on the food chain as possible.

At the Grand Union, the winner aisle was always the cereal lane. They had treasures inside some of these boxes, much like Cracker Jack and its wrapped gifts. If I was lucky and played my facial expression well, I was going home with the sweetest, crunchiest, most treasured box in the whole of Grand Union.

The treasures varied, and my quest was always for a car of some sort. I loved playing with cars. It did not matter if they were plastic and came in a cereal box; all that mattered was that they would have actual wheels and that I could roll them around and pretend I was the most fearless driver. These tiny gifts that came in wrappers inside cereal boxes were a joy for Osvaldito, and I looked forward to every trip to the Grand Union.

I had to continually strategize to get the treasure. I had to choose carefully and then beg as if my life depended on it. First, I had to check out all the boxes carefully. You might think this was easy, but try being about three feet tall and highly ambitious. The prize had to be worth the begging, and the cereal had to be worth the eating. Ultimately, all my strategizing meant nothing if Abuela was not in the mood for cereal that day.

I was focused, waiting for the cereal aisle moment. Oh yeah, I almost forgot that while devising this plot, I also had to control Hercules's pace as we walked up and down the aisles with occasional stops. Abuela's pace was much faster than mine, and the journey was a tug-of-war. She often pulled to hurry up my pace and interrupted my fantasizing—or I would be on the other side of the rope, waiting patiently and trying to keep composure while Abuela bought jamon, *bistec de palomilla*, or picadillo. Then there was the killer, the liver steak. I will never forget the smell of liver cooking, and with that, I will end this phase of la carniceria because I am afraid, I may still puke at the thought of the stench of liver frying in an iron skillet.

Life is never short of surprises; this I have learned. As I was contemplating the orchestration, the plot, the scheme, the chart, the map, and the graph in my little brown-haired head of how to align the heavenly stars to get the perfect cereal box with the most valuable treasure, well, life had other plans. My destiny, my archangel, and the Almighty himself had another design that would completely halt all the military science that even the most sophisticated CIA agent would have envied.

As I turned around at a slow-motion pace, there it was, bigger than life itself, at the front of the cereal aisle: a pyramid-shaped stack of laundry detergent boxes being promoted with a free book. I did one of those puppy-dog looks, the one a dog does when he turns his little head side to side. My plans slipped out of my brain like a slimy outpour of green Jell-O. Laundry detergent was not in the game plan.

Beethoven's Fifth Symphony filled my head and my surroundings; everything became illuminated with super-steroid fireworks. It was like that moment in a game show when the balloons fall from the sky with confetti, and everyone is cheering and applauding, jumping up and down in the most joyous rapture. It was a glazed doughnut fresh out of the bakery oven. It was winning the grand prize behind curtain number one. This was a virgin moment of excitement like no other, announcing the arrival of the good news. I was never the same again.

Osvaldito would become a better man because of this divine intervention. No matter how much we plan in life, sometimes the order of things turns out differently. Orange and more orange were glittering at me like rays from a galaxy far, far away, reaching out to the long-lost prodigal son. There was the black spot surrounded by orange that caught my eye, and the subconscious was struggling with my consciousness to focus.

Black Beauty—it was *Black Beauty*, a book by Anna Sewell. Never had my soul experienced such ecstasy. In this unexpected corner of the world lay a laundry detergent display with the accompanying gift of an orange book with a black horse on its cover.

God Almighty, I prayed, *oh, heavenly Father, I need to have this book by any means!* I knew about God because Abuela had a picture of him on the wall that lit up at night, and his name was Jesus. His eyes would follow me everywhere. No matter where I was in that room, Jesus kept an eye on me. At first, this was a horrifying thing. I would often try to trick God and see if he missed me, but no matter how much I tried, Jesus could follow me throughout that room without turning his head. I suppose he is God because he can see you no matter where you are. I can still feel his eyes today. Funny how life works, that God on Abuela's wall has kept his eyes on me throughout my entire life.

"Abuela, Abuela! Please buy this laundry detergent!"

Her reply: "*Estate tranquilo, nino. Que yo no necesito jabon de lavar. Siempre estas inventado.*" "Be still, child. I don't need no laundry detergent. You are always inventing something."

A different rendition of my original plea followed for what liked seemed centuries to me. One thing I have learned in life is that when your soul and heart speak louder than your mind, you must learn to persevere and follow their lead. If I have ever felt one, this was a calling from a faraway place whose origin was not understood but felt. I was not about to give up on *Black Beauty*.

"Abuela, *please*! I promise I will never—in my entire life—ask for anything again!"

"No!"

"But, Abuela, I need this book. Please!"

I believe in some predestination, and I will save you from a very long and pouting story. Suffice it to say that Jesus's eyes were at the Grand Union, looking out for Osvaldito, because he went home with a copy of what became his all-time favorite book, *Black Beauty*.

I did not know how to read. Not one of the grown-ups in my life ever had a book. Except for my mom's *Cosmopolitan* fashion magazines, and the occasional *Reader's Digest*, there was little printed material in any of Osvaldito's world. Unless you call a Cuban calendar and cardboard hand fans literature, there was nothing to read or learn from but the old, dusty Bible at the center of Abuela's vinyl-covered dining room table. Like the brochures of the fake tourists, this Bible was full of dust and remained opened to the same page for eternity. I learned it was a picture of the painting of *The Last Supper* by Leonardo da Vinci. I learned this many years later when I knew how to read. Like the brochures, it seemed to me to be on display for a strange form of attraction rather than any real practical usage. But on TV, on that tube that partly raised me, I saw smart-looking people carrying, reading, and having books on shelves. Was it nature, or was it nurture? Who cares? I had *Black Beauty*!

In my early thirties, I took what turned out to be a very impressionable and vital trip to Key West. While there, I entered a former house of the writer Ernest Hemingway. As it turns out, he lived very little in that house, yet his energy is everywhere. It is now a museum for tourists to roam about. As I left the museum, I entered the small souvenir shop underneath a set of stairs off to the side and tucked away in a little corner of the old mansion adjacent to the pool. It was a typical quaint souvenir shop. The cramped space was filled with artifacts so the fans of Hemingway could splurge and take home a piece of the man—or at least the history of the man.

Up until that point, I had never read anything that Hemingway wrote. I was not a Hemingway fan, by any means. I had never read anything he had written, and I was not particularly drawn to his type of writing. Yet, in this little souvenir shop, I read one of his quotes on a paperweight that I was compelled to purchase. The paperweight has a small stamp like picture of Hemingway with the quote: "Good writing is true writing." To this day, I own that paperweight. I eventually read *The Old Man and the Sea* and thoroughly enjoyed it. I have learned much about the man since, yet this quote strikes me as one of the most profound literary quotes ever written.

CHAPTER 2

I have always heard that a writer must know his subject. I know certain ingrained things, yet others are forever escaping me. The only truth about this writing is that I felt compelled to write, to live, and to share with others a little boy's story with a happy ending. I wrote because I finally understood that everyone is worthy, including me. I wrote because my loneliness propelled me to unite with that universal soul for which every artist yearns. That day in the Grand Union, the Almighty established a plan. Osvaldito had wanted a little plastic car to escape his world, but now Osvaldito had a book that he did not know how to read. He had something better than an-escape route: He found hope. He found the road to Oz. He found truth in an orange display of laundry detergent.

If I could read that book, I would be like the kids on TV who had a home, a mother, and a father. I took to writing much like I took to the book, though I had no intimation of how to decipher its code. I had nothing left to lose. It was the eyes of Abuela's God that kept vigil on my soul, the same eyes that followed me around and had once spooked me. It is the courage of a dead man walking that offers the nectar of truth to its own true destiny. The courage, love, and humility that I learned through *Black Beauty* gave me the window through which to learn about humanity, survival, the roach, and God himself.

My master plan had failed at the cereal aisle, but God had a better plan. He gave Osvaldito a friend, a best friend. He gave Osvaldito hope, faith, love, and compassion. Most importantly, he taught Osvaldito that his mother's words were the only truth he would ever need: "*Osvaldito, nunca estamos solos, clama a Dios que el nunca nos abandona.*" She told me that we are never alone, to always reach out to God, that he never abandons us. Until her last dying days, her words were loud and clear in her distant eyes.

No matter how much I have read and how much I will ever read, my mother's words will always remain among the most sacred and important pieces of literature this man has had the grace to learn. Indeed, Hemingway, good writing is true writing. What I write herein comes from my mother's conviction that we are never alone. Her legend was not left in gold but in her faith. Her words are not an impossibility attained only by the few privileged, the well-schooled, and the theological institutions. We are all God's creation, and in being so, we are never alone.

The best schooling of all is to know the frailty in our humanity, our dependence on a power greater than ourselves, and that we are love in its purest form regardless of our outer forms. If I can write at all, it is because it is my truth, be it the truth of a scared little boy lost in the wilderness of the Amazon jungle, or the fears of a grown man trying to confront his own inevitable mortality. The only truth worth writing about is love, and I found that love in myself. The best education starts with the heart, and it ends there too. Everything else is dust on unread brochures and Bibles used only for display. Evrything is true when it comes from the heart.

CHAPTER 3

The place of my birth is a trifling matter; it is where my heart emancipates that I celebrate.

—Osvaldo Calixto Amador

I was born in Cuba—Havana, Cuba, to be exact. I was born in the year of our Lord 1965 on the sixth day of September at approximately one in the morning. The delivering stork dropped me precisely on an island set roughly ninety nautical miles from Key West, Florida. I am confident that I was born from love and out of love, for my mother never missed an opportunity to let me know how much she and my father had wished for a male child. I was both my parents' firstborn boy. I was named after my father, Osvaldo.

In 1965, the Vietnam War continued to be a significant crisis for the United States, the Beatles released the album *Help!*, Lyndon B. Johnson was president, Malcolm X was shot and killed, and Martin Luther King Jr. took the American civil rights movement to the streets of this nation. By 1965, the relationship between Cuba and the Soviet Union was well established. On October 3, 1965, precisely three days short of a month after the stork had dropped me on my parents' doorstep, the new Communist Party of Cuba was inaugurated. As my parents celebrated the birth of their very first son, the dark clouds that were hovering over the island were too thick and dark to dismiss.

The political climate in which I was born would mark my life in ways that would take a lifetime to comprehend. For one thing, I was raised without a father. As a child, I never understood what having a father felt like. As an adult man, I know how important a positive male figure is for any child. As a gay man, I can't help but notice how often I have sought a father figure in my relationships. Undoubtedly, the gods throw some dice, and life is affected. This time, taking the place of God was a man named Fidel Castro, and that dice tossing would affect the lives of millions and the world itself.

My father was my mother's second husband and the love of her life. My mother was my father's first wife, and she was the love of his life. She had married young to her first husband and had a daughter named Georgina. By the time I came along, I had a half-sister and a sister born to both my parents, Teresa. I declare that three siblings have never been so "different" than in our case, a euphemism if I have ever known one. Especially Osvaldito, because Osvaldo Calixto Amador has disgraced all concerned, being that I am a full-fledged "*maricon*." I use the word "maricon" with painstaking purposefulness. It is a most derogatory term, used to denigrate its recipient to a level lower than a cockroach. It is not much different from "faggot" or "sissy." I was the recipient of all these unanimous words of hatred.

Cuba was under a dictator, so my family, which now constituted my mother, sister Teresa, and me, fled the island on one of the last flights out, the freedom flights. You are not missing a thing: Georgina stayed behind with her biological father. I learned I had an older sister when I first met her later on as a young lad of six or seven. My father also stayed behind in Cuba. When my mother, Teresa, and I left, I was barely nine months old. I was to meet my father again as a teenager when he was able to escape the island in the grand exodus of the Mariel boatlift.

The immigrant part of my life is not more or less tragic than most immigrant stories. My father and mother are my heroes, if for nothing else, for doing what seems to me to be the impossible: risking everything they loved to give their children freedom and a better chance in life. I can't help but wonder, taking away the horrors of Castro's version of Communism in Cuba, what a life with a father and an entire family would have been like. I never met any of my mother's side of my family, but I heard stories I treasure.

When the Cuban government official knocked on my parents' door to issue our departure documents, my mother opened it with me in her arms. The official entered a room where my father was standing behind my mother, holding seven-year-old Teresa close by his side. The authoritarian's voice blurted out that he had passages to leave the island in the name of Marta Virginia Amador Alvarez, Osvaldo Calixto Amador, and Teresa, and that we had two weeks to prepare for our departure to the United States of America.

My mother's trembling voice burst out the words, "You are missing my husband's name!"

The despotic voice, which reverberated through the Cuban enclosed porch with its "*medio punto*" (stained glass arched windows typical of Cuban architecture), responded, "*Estos son los unicos que se van!*" Meaning: "These are the only ones leaving!"

When my mother told me this story when I was a man, my heart broke. She revealed this story to the baby she was holding in her arms the day she heard the news that our family would be forever broken, never again to be whole as God had intended. Her voice trembled no more, but the sound of pain still echoed, if ever so distant and faded, from the chambers of her soul.

My father's voice issued its own stern directive with an ardent look at the woman holding the infant. "*Si, ellos se van!*" "Yes, they are leaving!" My father's voice was more powerful and resolute than the makeshift revolution's mannequin's inflection. The sun's glare kept half the room lit, casting shadows on the tongue that spoke the evils of a betrayed revolution. The same veranda welcomed the glimmering rays peeking through the Cuban stained glass, elucidating a potential brighter future.

She didn't understand, she couldn't, but she painfully understood. My father's command would impact our lives forever. He instinctively knew the decision had to be quick, without hesitation. It was a severe incision there and then; no time for blood loss when lives were at stake. There was no time for a family discussion, for devising a plan, or for indecision. Certainly, there wasn't time for cowardice. Some decisions are gut-wrenching, and this one ripped my parents' intestines inside out. She had two weeks to feel everything familiar to her for perhaps the last time. She had two weeks to pretend that all was well, knowing that nothing was. She would be boarding a plane traveling to another world, which political ideologies had forged ninety miles into interminable space.

My mother's last day with her mom was the best performance of her lifetime. The morning before she was to depart Cuba forever—she would never see Cuba or her mother again—she went, as usual, to have "*una merienda*," lunch, at noon. Sitting in her mom's kitchen, pretending all was well, she had a faintness in her demeanor. Her color was of a ghostly shade. This color can seldom, if ever, be kept from a loving mother. Her thoughts were in her "*adios*," in her parting words. How could she say goodbye to the woman who had raised her against all odds?

CHAPTER 3

Decades later, in a different world, I played the same ghastly role with the woman in this tale. Some goodbyes can't be uttered and are best left unspoken. My mother had decided not to tell anyone she was leaving, for she knew that the farewell would end the lives of those she loved. It was a chilling time for our family, and my mother navigated the uncharted territory with grace and courage. She mustered the courage of the Greek goddess Athena, wearing her lying eyes as the only armor against her pain. She would face this reality alone. She would learn later that this would be her destiny, a life without comrades in love, her family.

The harshness of such a brutal separation had no cure, and nothing could alleviate its pain. The kind of pain my parents felt and endured speaks of the kind of courage and nobleness inherent in our humanity. The death of a child, a family, a mother, the very tearing of our core is maintained by a spirit of which I choose to call God. In this world, nothing can alleviate the kind of pain that the loss of a loved one presses on us. From another realm, we are carried by concealed hands, invisible arms that allow us to remain without any semblance of life. If it were not for love, the nightmare of life would devour us.

My mother's endearing nickname was Mimi. "*Mimi, hija, que te pasa?*" My grandmother asked her: "What's wrong?" Something was wrong.

My mother choked on her tears, not allowing any to roll out of her big, beautiful Spanish brown eyes. It wasn't until she stepped out of her mother's house for the last time that she let the levee break. The flood of tears rolled freely, marking puddles of footprints in her native land for the last time. Walking out into the glaring Cuban sun, leaving her mother in doubt, she knew she may never travel the same country road that had led her home so often before. The small cabin by the river in which she grew up soon vanished, and so did her happiness. I could still feel her pain when she told me this story. Her eyes had quit lying, the were exposed to reality. I could feel the pain from when she said goodbye to my father as he stood behind the iron gate that separated those leaving the island and those staying behind.

Amid the crowd of spectators and government officials, they had their last embrace. My father let go of me, his nine-month-old child; my seven-year-old sister; and the love of his life, my mother. As he hugged and kissed her for the last time, he whispered in her ear, "When you walk to the other side of the fence, don't look back. If you have ever loved me, listen to me; keep walking—just don't look back." Her heart was heavy, tears mixed with her saliva and sweat; she wanted to look back, but what good would looking back do?

Carrying a hefty nine-month-old child, consoling a seven-year-old, and carrying a bag of rags, she walked over the invisible line of everything familiar toward everything unknown. She walked, vaguely feeling her legs with each step. She heard faint sounds of muffled cries, sorrowful moans, aircraft engines, and the soul of the only country she had ever known, her native land, Cuba. She wanted to look back—no, she wanted to run back—but what good would that do at that point? She gathered her strength to keep looking ahead, respecting my father's wishes; for she loved him, and now was no time for weakness. She walked under the Cuban skies for the last time in her life. She felt the same breeze of the palm fronds that had caressed her youth and given wings to her young girl's dreams. "*Yo regresare.*" "I will be back," she told herself in a last empty attempt to garnish hope, but she never returned. With a few steps, she lost everything that was meaningful in her life. Ahead of her now were only uncertainties in a foreign land with two innocent children to give her life any meaning.

As she took the last steps on Cuban soil, she felt a fainting spell coming over her. As her knees weakened, she resisted, for no one from the now Communist government on the tarmac would care if she dropped to her knees from emotional exhaustion. The newly formed government repudiated those who left and tortured those who stayed until they had no choice but to adhere to a strict dictatorship.

She was made of iron and tenderness. She was a woman whose name I will carry with me until my last breath. She would never see any of her family again. She left behind all her brothers and sisters, her childhood friends, her dreams, her makeshift toys, her mother, her daughter, and the only man she ever truly loved, my father.

I learned that my father never returned to our home after that day. He could not face my empty crib, the empty rooms, and his now empty life. He remained wandering from one friend's home to another, as a stray dog wanders incessantly without knowing where its next source of comfort will come from. He disappeared into a ghostly desert of emptiness for an eternity. He forgot his name, he forgot he was a man, and he had no one who could ease his pain, but he never forgot us. His only purpose for living became to reunite with my mother, my sister, and me. My father never lost focus of his only reason for living; he was gifted a mustard seed of hope, and he would hold on tight to it until we would unite once more.

Courage is given in the most surprising moments; unexpectedly, we traverse that which would seem impossible to endure if we had any foresight. No one knew the permanence of this voyage, the ramifications of our parting. If anyone could have seen it in a crystal ball, the pain would have devoured us all. I have often wondered if Osvaldito, only nine months old, felt any of the agony surrounding him during this significant event in his life. Did he feel his father's pain in letting him go? Did he feel the tension confounding this event for weeks or months? Did his mother's tears and sorrow communicate in a way that only a mother and child can communicate? What was it like for Teresa to leave behind her father, her grandparents, her cousins, and her classmates? What was Georgina feeling, knowing that her mother was leaving her behind? No government, no political ideology, no one man should ever have the power to tear a family apart.

Decades later, this tragic event remains. When families are being dissolved, separated, and even killed in their search for a better life, I can't help but know that I was among them. It's so easy to polarize political ideologies. Everyone wants to be right, everyone wants to have power, and everyone forgets that there are real human beings behind every political ideology. I do not pretend to have an answer to any of my questions, and I am only grateful to have empathy. Often, it seems to me, as distorted as this may seem, that unempathetic creatures roam free, at least in this world. One day, we will all know for certain; meanwhile, hope will keep us alive—like it did for my father.

After our departure, my father, Osvaldo Amador, lived a wretched life. Except for the brief period that he held his little family together in a decaying country, he knew very few moments of happiness. After we left Cuba, he was imprisoned for trying to escape the island. In Fidel Castro's Cuban prison, he was tortured and stripped of all human dignity. When he told me his story when I was a young man, I recognized a valor that I had so often dismissed. "*Los hijos de puta nunca me hicieron decir que viva la revolucion.*" I realized when he said these words— "The sons of bitches never made me utter the words 'long live the revolution'"—that I come from the best stock, an uncompromising stock that sticks to its principles even under the torture of Satan himself.

My mother was a beautiful woman with no formal education, but she was one of the wisest women I've ever met. She was a rag doll born into a twisted destiny that eventually stripped her of everything she ever loved. Despite the drain of her life, the agonies and injustices suffered, she was always a high-spirited woman who was adamant about forgiving all, even her staunchest enemy. I know without a doubt that she would have forgiven everyone who did her wrong, for this was the kind of spirit my mother was made of. Like mother, like son; I forgive all, even when hatred is much easier and justified. I don't believe my father was as forgiving as my mother, but he was a kind, gentle soul who reconciled with his destiny and remained a man of character regardless of the injustices life had thrown his way. I learned that no matter where he stood or how little he had, he proclaimed gratitude and a benevolent spirit wherever his feet landed. Like father, like son—I am forever grateful for it all.

Growing up, I had always thought Fidel Castro was the devil himself. All the grown-ups in my life referred to him in two ways: "*el hijo de puta*" or "*el diablo.*" The son of a bitch or the devil. I always pictured Fidel with horns in a visual of Dante's *Inferno*, accompanied by a fiery harlot as his mother. All cultures have idiosyncrasies, and Cubans have a unique way with words. We are especially fond of humor; no matter how severe the pain, we laugh. Some things in life require laughter, for if crying cannot remedy or cure a malady, at least, if we can summon some humor, it can help ease some of the suffering. Cubans come in all shapes, sizes, and colors. We have fat Cubans and skinny Cubans. We have loud Cubans and quiet Cubans. We have blonde Cubans, blue-eyed Cubans, and Cubans with kinky hair. If it were not for the love of the motherland, Cubans could blend into whatever part of the world they found themselves in. In fact, they do. One of the most predictable idiosyncrasies about Cubans is their pride in belonging to the Cuban clan.

I once saw a sign in a Cuban café that read: "*Si no fuera Cubano, pagaria por serlo.*" "If I were not Cuban, I would pay to be one!" This sign stuck with me because I understand the depth of Cuban pride. I must admit, after pizza and glazed doughnuts, Cuban food earns exceptionally high marks on my list of favorites. I encourage you before you die to have freshly baked Cuban bread tostadas with butter. If you can add a café con leche done with *leche evaporada* (evaporated milk) to dip your Cuban tostadas, this, my friend, is a taste of heaven on earth.

Our desserts are simple—try an old-fashioned homemade flan or a flan made with cream cheese and mango, and after tasting it, revisit the meaning of the word "simple." There is also, of course, our music with its mixture of African rhythm and Spanish guitar, an irresistible temptation for any hips with soul. Let me not forget the intoxicating invitation of the handmade Cuban cigar. A Cuban cigar, a Bacardi rum, and the sounds from the "Queen of Salsa," Celia Cruz, and we have a conga line.

A Cuban conga line is an invitation to hook up to a chain of hips moving to the sounds of conga drums. Here is where the old, the young, Black, white, Jew, Christian, Muslim, gay, straight, and all strangers alike become a part of our Cuban soul, even if for just a few minutes of elation. It does not matter where you come from, what you believe in, or what you look like, music is the rhythm of the soul—and Cuban music raises the dead.

It often saddens me that I do not know the land in which I was born—the land where my father and mother grew up and fell in love, the land where José Martí wrote some of the most beautiful verses in the history of poetry. I would love to swing from a handmade hammock next to the river where Mami spent her youth running around shoeless in a Cuban paradise. To have met my maternal grandmother, whose soul I recognized through my mother's beautiful hymns. To feel the breeze coming through the crashing waves of the Malecon or the white sand of Varadero Beach under my naked soles. I am an islander. It is in my genes; this is something that cannot be explained, but I can attest to it without a shadow of a doubt. You can take the boy out of Cuba, but you can't take the Cuban out of the boy.

I regret not meeting my mother's favorite brother, my uncle Gabriel. He was a handsome man born blond with blue eyes and pearly white skin. According to my mother, he resembled me in spirit like no other, despite the fact we were only united for the first nine months of my life. He was a "maricon," and my mother loved him without ever questioning his love for men in a time when being gay in Cuba could have cost him his life. He was gifted to teach and cure, and he went to the best schools on scholarships. He eventually went on to the university on the benevolence of the nuns who fell in love with his angelic spirit. How I would have loved to sit and talk to him about his love of books, his love of opera, his love of children, and his innate ability to heal the sick, both in spirit and body. There was never a day with my mother that she did not remind me how much I resembled Gabriel. "*Increible, Osvaldito, me parece que lo estoy escuchando a el.*" "Incredible, Osvaldito, I feel like am listening to him when I hear you speak." The universal soul transcends space and time, more importantly, death and life. It is called by many names; I call it love.

Except for the folk stories I have deliberately been told or overheard as a child, what recollection can a nine-month-old baby have of his birthplace? I learned much of what I know about prosaic Cuba by eavesdropping on conversations on porches. While the adults savored the strong Cuban coffee and used paper hand fans distributed freely at the local bodega (neighborhood mom-and-pop grocery stores) to advertise their imitation artifacts from the motherland, I observed with my ears the delicious memories of a country I have yet to know.

The much-relished simple hand "*avanicos*," or fans made of cardboard, almost always had a Cuban flag imprinted on them—it was necessary to remember what was left behind. These avanicos helped much with the hot Miami summer and the communal pain. The reminiscing, the romantic tales told sitting in rocking chairs on Florida porches, alleviated the sting of loss. Cubans lost everything familiar along with their dreams. Most, if not all, Cubans had family remaining in the island. Most believed that they would return sooner rather than later. Most cleaned floors, washed toilets, or made *cantinas* (homemade food) to earn a living regardless of their titles in Cuba. They started from scratch, point zero, and worked their way up with sweat and tears. At one point, they gave their lives in a botched attempt, during the Bay of Pigs, a clandestine rescue mission to free the island from the tyrannical grip it was imprisoned in.

Life in the new promised land slowly converted to a harsh reality as the days, weeks, and years passed without any hope of ever reuniting with the geographical place called home. The exact meaning and origin of the word "Cuba" are unknown, but some believe it originates from the Indigenous Hatueys, who called the Cuban soil the abundant fertile land. It was abundant until a perverted revolution dried the land under the auspices of benevolence. The pseudo-humanitarian tyranny robbed the soil and soul of the abundance found in Martí's verses. Cuba has been an island raped over and over again by conquistadores, authoritarians, dictators, fascists, and reckless, soulless mobs with a total disregard for the heart of its people.

My father's family had been able to escape the grasp of Communism and were now living in Miami, Florida. Upon arrival in the promising new country, my mother, who was in her mid-thirties, had no choice but to live with my aunt (my father's sister) and her family. I never met any of my mother's side of the family; they all stayed behind on *la isla bonita*. My father's side of the family I named "the beasts." I have forgiven the unforgivable, but forgiving is not forgetting. I have learned to use manure as fertilizer, but hurt was caused, and like the lotus flower, I grew from the mud.

Living with my father's family exposed me to the kind of evil that can destroy even the strongest among us. I experienced the kind of hatred Tom Robinson experienced as the "Negro" in Maycomb, Alabama, *in To Kill a Mockingbird*. I learned that prejudice and racism were real before reading Harper Lee's monumental work on the clash of races in a small-minded community that represented the larger society that sanctioned its injustices.

I learned early on that it was not only Fidel Castro that was the devil—but so was alcohol. My father's side of the family were almost entirely alcoholics, with the exception of my father. Living with the effects of the disease of alcoholism made me an observer and sharpened my survival skills from the time of my earliest memory. There was no choice; when one lives in an alcoholic family, one learns the skills it takes to survive fairly young because the neglect and abuse can be deadly if one does not develop the survival tools.

Alcoholism, I learned later in life, affects the whole family system. It does not matter if only one person is an addict; the addiction—in this case, alcoholism—affects all those who love the person with this malady. In turn, most become dysfunctional in one way or another.

I learned what I did not want to be, and this meant I did not want to be like the beasts. I learned to recognize the real face behind every mask. As a mature man wearing glasses, I was told by my ophthalmologist that I had the best peripheral vision he had ever seen in his whole career. I thought, *when you are raised as I was, not only do you develop peripheral vision; you also learn environmental cues that no one in hyper-survival mode can afford not to see.* That's how I spent my childhood, in a traumatizing war zone that required me to leave any fancy notion of a childhood behind. As an adult, I learned much about children growing up in alcoholic households, and the stories are sad and traumatic. I also learned that we survive and that there is plenty of help, free help, often given altruistically from those who have suffered from the same upbringings. Twelve-step programs have helped millions around the world, and it helped me understand the disease of alcoholism. There is hope, and as my mother would say, we are never alone.

In the early years, while living with my aunt in the newly promised paradise, my mother suffered from severe depression. She had lost everything, including the hope of ever reuniting with my father or my sister again. She cried constantly. There was little communication between the US and Cuba, and few letters or phone calls were accessible due to the iron wall created by opposing political ideologies. Only in Miami, a place so close to the island, can ninety miles seem so far away. For the rest of the world, Cuba is close enough; for Cubans, it is as far as the most unreachable star.

She was not allowed to cry. Grieving was not allowed in a household where alcohol and chaos ruled. My mother suffered the indignities of a dysfunction gone haywire. In no uncertain terms, my aunt, a raging alcoholic, told my mother she could not cry and that she would not tolerate a depressive person in her home. My mother walked the lonely streets of the now Cuban enclave alone to find the freedom to cry. My mother left my sister and me behind. She, in the new promised land, did not have the freedom to shed her own tears of grief. Like my father, she forgot her name, she forgot she was a woman, and she forgot she was a human being because she was torn apart by a game of dice—and the winners usually take it all, including your soul.

By the time I was one year old, I had been taken away from my father's loving arms, left behind a revolution, and lost a mother to depression. I was living under a roof full of alcoholics without recovery, my father was imprisoned and tortured, and Teresa and I were at the mercy of the beast. The exodus was not a triumphant one in all respects. Life can be flawed even in the promised land. One of my most treasured possessions is a little cardboard cutout birthday card my father made for me while in prison: "For my son Osvaldito on his birthday." I can't imagine what troubles and risks he took to make and smuggle this little cardboard cutout birthday card, but I can tell you that it is the only card I have ever received whose value cannot be measured.

During the time he was in prison, he was given electric shocks as a form of torture to get him to say, "*viva la revolucion*," or "long live the revolution." He was placed in a bed with his wrists and legs tied while a constant drip of water fell on his forehead for an eternity. He was placed in isolation cells where he lost all sense of time. These tortures were meant to weaken his spirit. My father was denied access to his humanity, yet he managed to make me a cardboard cutout birthday card. Love lives in the darkest places, and it never leaves us—not even when we can't see our own reflection. He scraped, searched, and turned a Cuban prison upside down so I would have a memento to remind me that I had a father who loved me.

In this card, he left material evidence of his gentle, delicate, poetic, and artistic nature. He was a man who never lost his sensitivity and never gave in to torture, and his only crime was wanting to unite with his family. He went to all ends to gather up the best piece of cardboard. Perhaps he got it from a food container. Maybe he had to bargain for the color pigments. He would have sold his soul to the devil if it meant his firstborn son would receive this token of his love. He drew this in the dark because evil was always lurking to devour love. The prison guards would have devoured his desire to send his son a birthday card. These Cuban guards were ordinary men, Cubans like my father. Perhaps at some point, they may have even known each other—they may even have been neighbors—but a political ideology turned them against their own. Hatred is the most primitive of human emotions, ignited easily and followed competently regardless of the damage caused to the recipient and the perpetrator.

This is what I know about Castro's Communism: It was cruel. I learned this only through its side effects. Those who remained on the island, through no fault of their own, joined the enemy to survive or suffered greater human indignities and deprivations as a consequence. There is no theorizing here: This is the fact of just one family's life as affected by that utopian ideology whose godfather is Karl Marx. The form of dictatorship that Castro implemented terrorizes me. Many believe that Castro's regime was not Communist; they believe it was a radical form of dictatorship that oppressed its own people, creating an enemy of a land that stands for the ideas of democracy and human dignity.

Any form of radical thought is not a comfort zone for me; I prefer, as with my paintings, to find the middle way. A staunch, stoic, frigid form of capitalism can be as cruel as any other form of extremism. It never ceases to amaze me how plain good ideas can become powerful evil tools in the hands of egocentric power-hungry individuals who eat the fat of their own people while the populace goes hungry and starves for human dignity.

In my adult years, I learned of the countless stories of families being separated, people being tortured, and the many holocausts that would shrink any man's heart. The history of humanity is an-enigma to me, and it shall always remain that. I do not believe I will ever find synthesis in its contradictions. I am not amenable to Darwin's theory and am afraid of my contribution to it. Even Christ cried out on the cross, "Why hast thou forsaken me?" All the pain is worth it because there is only one answer for me: love. There is no other definition fitting for a God of my understanding or remotely viable to my human intellect, soul, and, most importantly, heart than love.

Cuba has always been a mystery, a riddle to me. Being born in Cuba has had its advantages, and even if I could, I would not ask for another heritage. The history of Cuba is complex and sad. Leaving Cuba was not a choice I had to make; it was made for me by a man with iron courage. But I am glad I did not suffer the degradation of Castro's regime. Just to name one thing, the treatment of gays and lesbians was egregious to the extent of them being sent to concentration camps during the Castro regime.

CHAPTER 3

If you were a man and there was the slightest suspicion that you were a "maricon," you were incarcerated and sent to concentration camps, as they did later in the eighties with AIDS patients. I refuse to enter a fruitless conversation about Communism, Capitalism, or any other political ideology. Although politics is an extremely important aspect of a so-called civilized society, the reconciliation of opposing views can only be respected once human value is never a variable up for discussion.

No matter what the political ideology is, once a life is in peril because of that ideology, it ceases to imply a humane proposition. It's not that I do not have a point of view—we all do—or that I believe one point of view is radically different and/or better than another, for that was a fantasy I once held. Anytime blood is spilled, families are severed, people are put in encampments, and child labor or racist dogmas are part of the equation, I could never be impartial. This topic is beyond the scope of this writing, but when radical empathy takes over the human desire for power, it gives a new meaning to the word "civilization." Until then, many are at the mercy of the dice throwers.

I am confident my mother would not have abided by my father's decision for us to leave Cuba had she thought she would never be reunited with her daughter, her family, and my father. The word "Georgina" was never far from my mother's lips. Throughout my entire life, Georgina's name was always present; she was her firstborn, and she loved her so much. Not unlike my father, my mother lived a wretched life until her very last day. At my birth, she declared she was the happiest in her life. This happiness lasted nine months. Was it worth the pain? I can hear my mother's answer as a resounding yes—without hesitation.

Politics ripped my family inside out, like busy little termites eating away at the foundation of the most sacred God-instilled institution: family. I shy away from too much pride in any nationality because there is danger there for the likes of me. In America, many years later, as a graduate student in my sociology classes, there were two schools of thought. In one, I was Cuban American, which basically meant my heritage was Cuban, but I was socialized by listening to Madonna, I would have enough roots to move to Celia Cruz's rhythm, eat *lechon asado* on *Nochebuena*, and enjoy my once-a-year Cuban Kiwanis Calle Ocho celebration of Little Havana in Miami. I would grow up in the American melting pot and become *un arroz con mango* (rice with mango—meaning "wild mix"). In this school of thought, I would retain my heritage and still be able to assimilate comfortably.

Another school of thought was that I would become more and more Americanized, and as I aged, my roots would become frail and wither away, becoming extinct. In other words, the capitalist machinery would absorb any Cuban-ness as the years grew into decades, and decades of obsolete American dogma would eradicate any Cuban traces. This system would wipe me and deny me the one true American value I treasure: the potential to be a true individual with certain inalienable rights. The academics proposing the extinction did not know how strong Cuban coffee is! And just like our coffee, the roots of the Cuban people are deep and unrelenting.

The students and professors in my sociology classes were intellectuals, seekers of the truth, compadres, empiricists, and absolute scientists. We all venture long and far into distant lands for what we can find in our own backyards. All in all, many scientific evolutions and, at times, a much-needed revolution were boiling under the guise of advanced learning. Much can be found in the shelter of the university.

"Ask and thou shall receive," they told me, on this day, I detested the question; it was meaningless to me, my classmates asked the question of what it means to have been born in Cuba and raised in the US. I was impatient and detested the endeavor that we had embarked on. I was searching with an aching heart, not a logical mind. I had long dispelled the veil of intimidation clustered by the walls of science. The answer is not needed any longer. Often, I find the whole endeavor rather arrogant and egotistical. What's in a flag? In a nation? Flags often scare me—nations do. Yes, I was born in Cuba. Yes, I was raised in America. Does this make me a Cuban American or an-American Cuban? Let the dice find an answer.

What it means to be a human being is a much more interesting and sensible course of study for this man born in Cuba and raised in America. I do not dismiss my heritage for one second. A little fact about my background, my DNA shows that I am mostly from Portugal and Spain! To my surprise, I am even Irish and Scottish. To this writer, this proves that where we are born, where we are raised, and what our biology says about us, none of these are as meaningful as how we choose to live our humanity.

I do not deny my gratitude for the United States of America, and I feel as much American as the guy that came fleeing oppression in The Mayflower. But I here confess that my true interest lies in my true nationality: being a human being. I am interested in what unites us rather than what separates us. I am mystified by all attempts to define what being a Cuban is. I am mystified by all attempts to define what being an American is. My true journey entails what being a good human being is, and this is where my heart opens and emancipates. Where I was born is but a trifling matter, and where I was raised is not more or less important. However, without the ideals of freedom, no man has a chance to fully become, and those ideals are in a place called America. More specifically, The Unites States of America.

Science is a god, and God allows all inquisitions, regardless of their fruitless endeavors. God even allows the absurd attempt at defining God. All definitions are attempts to understand ourselves, our environments, and God. I long ago stopped trying to define God, for to define

God is to box God in an idea, which strikes me as the most arrogant and egotistical of all our human endeavors and the root of much evil. Not unlike nations that form borders to differentiate between races and economic raw materials given freely by Mother Earth, man's arrogance creates separation. Labels can bring darkness and evilness even to the gods we worship. I believe the question worth exploring is in front of my mirror every morning: Who am I? I am a man of flesh and bones, no better and no worse for having been born in Cuba as a "maricon." The dice are thrown, and definitions are stamped—and we begin to incarcerate the innocent with bourgeois good intentions, we form nations, political ideologies, religions, and hatred. We form God from our own image, from our own narrow indoctrination.

How do I contribute to this world where charity and love are mostly out of stock? Am I practicing what I preach? Am I preaching what I practice and hope to practice? Or am I a hypocrite like Maycomb's churchgoers in *To Kill a Mockingbird*? Does my being a gay man dictate my whole existence, not unlike a straight person who dictates theirs based on societal sanctions of their sexual preference? I refuse to be boxed in like the gods that have been encapsulated in a massive iceberg by their devotees.

Every creature is a mystery on its own and those that can, defines its world on its own, and if I label myself anything at all, I am a "wannabe." I am a man in constant transition, evolving with every breath; nothing is ever the same—nothing. Everything is water and air passing through our hands. Sociology is the study of the individual and his environment—the environment and the individual. Karl Marx questioned whether the environment created the individual's consciousness or if the individual created the environmental consciousness. Throw more dice, and you may have an answer. What mystifies me the most, and I predict it will continue to mystify me for all my remaining years, is what being a human is.

CHAPTER 3

The fact remains that I was born in Cuba and traveled on a jet plane to a city the Tequesta Indians called "the enormous body of water"—Miami. The gods threw dice, and I was socialized by a herd, a pack that thrived on labels. My family traversed a big body of water to arrive at an evolving Miami skyline. To my dismay, I have dreamed of an identity that would include rather than exclude me. I would spend most of my life trying to fit in. Later, I learned that fitting in was never my destiny. My destiny has always been to try to understand, accept, and circumvent the face of evil. In my reality, I learned to fuse the goodness of Mother Teresa and the Satan in those I love. Where I was born is not as important as how open my heart remains. For it is in this realm, the realm of love, that I find comfort and affiliation.

History can be a funny thing—if it weren't for the fact that it's truly so very tragic. It serves to teach us what we as a species can't seem to get right. I belong to the universe, to all places and none. I feel comfortable among people of all races and nationalities. My own place of comfort is never found among ignorance, hatred, and labels that can lead to bloodshed.

While having been born in Cuba has marked my life in undeniable ways, I am a better man for knowing that true freedom lies in my own self-made nationality. What I have learned I have been able to learn because of a place that emphasizes individual freedom: the United States of America. Perhaps no man and no country are truly, totally free, but I am content for having the opportunity and the ability to struggle to reach this ancient experiment handed down from our Greek forefathers. My search for my own personal freedom would have been castrated by the Cuban government. If I had to choose, I would have chosen my father's decision: He is my hero, and I owe him any form of freedom I have been able to savor. I can never take my parents' tears and struggles for granted, for I know the pain of loss. Wherever I stand, I stand for all. If I judge as a human, I allow myself a temporary reconciliatory judgment—and not the kind that preaches the salvation of anyone's soul. That is between each individual and their god, their conscience.

> *Everything that divides men, everything that specified, separates, or pens them, is a sin against humanity.*
>
> —José Martí, "My Race"

CHAPTER 4

Home is an open heart, ready to live again and again, an ocean of beingness. I was planted in the noble garden. I belong among the weeds and the gardenias; my aroma is earth.

—Osvaldo Calixto Amador

Half asleep one night, in a dreamy state of mind while watching *The Wizard of Oz*, I heard Dorothy ask Glinda, the Good Witch of the north, "Oh, will you help me? Can you help me?"

"You've always had the power to go back to Kansas."

Kansas, of course, is home for Dorothy, and we all know there is no place like home.

"I have?" said Osvaldito…oops…said Dorothy with more than a great dose of surprise.

At this point, the Scarecrow jumped in, and Osvaldito heard him say with much astonishment, "Then why didn't you tell me before?"

The answer is obvious: "Because Osvaldito wouldn't have believed me. He had to learn it for himself."

I had to learn it for myself.

I have dared to tread deep within my subconscious mind, jump in with faith, and dive with God's own breath. Since I never really had a home, I had no home to return to. I had to learn to define my own meaning of home. In the middle of my life, in Campina, I found a concrete foundation for the sense of home. It was not the location or the building itself I was most grateful for; it was the idea of home. I love nature, I love the idea of God, and I found God in the blue jays that visited my yard, in the cardinals, in the slimy yard snakes, and in the piece of earth I had been loaned.

The journey home has been painstaking, but I feel enormously blessed to have been allowed to experience it. Despite my reluctance and negation, life persisted like the weeds that grow stubbornly against all odds out of an old piece of cracked pavement. Having dived into denial head-on, I concluded that—not unlike Dorothy—that I had the answers all along. If Zeus himself had struck me with a bolt of lightning, I would have been skeptical. Everything I needed to know had been stamped in my heart from time immemorial. My DNA is not made of the known sciences alone, it carries deep within the nucleus, a spirit that knows the way home. Fortunately, now I know, I will always find my way home.

Nothing written within these pages belongs to me. The journey toward real freedom is as old as the beginning of time. We are all united by a force that surpasses species and universes. We are the universe experiencing itself through human consciousness. The answer becomes known when the question ceases. My mother once told me, "*Con tu arte vaz aprender mucho de la vida.*" "With your art, you will learn much about life." Such wisdom from a woman from *el campo* (the countryside) and only a second-grade education. Indeed, Mami, art has taught me much more than I could have ever imagined.

CHAPTER 4

I love the art of abstraction because it is creation from seemingly nothing. I stand in front of a blank canvas and let myself go completely. To be led and transported by my inner self is a freedom that only true humility and surrender have granted me. It is a game with God, and she maneuvers the whole creation. I am only to be emptied of uselessness, and a lot of my contents, my thoughts, are useless. It is only then that I become the medium, the instrument for her royal majesty's divine plan. The result of any painting I have ever done assures me that a force I call God exists. Gracias, Mami. As usual, you were right.

Campina grew around me, or I grew around it. Soon, I felt more at home than I have ever felt anywhere else. Enter Teresita, Teddy, my wiry-haired blonde terrier mix. Teddy was an angel in disguise, a savior given to me by my mom. She was a mutt who had the blood of royalty. She came to me with only a few months on this earth, but her heart was as old as the big bang itself. Toto was my life's love, and I can confirm that love is the most powerful force in the universe. Parents with more than one child may understand what I write about here: Love is not limited. I could love Toto with all my heart and Teresita with all my heart. That is a lot of love for one heart, yet it never tires of giving and receiving the most priceless of human gifts. On the contrary, the more love I felt, the more love grew.

It was hard for Teresita to understand that Toto was not amused by her. In fact, she wanted nothing to do with Teresita. On the other hand, Teresita wanted everything to do with her older sibling. She teased and prompted Toto from afar; she wanted her attention, to play, to run, to amuse and be amused, but nada, zero. Toto was adamant that Teresita had no part of her world. Of course, Toto was at the end of her journey, and Teresita was at the very start of hers. Toto required peace, and peace we gave her. On many occasions, I sat with Teresita and explained the need to accommodate her sister.

Although she was a puppy, she had the counterfeit expression that she understood her daddy. To her credit, she was a good puppy, and I never had to raise my voice—except for the one time when she ran across the street, to my near demise. It was one of those times I saw the pearly gates.

I believe in humane euthanasia, but it is hell to make the decision! I prayed, consulted, prayed some more, and consulted some more, but it was still the hardest decision to make. Even now that the world has moved on, I feel the pangs of my last memory with Toto. I am so blessed that our paths crossed in this lifetime, and I am certain our paths will cross again. I have her ashes, but I have not been able to look at them except when I received them. Silly of me, for I know she is not in the ashes any more than she is in her body. I feel her in my heart, and I miss her so. She helped save the young man who felt all alone in this vast cold world; she was God incarnate. As I write this, I am surprised at the avalanche of tears that have surfaced. I feel her here, next to Ozzie, cuddled in his lap, gazing at him with her adoration.

Teresita arrived at the perfect time, and as usual, those things in life that are meant to be require only an open heart and total trust in God's timing. I have experienced that even death, no matter how much I have wished it and prompted it, will not come a breath sooner than when the divine fancies it. Learning to live with unconditional love for all sentient beings, and accepting that death is always a breath away, allows me to be grateful for every microsecond of life. In the end, and I have been to many endings, love has always saved my soul from disintegrating into the opposite.

Teresita lived with a more equipped Ozzie than Toto did. She enabled the grief of Toto's death to be palatable. She was a godsend. She was a joy, and she would have been the smartest in the doggy prekinder, I am sure of that. Her attention span was that of a supremely enlightened Buddhist bodhisattva. As you will learn, I eventually had seven furry bodhisattvas that became my gurus. I have never felt the need to travel to an ashram to find enlightened beings, for they have all been provided in the exact time and space that the student in me has been suited to receive the ambrosia from the gods. Some people travel the world and the seven seas to escape, find, enjoy, relax, vacation, and disengage to and from themselves and their environment. God is here and now and will always be. What we are all at one point or another trying to escape travels with us as carry-on baggage—not even a worry it will be lost in the voyage. You can traverse to the outer limits, but you will only find yourself, joy and misery alike.

Jesus traveled on foot everywhere without missing the enlightenment inside himself. Some of us travel far and wide to learn that it has all been within our immediate possession. The longest and greatest journey to undertake is the exploration toward the inner true self. This is the longest and perhaps the toughest journey, yet it is the most fruitful one. Every road leads to ourselves, and how we choose to travel depends on our free will or lack of it. I have learned in my life that doing my part with the best intentions is pivotal in my journey. Feeling every feeling, denying no human emotion, and spreading seeds of love gave me a Garden of Eden that no foreign expedition could have supplied. Any form of awakening I have experienced has required an inner voyage. This is not to say that a good trip to Bangladesh couldn't give me a tool toward self-realization, but this is to say that I am wherever I find myself, and that is here, right here and right now.

Teresita was a dear, sweet creature. As much as she could focus, she could play. When she wanted to play, it was: "Run after me, Daddy, or I will run after you!" I had the energy and the desire to please her, for I was young, and no matter how the world had tried to defeat my spirit, I stood up like Black Beauty and galloped happily. One night, I wanted to draw her in pencil, and I thought, *play with her a bit, then she will tire, and you can draw her*. Oh boy, was I ever wrong! The moment Daddy picked up his pad and pencil, something in her went extremely eccentric and funky; she knew her royal portrait was about to be made, and she wanted no part in it. I am an abstract painter, and I do not care for drawings, but the few times I have been inspired to draw, the inspiration was always powerful, and this was one of those few times.

I followed her around the house with the pencil and pad as she played catch-me-if-you-can! It was so much fun; it was the most fun I have ever had doing a drawing. I crawled on the floor, jumping on furniture right behind her, running from her as she wanted to pick on Daddy's ankles, all the while trying to get her essence in a good drawing. I laughed out loud and wondered how mad I would have looked to any outsider peeking in. I am glad I persevered because it is the most authentic drawing I have ever done under the most laborious circumstances. If I remember correctly, there were times I was drawing upside down!

My home was slowly but surely blooming, as was my garden. My soul required much more tending, but it was nearing the light, and Teresita's joy was a very needed ingredient.

Teresita and I fully enjoyed our borrowed territory. She was curiouser and curiouser like Alice in Wonderland. She was flourishing into a respectable young lady, and the car was a new discovery that became the extension of our home. She cherished the drives in Daddy's brand-new German convertible. During our rides, she would extend her proud little body as far out the window as Daddy would let her. Her majestic and assertive posture spoke to the world in identifiable terms; she was the main bitch, and I was her leading man. The world was a banquet, and we were bombarding it with boastful self-confidence. We drank out of the golden chalice; we had found the holy grail. The air exuded the fragrance of love; it was a new day. What a pair we made, just the two of us. I was Charlie Brown, and she was Snoopy; I was Mary, and she was my little lamb. When one door closes, another one opens—"*Dios nunca nos abandona, Osvaldito,*" as my mother would say: "God never abandons us."

Weekends came, and weekends went. Sometimes I drove her around with the top down, and sometimes not. Teresita loved feeling the breeze on her face during our adventures. Our field trips next to the wide oceans of the Florida Keys, the glaring summer sun, and the arrival of hope gave us fuel for all eternity. We drove, boundless, with this new recipe I had concocted. I had baked the cake, and I had not left it out in the rain. These rides needed no added ingredients. Her childhood was my childhood. I was being given another chance at happiness. We start over every day, with every breath. Life is constant change; the secret is that there are no secrets. The only secret I have learned is to surrender it all and allow the next chapter to become the story it was always meant to be. Everyone's story is already written in the archives of heaven.

***

The limitless soul is ageless. Every soul has a purpose; everybody under and above the ground has an individual meaning for us to discern. Giving up, surrendering, in the sense that I have come to understand it, means to begin again. Where one was born, where one wants to go, where one is, none of this is as important as how we tender our hearts and the hearts of all sentient beings. Letting go for me means having faith, trusting, hoping, having confidence, changing attitude, taking a breather, a step, doing what I do with love and then, with the confidence of a skydiver, I let go and let God in, knowing I have the best parachute in all of creation. It is not even over on our last breath; it is yet another beginning. Life is a round of circles; you are always due for a new beginning.

I had my first art exhibit at a time when most people would call it quits. I decided to expose my voice at a time when most people are thinking of retiring. It isn't over until our last breath, and even then, it's about another transition, perhaps our most spiritual and blissful one. Every morning is a new beginning, even if just to sit and watch the blue jays do their happy dance. Everyone has a lost and found story; we are the heroes. Everything personal is universal, and everything universal is personal. I was never alone; even amid my most severe pain, I have always been in the best of company.

All the grand masters that have come before are my teachers: Jesus, Buddha, Muhammad, the poets, the writers, the butterflies, the rebels, the philosophers, the gods, and God. The best of all my teachers are those who have betrayed me, hurt me, and taken from me savagely; those have been the most sacred angels. They have all pointed to a new beginning, a new cycle. What was meant to denigrate me, God used to boost me, make me stronger, and help me learn about myself. Ultimately, God used the vileness to teach me about self-love, courage, strength, and the meaning of the miracle in all life-forms, including my own. Nothing any man can do can break your destiny—nothing. Nothing ever truly ends; everything changes form, and all is oneness.

When my mother wisely gifted me Teresita, she told me the story of the litter where she had come from. It was a sad one, meaning that no one wanted the mutts, and those who did take one would eventually abandon them. Teresita and I were among the lucky ones. For every Teresita in a brand-new German convertible with her daddy, there are too many more in cages of abandonment. For every Ozzie opportunity to create a home, there are too many more homeless in our wide, abundant world.

Here, I'll talk about manifestation. When the family did not take me up on the offer to spay Teresita's mom, I knew there would be another litter soon, and if there was another litter, I would undoubtedly take another Teresita, which would be white. Lo and behold, a year later, my phone rang, and my mother said, "*No saben que van hacer con todos los perritos.*" "They do not know what to do with the puppies!" I already knew there would be a white female, and I would adopt her as a companion for my little girl.

I went to see the newly born litter and held the smallest puppy I have ever held in the palm of my hand. When I held her, I felt her soul, which was like holding air itself. Of course, God had another plan. I told the patriarch of this family I would take this white angel and that I would wait until the time was right to wean her away from her mommy. I kept abreast of her development for weeks and prepared Teresita for her arrival. Teddy may not have understood my verbal language, but I assure you that she understood the language of the heart.

The day came to pick up the white angel, and this was when God threw more dice. It was challenging to walk into the place and see all these puppies in a cardboard box; most had no destination and little destiny. Not unlike preparing Teresita, I prepared myself. I was going to walk in and take the little soul as expeditiously as possible.

What happened next was unexpected. The moment I walked into the hot and humid crowded garage with the cardboard box full of puppies, a small ball of fur jumped out of the box and came running over to me. She was all fur, pleading at me with all her little might to pick her up. This part was a nightmare. Between the hot air, the foul stench, and the cries of all the puppies, this little helpless ball of fur begged to be rescued. I had planned to take the chosen one and run out, but I did the inevitable and picked her up. She licked my face in a frenzy, and she cried, and I could hear her distress loud and clear. My heart was breaking, and I couldn't be a deserter of my committed chosen one, but I had not planned on three dogs! I did not know what to do. Again, not unlike my father, I made a quick decision.

"I'll take this one," I heard my voice saying. Who said that? I was surprised to hear my own voice out loud, making such a drastic decision in microseconds! I needed an escape fast, so this bouncy fur ball came home rather than the chosen one. It was Sophie's choice in real life, not that Sophie really had a choice. It was a no-win situation for Meryl Streep's character in the movie *Sophie's Choice*.

We came home, the courageous furry ball and me, and she was a stunning puppy. As lively as she had been in the stinky garage, she became very mature once she arrived at Campina. Teresita received the new stork delivery gracefully, just as I knew she would. She was a perfect older sibling, giving the fur ball her space but giving her love and affection as well. It was endearing to watch Teresita lick her little sister with the gentlest of strokes from her little tongue.

Although Teresita and the fur ball had sprouted from the same mother and father, that was where the similarity ended. Teresita was very much a terrier, and the fur ball resulted in being very much a shih tzu. A few weeks passed, and the shih tzu fur ball had no name. I thought she was so prissy in looks that I should give her a formidable reputation to bewilder any would-be bandit, and I called her Cujo. *Cujo* is a film about a dog who gets rabies and becomes awfully mean, and, yes, Cujo was fitting! Cujo was the most loving and adorable little ball of hair whose only menace to ward off any predators would be her name.

My phone rang. "*Nadie quiere la primera perrita que escojite.*" The voice on the other end was my mom: "No one wants the first dog you chose." It had been over a month, and I had prayed for a good home for that angel I had held in the palm of my hand. I learned later that she was the runt of the litter. The good news was that they were able to give all the other puppies away, except for the one I believed I had manifested. Instinctively, I had a "knowing": *I'll take her, Mami.* This knowing I feel I have is a gift and a curse. For as long as I can remember, some moments have come from deep within me and defied any reason or logic.

This is the first time I have admitted this to anyone other than my soulmate and mother.

My mother told me a story that I vaguely recollect. When I was around the age of four, she took me to a big celebration in a home owned by a bourgeois Cuban family. The house was crowded with the Cuban tribe. It was a scattered party, and people congregated in every corner of the middle-class Little Havana home. Many of the Cuban diaspora that flourished in Miami in the early days of immigrating settled in an area that would be known as Little Havana because of the concentrations of salsa and merengue that inhabited its arteries. There was Cuban music and Cuban food, and then there was Osvaldito. As if by magic, Osvaldito sat on the kitchen floor and told people their fortunes. Suddenly, the music ceased, and the congregation was in the kitchen. What was I saying? What was I doing?

"*Mi hijo todo el mundo estaba escuchandote.*" My mother told me that she genuinely did not know why people were listening to me, but the party came to a standstill. Mami was bemused with this four-year-old boy sitting in a Buddha position on a cold *piso de granito* (granite floor). I remember a party, sitting on the floor, and saying things that my vocal cords orchestrated into a sort of language. That's it.

Was this some prognostication of the knowing that I later began to slowly recognize as a spiritual messenger? I do not know, and it's OK not to know, for not knowing allows me the openness to know more. I believe we all have the power to know beyond the reality that comes into our conscious awareness. I believe in a force that defies all reason and logic. Personally, the knowing is not something I choose or get to control or use in any way. If I did, I would have selected the big lottery numbers long ago. It's a knowing—when I flow with it without hesitation, then I am in the knowing. I believe children and animals have this. It can be called by many names, but not unlike the Tao, if you can name it, it's probably not it.

I can take care of three dogs; it's a lot, but I can do it! I said to myself, and I understood that the white angel I had held in my hand was meant to be with me. She chose her name by her very own personality: Raggedy Ann. Eventually, I ended up with seven precious gurus, all of which came into my life in God's unique gift wrapping. Each was a new beginning, like the day; with every beginning, there is an ending. Except for in matters of the heart, there is no end, and the heart does indeed go on. They all remain with me with their jovial wagging spirits.

I went to pick up the runt with elation and absolutely no trepidation. The number three, which eventually became the number seven, was to continue creating the meaning of the word "home." When I picked up Raggedy Ann, I was so euphoric with gratitude and happiness that I could hardly contain myself. God had created his miracle in his own way! I was meant to find Cujo's love, and I was meant to have the runts, the Wilbur in *Charlotte's Web*. God was showing me the laws of manifestation. Like the Doorknob told Alice in Wonderland, things may be impassable, but nothing is impossible. If you believe this, then all possibilities are wide open to being possible.

Raggedy Ann came to join Cujo and Teresita. Teresita immediately took a liking to Raggedy. Perhaps she felt her runtiness—or perhaps blood is indeed thicker than water. Whatever the case may be, Teresita became a wonderful big sister to both Cujo and Raggedy Ann.

CHAPTER 4

How did I come up with the name for Raggedy Ann? It was easy! Her nature was one of being disheveled. Her hair was wooly and wild: She was Keena. Her hair remained unmanageable all her doggy life, and she liked it. No matter how much I tried to keep it neat, she wouldn't have it. Several adjectives were befitting right from the start because her personality was unique. Before I go on, I must make the emphatic admission: She was a beautiful white-haired mix of a terrier with bright hazel and often green eyes. Her eyes changed with the day's lighting and her moods, but they always watched intensely.

Raggedy loved Cujo and Teresita from the start, and they all played wildly in Mother Earth's terrain. It was usually Raggedy who initiated the greyhound race around the farm; the Road Runner had nothing on her! As soon as she got to Campina, one of her ears was permanently flipped back, as if she purposefully wanted it combed away from her face. She had no vanity. She was not into fancy hairdos; she was Keena all right. This was to be one of her signature styles, for she had no interest in being in a beauty pageant of any sort. She was better at quiet observations, and she studied us in her mental lab. She was still one moment, and then she'd start out like the Road Runner in an instant—and her sisters would follow the leader. She was a trailblazer, a tomboy, a goth, a maverick, and a rebel without a cause.

"*Una muneca de trapo es lo que parece.*" "She looks like a rag doll," my mother told me, and instantly I thought, *Raggedy Ann!* Amazingly, she was the runt of the litter; amazingly, she did not become the alpha knowing that she could have, and amazingly, she was strength mixed with a severe dose of independence and vulnerability. Raggedy did not set out to be peculiar or distinguishable—she just was. She had the strength, the chutzpah, the extra X factor required to be the leader of the United Nations, but she was content to be left alone. She was Greta Garbo incarnate from the very start. She did not care to manage, coordinate, or dictate the lives of others; her own world was full enough for her. Her politics were simple: Don't cross the boundaries that dictated her freedom to be an individualist.

Being a leader was not on her list of priorities. She had many other to-dos that took precedence. For example, rolling in the wildest, muddiest strip of land on the farm was of the utmost priority to her soul. After spreading herself wild around the fields of the countryside, she allowed little wildflowers to adorn her hair as if she were going to San Francisco. She was the endless nature flower girl. Freedom was her goal. She despised dogmas and routines, she cared not for the populace or their theories, and she was her own religion. She had made up her mind while incubating her runtiness, and her mind told her to walk on the wild side of life without regrets. She feared no one, and she straddled her masculinity with the gusto of John Wayne. She flirted her femininity as blatantly as Mae West, and she never let you forget that she was a petite petunia, fragile and docile at her whims.

Many times, half of me wanted to cry because she did color so far outside the lines. The other half of me had to laugh out loud because she was as happy as an LSD hippie in the sixties on their way to Woodstock. Her adornments were nature, weeds, hay, and tiny sticks, which made her feel the glamour of the stars. She enjoyed the freedom of nature like her dad, and "perfection" was not a word that interested her. It was in her imperfection that she was most at home. Your judgment meant little to her—and your opinion even less. I have never met a creature more comfortable in her own fur than Ms. Raggedy Ann Amador.

Cujo admired Raggedy's individuality and followed Raggedy's lead. No matter how wild and crazy the expedition would be, Cujo followed unrestrained. I believe that it was then that she felt the most alive. Teddy was a boundary alpha and took this responsibility faithfully. She joined in the adventures, but she was the voice of reason. She remained faithful to her duties to the very end, a royal queen of true-blue blood if there ever was one. Cujo had a high doggy IQ, which made her susceptible to much anxiety. There is no doubt in my mind that she was genius material, but like a lot of true geniuses, she lacked self-confidence and suffered from depression and anxiety.

Raggedy gave Cujo the wild streak she could not bring herself to set free on her own. Watching Cujo and Raggedy play in the Wild West was like watching an old clip of *The Little Rascals*. Raggedy led Cujo to adventures and destinations that Cujo would have never dared venture into on her own. Cujo colored strictly within the lines; only with Raggedy did she dare splash paint in wonder as every child should have the chance to do. They say opposites attract, and Raggedy and Cujo were Laurel and Hardy, Fred Flintstone and Barney Rubble, and Thelma and Louise. Cujo knew she could do anything her little doggy mind set itself to do, but she was content to let Raggedy take the baton. I suppose Cujo wanted perfection, and following allowed her the liberty of not making any errors in the farmhouse.

Campina was buzzing with youth and playfulness— "my cup runneth over" was filled with magic from above. It was the oasis of the misfits, the runts, the fountain of the unpremeditated avant-garde. It was Austria's Bohemia in Coral Gables, the Renaissance of the Wild West. It was St. Francis without religion and Old McDonald's farm amid a torrential springtime. Campina was Ringling Bros. and Barnum & Bailey without the cages. It was the feeling of that first childhood field trip to the Museum of Science, where everything is a wonderment. The road to Oz was paved with balls of fur and radical tenderness. Home was near now, and the Tin Man needed nothing else, for his heart was expanding thoroughly, bursting at the seams with joy, emancipation at last. Osvaldito was learning of a new beginning that he had forgotten at the old lost and found. He was painting and playing in the scrubland, running around with the pack of rascals whose hearts allowed him to gain a sense of his lost innocence. We were certainly not in the land of the beasts any longer.

Eventually, the four-legged pack would include Teresita, Cujo, Raggedy Ann, Lusito, Little Man, Kika, and Blackie. The feathery part of the family would consist of my beloved cockatiels, Lola and Pancho, Junior Cockatiel (nicknamed CJ for Cockatiel Junior), and Freckles. The lovebirds were Junior (nicknamed LBJ for Love Bird Junior), Peachy, Miracle, and Sunshine. There were a few Lolas and a few Ponchos, due to the early demise of one or the other. Campina was brimming with life; if there were ever a funny farm and a happy time in my life, these would forever go down as the most joyful moments in the history of my world. The funny farm was a loving one full of God's heavenly beings, often funny and often tragic, but never empty of nature's own recyclable fuel: love.

I had an ongoing dialogue with nature, and nature responded with its unparalleled outburst language called "harvest." I had forgotten what it was like to be happy, and nature brought me back to life. I gave to the little abandoned piece of land, and it gave back exponentially. As you give, so shall you receive. I wanted time to stand still, but if there is such a thing as time, it does not obey anyone's command. I was good enough, and I was more than enough, but I had to let go of the darkness that spoke of self as a solitary entity in a vast ocean of separateness. The mask of loneliness was but only a mask among many others. All that was needed was to plant that mustard seed and the innocence of Osvaldito and paradise would be found. I learned that it was OK to have the tears of a clown, as long as I remembered that I also had the mask of Aphrodite: happiness and pleasure.

If I am lucky, I can retain the memories of those fleeting moments of exultation that give rise to hope. The short memories suffice for the obstinate anguish for which the pendulum of life trends with the winds of destiny. Home is where the heart is, and my heart was full of love. These memories I would plead to take with me upon departing this form; it is the only baggage I will claim at the checkout counter on my final voyage where every man is destined.

Man may have exited the Garden of Eden, but I am here to tell you that there is a return. My Eden had mockingbirds, blue jays, runts, and roaches. It was up to me to create or destroy. If I have learned anything at all from my creator, it is that I am often given the illusion of free will. It is then that, like my father, I choose to create rather than destroy. I choose to love rather than hate. I choose to nurture rather than kill. I must never forget that I am a mere mortal with a soul and that all my thoughts and actions should be filtered through the lens of love, the only conscientious lens that will ever suffice. I was learning to define a home. It had a geographical space called Campina, but what made it a home were the misfits inside who had been shunned by a world of perfectly square pegs. This was our time to walk boldly in the garden from which we had been expelled. There is no place like home, and I thank God my home is love, for it is a mansion transcending space and time.

Now that I have a voice, a hymn from the celestial sphere, I forget myself no longer. I am alive; I know my name. Like the ocean's waves, I sway gently, sometimes crashing, sometimes ending, but always flowing gracefully with the winds of change. Home is an open heart, ready to live again and again, an ocean of beingness. I was planted in the noble garden. I belong among the weeds and the gardenias; my aroma is earth.

CHAPTER 5

> *Do you know why this world is as bad as it is? [...] It is because people think only about their own business, and won't trouble themselves to stand up for the oppressed, nor bring the wrongdoers to light [...] My doctrine is this, that if we see cruelty or wrong that we have the power to stop, and do nothing, we make ourselves sharers in the guilt.*
>
> —Anna Sewell, Black Beauty

Garvenia was a private school paid for by an immigrant's hard-earned currency. It was not the first school I attended. My first day in kindergarten was in the public school system. It was traumatic. I have constructed the story of Osvaldito's first day in the garden of education.

Osvaldito was a pale, brown-eyed, beautiful little boy with full red lips and dark hair, a descendant of the ambiguous Spanish Mediterranean stock. He was the male version of Snow White. At home, he spoke Spanish and heard echoes of anger and hatred. Although unable to understand, and much less articulate, his feelings, he missed his mom and certainly his father. Not knowing who to turn to amid the storms, he felt orphaned.

On the first day of kindergarten, his grandmother walked him to school with a brown lunch bag. They arrived at a square cement building called kindergarten. Have you ever wondered why some schools look more like prison cells than cozy farm cottages? Perhaps someone missed the memo that schools should feel welcoming and not be square cement chambers that echo with the screams of an uncaring civilization.

The etymology of the word "kindergarten" is German: "*kinder*" meaning child and "*garten*" meaning garden. Children, like plants in a garden, should be carefully esteemed but most importantly loved. Teachers are the most trusted and treasured of gardeners, for never will there be a more profitable harvest than the tender offspring of humanity.

Sitting at the back of the classroom, Osvaldito understood little of his surroundings. The teacher, a giant woman, looked frightening, and he could not understand the noise coming from her mouth. Something about this stranger scared him, and when he was spoken to, he could not answer. He felt alienated in that land he would come to know well: terror land. Papers, crayons, and unidentifiable directions were given. Osvaldito was now in panic mode, understanding less and less.

What language was this, which this giant, right out of "Jack and the Beanstalk," spilled into the unfathomable congested air that enclosed my freedom? How was I to breathe freely with these voices whose code I could not decipher? What were the rules that the others so casually discerned? What was this predicament that had been laid forth upon my little intellect, which gushed such fear into my immature cellular structure? *Be still,* I told my freezing bones, *for you have sailed the turbulent dark seas of this matter before.*

Nothing lasts forever—or does it? *Shall I remain Sisyphus from kindergarten on?* my old insides asked. El viejito, the old man in me, questioned as he peeked through my young skin now full of bumps called goose: "What language speaks this giant?" From within the freezing bones of the celluloid spectacle, I had more fearful questions than a little boy could grasp to ask, much less untangle into mere reason. I was thinking my questions in the language of the Spanish conquistadores for which the state I had been flown to, Florida, had been named. How would I transfer my thoughts to this ancient code from the Anglo-Saxon tribe with which Shakespeare patented much of humanity's emotions? I knew none of the codes going on in my little brown head, or outside in that cold, blockish pirate ship that had abducted me to take me to exotic lands where I would never be found again.

The teacher was tall, rigid, and militarily brusque, giving orders expeditiously and expecting results, certainly not questions from a Cuban dwarf with hand-me-down galoshes from El Refugio. She grew taller and taller with every shortness of my breath. The mammoth made of steel was harshly passing orders unto me in vain, and I didn't know her language. One more look from her fiery eyes would melt me like supple flesh under spitting lava from the most wicked volcano. Fly away, my little legs. Become wings and be free. Rise up in arms to fight this windmill in the shape of the grotesque symbol of dryness, frigidity, and unearthly anomaly. Run until you can fly, feeling the air beneath you raising you up like the child of God that you are. Save your immortal soul from the stench of this witch's brew that is no gardener, indeed, but a foul fertilizer of the most innocent tribe: children.

I can remember this little boy's fear with unmistakable clarity. The one sure thing Osvaldito knew was that he needed to rush out of this prison before his heart popped out of his little chest. The pressure cooker inside my body was about to explode, but before I knew it, my body got up and flew away. Osvaldito grabbed the brown paper bag that contained his nourishment and ran out of the cluttered room like a true thoroughbred horse. Without any sense of direction, I ran, I cried, and I continued out of the field where the gardener was spreading foul manure. The streets were now full of a buzzing populace. Adrenalized, my terrorized little legs kept up the speed of light. Fight or flee, I chose freedom. I knew not what I was fighting or how to fight: A war had been declared, and I had not shot first.

If fear is instinctual, my instinct was in alarm mode. The scarce oxygen in my veins noted my desperation and prompted me to dash faster and forward. Like my mother, I did not look back. My palpitations were leather whips against my innocent soul. The whip holder was the gardener who inflicted spur straps, the all-too-conventional methods handed down for generations for the mere pleasure of the brainwashed who find enjoyment in these societal rituals against some of nature's most innocent sentient beings. I have never understood the slaughter of innocent lambs in religious contexts—or any animal for that matter. The God I know would never demand the sacrifice of life. Undoubtedly, humanity plays God at its whims and in the name of whatever god or gods they have been programmed to believe in. On the day that love and compassion become the only God, mortality rates will diminish drastically.

> *"There is no religion without love, and people may talk as much as they like about their religion, but if it does not teach them to be good and kind to man and beast, it is all a sham. "*
>
> —Anna Sewell

I do not remember how I returned to the clan, but I did. I hid outside the building where we were housed, trembling and hoping no one would ever find me. I had no plan. This was not well thought out; the only thing I knew was that I did not feel safe in that place they called "kindergarten." It looked like a prison, and the gardener's eyes resembled those of the racists I learned about later as an adult. The ones who march with white robes and spew hatred, and the community of Maycomb, Alabama, whose masks were painted on Sundays—and on Monday confronted Atticus to "kill the Negro." Hatred, like love, does not need words to feel it; one instinctively feels it. Every species under this circus canopy feels love and hate without the need for articulation or books of law.

After that first day, Osvaldito felt panic at the mention of the words "kindergarten," "school," or "teacher." He was taken back the next day, and this time, the giant in front of the class was more frightening than before. There was no peacemaking from the gardener, no softness opened in her; if anything, her nature became indignant, and her nostrils flared wider. She looked like a mean old dragon. Osvaldito never saw a smile from this gardener. Instead, Osvaldito felt a cold breeze, an arctic chill that shook his very foundation. Osvaldito was a gentle, kindhearted, shy little boy, and I am confident that if he had received some compassion and understanding, his fate would have been quite different. The labels from the beasts started immediately: "*No le gusta la escuela. Es un vago!*" At home, Osvaldito started to hear: "He is lazy, and he does not like school."

No one stopped to explore or ask why. No one troubled themselves to dig deeper or put themselves in this little boy's shoes. I did not understand English, for one, and I feared being abandoned as I had been so often before. I had been ripped from my father's arms, separated from my mother, and tormented by a drunken herd. I needed, at the very least, some love and compassion that would assure me that I would eventually understand the orders being given at the front of the icebox-shaped room. I needed to know I would be picked up and not left there as I had been left in so many strange places before. Perhaps this would have helped my anguish that built up with the lack of patience from the frigid giant called a teacher.

There was something wrong in this kindergarten, and perhaps there was something wrong in Osvaldito; most likely, there was something wrong with both. However, no one stopped long enough to delve deeper into these events that would shape the life of a little boy.

Leaving a child at school for the first time must be a devastating ordeal for any parent. Here is where our societal systems fail. We send humans to learn theories upon theories on education, much of which will benefit the teacher and the child, but where does the human variable come in? How can we make sure teachers are not just robots regurgitating theories? Unfortunately, I do not have the answers, but—as a society—we must put our money where our mouths are. If we preach from the pulpits, the capitols, and the PTA meetings that children are a priority, it is a principled matter that we find the answers. It all starts at the beginning, and a child is the very beginning of hope for humanity.

In my later years as a teacher, I observed this incapacity for tolerance and humanity by a small number of tired, restless, and neglected professionals whom the system had failed. In turn, they inadvertently failed the children. Life goes round in a circle, and I feel sorrow for the person who cannot see they will eventually end where it all begins and begin where it all ends.

The clan had found a scapegoat. Meanwhile, Osvaldito had started the journey toward the depth of his interior, a journey that would never cease. Every night, I cried. I asked for my mother, and was told I was "*un malcriado.*" Another label had begun; I was misbehaving when I asked for Mami. Not unlike what my mother was told when she cried, I was told the same and by the same monsters. By the age of six, I was lazy and ill-behaved, and I was not allowed to miss my mother. Meanwhile, I was clueless, but my insides hurt, and they never ceased hurting for decades to come. I was homeless, an orphan, and none of it was my war. I had no choice in the garden where I was planted. I was a mockingbird preyed on like a blue jay.

Can innocence be protected from its own tribe? Or is our own species the worst predator unto its own clan? Sadly, it is evident through history that our very own species, often those closest to us, harms not only the innocent but also all of nature. Man can be the most dangerous animal in all jungles, and it may have started when we believed we were the center of it all, made in the image of God. I believe this requires, at a minimum, revision.

If there were school counselors, I don't remember any. You can't teach empathy to any professional, but you can observe empathy or the lack thereof. A curriculum of inclusivity is currently being taught across the United States and, I am certain, around the globe. The world needs a radical revolution, and that revolution starts with self-love. If we are taught to hate or to avoid redirecting its energy appropriately, it will add to any Darwinian DNA we may have. On the other hand, if we are taught to walk in the moccasins of others, we may learn to alienate, or even irradicate, the deep-rooted sense of hatred that stems from fear and a lack of self-love.

This was at a time, with no counseling at school and no comfort at home, when you sank or swam. The next day was exactly like the one before, and I escaped school every chance I had. I was Houdini, the escape artist, and the school, the teacher, and the monsters at home began to get louder and louder. I still did not understand any of it. I was in fright mode all the time, and no one de-escalated my fear; they went out of their way to escalate it.

The solution was to transfer Osvaldito to a private school in Hialeah. There was going to be a move, and everything got discombobulated, but I held onto Blackie, a stray dog who became my best friend. The same dog who trembled in the bathroom when my grandfather took out his gun and pointed it at us without rhyme or reason—in a drunken stupor, I was to learn later. My brave little boy withstood it all, as did Blackie. Blackie and Osvaldito had done the unforgivable; she had peed on the terrazzo floor, and it was Osvaldito's fault because unknowingly he had allowed it. In Tata's police mentality, a good wave of a pistol, a stern yell at both Blackie and me, would prevent this incident from ever happening again. After the event, he sat down in his recliner and continued to drink his whiskey as though it were the most ordinary of days, watching an episode of *Bonanza*. Blackie and I went outside to hide under the wooden shed that was raised on bricks. We stayed there until we both felt saved by the earth itself.

Four things gave me comfort in those days when it seemed my innocence was being drained with every passing moment, and the thought of seeing my mother was at the top of the list. I knew Blackie loved me, and I could hold onto her when the rum and drums became too scary to withstand. There was my pacifier, which Freud would have had a field day analyzing since I couldn't give it up for many years to come. And then there were the cartoons, the colorful pixels that made it all magical and taught me much about colors, morality, and the language I learned to call English. Although I loved Teresa, she wanted little to do with her little brother. Teresa was, after all, fighting her own demons, and forming solidarity with her weakling brother was not her priority or in her best interest.

Every day, I was taken to school, and every day, I found new ways of escaping. I learned to hide under the houses that sat on top of bricks. In these crevices, I learned to find safety. If the drunken noise ever became too frightening, it was the dirt underneath, the land itself, that cuddled me into a warm embrace, assuring me the overground monsters could never reach the small spaces Blackie and I could fit snugly into. I learned to escape while the chaos of the cafeteria disregarded the roaches running around the crevices of the old school auditorium that served as the lunchroom. I learned to run like Black Beauty with blinders, looking only forward and at full speed. Later in my school career, or lack thereof, I won awards for running track because I was always the fastest kid in school. I wasted no manure; it all had become fertilizer.

The clan speeded up the move, and I knew I was not going to be attending that school anymore. I was told of the move and the new school, and on my last day of the Alcatraz called kindergarten with the monstrous dragon, I did not escape. I was happy, for I knew I would never have to see the fire flaring out from her nostrils ever again.

When I got back to the house, it was practically empty. A few boxes were scattered here and there, some empty, waiting to be filled, and others closed meticulously. I looked around; it was the first time I had seen what emptiness looked like outside of myself. I sauntered as if discovering a new territory never explored. With each step, the outer void united with the inner desolation, the hollowness of the internal was facing the blankness of the external. A ghostly feeling started to arise in me as I widened my eyes and suddenly realized that Blackie had not greeted me with her rambunctious joy. I was so perplexed at the emptiness, entering the rooms that now resembled a haunted house full of cobwebs in every corner, that I had forgotten my only comfortable ritual: Blackie's love as she welcomed me back. Something in me reluctantly awoke the awareness that Blackie was missing. A supersonic turbo blender was stirring up in me, making a puree of my feelings and any strength that kept me upright. "*Donde esta Blackie?*" I asked my paternal grandmother: "Where is Blackie?"

"Blackie was killed by a car," screeched her boisterous voice.

The sound of those words felt like the squeaking iron wheels of a runaway train flaring black coal smoke all over the empty living room. Her tone dug a hole inside me, filling my soul with the ghastly smoke from the black iron phantom locomotive making it hard to breathe. This was more painful than the soot from the flaring nostrils on the dragon at Alcatraz kindergarten, and my little body wanted to fly away once more, never to return to the land of the living. Instead, I darted in and out of each room in disbelief, crying out words meant to persuade the cruel audience of this tragedy that Blackie could not be gone. If I screamed Blackie's name loud enough, she would return, she would hear me, and she would run into the door with her joyful wagging tail welcoming me as she had done so many times before.

"*Donde esta Blackie?* Blackie! Blackie?" I called out for Blackie in pure desperation: "Blackie! Blackie! Where is my Blackie?"

I ran outside, I ran back inside, and I was like a hamster in a cage, rolling around in the same vicious wheel, not knowing where to go to stop the aching that immersed me without cessation. I screamed her name out with all my might: "*Blackie!*" I ran, and I called out her name. I cried with such agony that it made this memory one of those sepia-toned snapshots of my life that, unfortunately, I will never forget. I did not know where my best—my only—friend had gone. I did not know where to look for her, and I did not know the truth of what happened. I died that day, even if just a little.

The next thing I knew, I was on the lap of a teacher who put my little hands on his privates. I learned to be silent, and I learned that Blackie would never come back. I learned my grandmother had lied. Blackie hadn't run out and been killed; it would have been impossible for this to happen. Blackie was not allowed to go where the clan was moving, and as easily as God giveth, God takes it away. The dice had been thrown.

I eventually stopped crying when the well ran dry. I crashed, exhausted, that night with my nose and eyes full of mucus from my pain.

I think of Blackie often; I wish I could have saved her, and I wish I could have saved myself. I have paid that debt for years, thinking of my guilt, leaving Blackie, and not being able to save her. But, I did not know how. For years, I thought if I had never left Blackie with the clan, I would have been able to save her. I had shame as my attire, and it was the heaviest weight on a small child's bones. No words can ever express my loss that day; "sorry" is the sorriest word, and it often feels like the most incompetent of all of them. Later, I would learn from my mother that I was a very happy infant who never cried. She told me that during the time I spent with her in Cuba, she barely remembers me crying at all.

I never escaped from the next school where I was placed; I just quit. Something in me ended. I know this because this is the only memory I have of those days. Years later, in therapy, we tried everything to have me recover some of the gaps in my memory, but it was fruitless. These memories I write about are only faded photographs blurred by the kindness of time. Nothing more remains of those years: Osvaldito forgot his childhood. Innocence can be stolen, and it was.

"*Yo quiero hablar con mi mama.*" "I want to speak with my mother," I would say to my grandmother. My cousin would interfere with a burst of roaring laughter, and with eyes wide open, she would bellow, "*Tu no tienes mama! Ja ja ja ja!*" She was in her late teens when she dished out such evil: "You don't have a mother! Ha ha ha ha!"

There was never a scolding from either of my grandparents for her behavior toward me, but I knew she was wrong. I knew I had a beautiful mother who loved me, although I missed her and understood so little of the rationed time with her. In his *Confessions*, St. Augustine, named by many as one of the founding fathers of the Catholic faith, recalls a time in his book, a theological autobiography, when he stole pears for no other reason than the act of doing wrong for wrong's sake. This seemingly innate desire to do evil for evil's sake puzzled Augustine. Where does evil come from? What is its root? Why would a child of Reina's age want to hurt an innocent little boy who had done her no wrong? I do not know the answer, and I am glad. Reading St. Augustine helped me to reconcile myself with the frailty of my humanity and the divinity of God.

My imagination became my refuge. My refuge became the orange book with the black horse on the front that I did not know how to read. Anna Sewell had no idea of the many lives around the world that she would eventually touch, and she did this through her pain and her radical empathy. She never did get to live to witness any success of her book, but her home is now a charitable foundation—and horse sanctuaries have been established worldwide in her name. We can choose to destroy or create, and she chose to create. If evil exists, and it did in my world, so does the power of an all-loving God. It is we, through our consciences, that create this world or destroy it. Denying evil prolongs its existence; confronting it, at the very least, shows us our choices if we are courageous enough.

My homeroom teacher at Gavernia, not the monster who gave me stomach cramps, called my grandmother to let her know that I was a sweet little boy and behaved "perfectly perfect." He never talks, he never causes any disruptions, except that he does not do any work. He gazes out the window and often pretends to be paying attention, but in truth, he is far away. Something is wrong with his learning abilities, she said. Osvaldito must have some learning disabilities, and I suspect highly that if taken to a doctor, he would diagnose him and find the appropriate tools. Well, if this teacher thought she would get an unmitigated, sympathetic, allied response from my grandmother... If she were standing, she would have fallen flat on her ass at my grandmother's response.

"*Que mi nieto es estupido! Tu lo que eres es una mala maestra. Mi nieto no tiene que ir a ningun medico. Vete y aprende tu hacer mejor maestra.*"

Yes, that was my grandmother. She could turn from Satan to Mother Teresa and my biggest advocate all in a nanosecond: "Are you telling me my grandson is stupid? I'll tell you what this is about. You are a bad teacher. My grandson does not need any doctor. What you need is to go back to school and learn how to be a teacher."

I was moved again, on to my third school while still in the first grade. I do not know why the thought of a doctor insulted my grandmother and caused her to burst into evil flames. Perhaps, in her mind, it pointed some fingers, and someone was responsible for my lack of interest. Lord knows it couldn't be her fault! "De-Nile" is not just a river in Egypt, so I have learned. Denial can help save us from what we are not ready to see, and it can help destroy ourselves and others as well.

Another school meant little to me at this point. I had learned that the only use of school was time to draw and venture into my imagination. Besides, I had *Black Beauty*. I had made a pact with the horse on the cover: Yes, I secretly spoke to the animal kingdom early on. Blackie had understood me, and I knew for certain that Black Beauty on the cover did also. I spoke to Black Beauty on the cover, and Anna Sewell's spirit heard: "Osvaldito." Please, I asked him with the unquestionable faith of a child, let me read you! If he would let me read the secrets codified between the orange covers, I would love him forever—and I would take him with me on all my wild expeditions for the rest of my life!

I kept my promise, for Black Beauty is part of my skin. I was genuinely begging him to be my best friend; he was my childhood god, and my pleading was my prayer to the animal kingdom, the only world that had not hurt me. We could both escape to the Okeechobee Waterway and make a raft big enough for us to sail the narrow stretch of water going everywhere and nowhere, and like Huckleberry Finn, the vagabond child, and Jim, the enslaved person, we would find our own cosmos and visit E.T. and the rest of the Little Rascals. Thank you, Anna Sewell; thank you, Black Beauty; and thank you, God, for always showing up in the most unexpected ways—even in detergent promotions.

Another school, another label. Duck, sissy, *pato*, quack, and the beat of the relentless voices dissipated into my cloud made up of Blackie, Black Beauty, and all the farm animals in my make-believe Campina by the meadow. They were my temporary reprieve from cruelty. I was called these names gratuitously, for I never knew what I did to earn them. I soon figured that it meant I belonged in the girls' lines, that I was never to be picked to play on any team, and that I would be last. Even then, I had to endure the disgruntled team's acute complaining agonies, spiced with the type of hatred no child should ever voice or hear. "Where does this come from?" asked St. Augustine. As for me, I learned as much from evil as from its opposite. Often, much more from the opposite of love was granted than pure love itself. Who am I to question creation? I can only humbly hope to better myself and not stand at an altar condemning injustices for the sake of condemnation itself.

> *"And I kept seeking for an answer to the question: Where does evil come from? And I sought it in an evil way, and I did not see the evil in my own search. "*
>
> —**St. Augustine,** *Confessions*

Another school, and Osvaldito was lost in academics. What was the alphabet in English? What was addition? Why did they keep giving me spelling tests for words I could not pronounce? Why was I punished when others bullied me? Why was I so visible when my whole endeavor was to be invisible? Did I walk like a duck? Did I act like a girl? I never did figure any of that out. What I did know was that I caused repulsion wherever I landed exactly like the roach.

I came home to an angry grandmother who was obese and obsessed with food, and I often suffered the indignities of an enema because she demanded my bowels move at her whim. "*No, Abuela, no, por favor!*" "No, Grandmother, please, no!" I pleaded with her to relinquish the unnecessary, painful, ceremonial ritual of the enemas, but my pleas for mercy were rejected for years. The enemas were not necessary. It was a ritual that gave my grandmother and my cousin, who reigned like Bloody Mary, the consolation of feeling in control.

After the aforementioned events, if I looked at either my grandmother or my cousin in a way they might have perceived as disrespectful, it was sure to be off with my head! My head had already been chopped off at school, not just by my classmates but by the whole school! The hatred was rampant, and it spread like a wild forest fire. My only consolation was my imagination, and I soon found the perfect place: a small closet in the hallway that my grandmother was happy to have me disappear into at my very own leisure. It was glory for me because I was alone with all my thoughts without interruption from the madness outside. I had evolved from the underground space of Mother Earth to a narrow hallway closet aboveground. At last! Freedom! Thank God Almighty!

As a young man, I had no trouble coming out of the closet or going into it; it seemed to me that the closet was a symbolic place in my head that I could always disappear into and reappear when I was strong enough to face the masses, the paparazzi, the voyeurs, and the malicious Peeping Toms. I have never wanted to be famous because I know what an excess of attention can do to a psyche and a soul, not to mention a fragile heart. I like my alone time; I like my crawl space to think, write, and paint. It allows me that sacred communion with the spirits, to witness its energy and be fueled by it. Harper Lee, the writer of *To Kill a Mockingbird*, was a private person, according to some who knew her. She was a recluse and certainly did not welcome all the attention her Pulitzer Prize–winning book earned her.

According to the Library of Congress, *To Kill a Mockingbird* came second after the Bible as the most cited book ever. To paraphrase a quote from Ms. Harper Lee, I wouldn't want the kind of fame created by *To Kill a Mockingbird* for all the money in the world! What I have learned about Harper Lee is that she was an observer from early on. She loved her books and her privacy. I am not surprised, for it is my belief that those who have been relegated to the island of creation must have an extrasensory perception gene that requires a most controversial solitude. To this day, my solitude is required. I love people, and I love them best individually. I am not the most comfortable in crowds. Something is lost in the connection between human beings when we start to group. I prefer one on one, my dog, and the truth I seek, know, and hope for. I know I will never find truth on earth. It's very much the way I feel about abstraction and the techniques in my art; once I find a technique, I've lost everything. I will cease to explore, search, and reach; therefore, I stop evolving. My evolution requires constant revisions.

I cherished the phone calls from Mami. They were tapped, scrutinized, and negotiated by the Cuban Mafia, Abuela, but it did not matter. I still got to hear my mother's angelic voice. I always knew when it was Mami on the phone because my grandmother's voice would shift gears faster than a Ferrari, going from the Grinch to Andy Griffith's Aunt Bea's voice, from zero to sixty in less than a second.

"Mami!"

"*Mi hijito, voy a verte pronto. Estas comiendo bien?*" The most angelic voice on the other end of the phone asked if I was behaving and eating well, but most importantly she would be coming to see me soon!

The calls were always bittersweet. Yes, I got to hear her voice, but it only reminded me how much I missed her. Then there was the anticipation of a visit that often did not materialize. I often felt forgotten by Mami. I know today that Mami never forgot me; life forgot us, and she did the best with the memories she was able to salvage. Her love for me was relentless, and it shall always be. I feel her today as if she were here; the strength of her love for me was so powerful that it has enabled me to keep witnessing it in everything I am.

"*Este nino va hacer un basurero. No le gusta ninguna escuela! Ya no se que hacer con el!*" It never failed. My grandmother's relentless martyrdom voice: "This kid is going to be a trash man. I do not know what to do with him. He does not like any school!"

No, Abuela, I didn't like school! I didn't like being molested by an old man. I didn't like being called a faggot! I did not like being unpopular from the time I got on the bus to the time I got back off for being a sissy! I did not know my lines, my character, the role, the play, or the director. I did not sign up for this role, and you are all making me go through the most abhorrent audition, but I would inevitably gain the Oscar again and again because the fans of this tragicomedy loved to hate me. Time for another school! And another, and another. And the Oscar goes to…!

As a young man in therapy with Angelina, we both questioned precisely how many schools I had been to. I did some research with Miami-Dade County Public Schools, and according to their records, I attended sixteen schools from kindergarten to seventh grade. Of course, this did not include the two private schools, which brings the total to eighteen schools from kindergarten to seventh grade.

By the time I was in seventh grade, I did not know how to multiply, and I could barely add or subtract. I had and still have the worst grammar. I was sixteen years old, an embarrassment to all; the self-fulfilling prophecy had taken root and was now a full-fledged reality. Yet it was Black Beauty who opened his world to me, and he, my god, a black stallion's story written by a disabled girl, allowed me the privilege of entering the magical world of words. No one else heard my silence; everyone stood by watching the spectacle in amazement with binoculars, and they became witnesses to my own private holocaust. But they did nothing; they stood by as spectators of a horrific highway accident. Why watch, I have always asked myself, if you can't do a thing? Is it the horror that we enjoy? I certainly do not watch a horrendous reality and stand by idle. I prefer not to know—perhaps this is my blatant form of denial.

Anna Sewell, the author of *Black Beauty* (her only book), slipped and severely injured her ankles when she was fourteen, which kept her from being able to walk without crutches. Part of Ms. Sewell's blessing was to have had that extra-perceptive DNA that lovers of love seem to possess. This mystical sensitivity gene enabled her to recognize the nobility in the animal we call horse. Unable to walk, she used carriages to go back and forth in her small world. She was young, she was disabled, and she died way too soon, but while in this realm, she'd had the choice to destroy or create. She chose to create. Through her humane observation of the cruelty a human being can inflict on one of the strongest and most noble animals, she was used as an instrument by her higher power to save the lives of many Black Beauties, including Osvaldito. Ms. Sewell spread diamonds on the road toward love for those who came behind her and understood.

The first chapter of Ms. Sewell's genius work is "My Early Home." How fitting for Osvaldito, and what a monumental task it was to learn how to read in the privacy of my narrow closet in Abuela's long corridor. I was lucky enough to have a battery-powered flashlight that somehow landed on earth for my terrestrial cultivation. The whole endeavor was a covert operation, and strenuous, for it had to be done in hiding from the Cuban Hialeah Mafia (CHM). If my cousin were ever to see me, she would certainly make a mockery of my attempt to become literate.

At school, I wrote the sound of words even if I did not know how to write. I wrote what I knew, what I thought I knew, and what made the most sense to write, much like I am doing right now. I created my own combination of letters, which made up my own words to sound like what I heard the others read. Listening became essential in my silent world. I never dared speak or read them, for laughter and ridicule were sure to follow. Just like I had never dared to write for the same reasons. Besides, my goal was never to be seen or heard, and so the teachers, not unlike what I believed of Mami, often forgot me. Strangely enough, although my goal was to be invisible, it seemed that the more I tried to go unnoticed, the more the venom from the predators and bullies forced its way in. I always felt under threat from the cannibals, a.k.a. the bullies.

Being moved from school to school, I could never stay on one task long enough to learn anything of real value at school, but I learned, without a shadow of a doubt, that I was abhorred wherever my little shoes landed. I learned to observe and be invisible, and although I did not know it then, I was learning to be my own best friend. The real lesson I was learning was to trust in God. I was learning how to love myself regardless of what others said or did. If God stood with me, no one could hurt my spirit. My soul is God's territory.

I always thought trauma had to do with war veterans and severe disasters such as a tsunami or a genocide such as the Holocaust in the Second World War. Later in life, through much therapy, I learned that much of my life was lived through a traumatic lens. I always knew my life was less than normal, but I never actually thought of myself as a victim. It would have never occurred to me that neglect, verbal and physical abuse, sexual molestation, abandonment, and growing up in an alcoholic, violent household could be considered traumatic for a child. I am glad I did not see myself as a victim because it allowed me to believe that I could—and I did.

I eventually received a graduate degree with outstanding grades, I was accepted into a doctorate program, and I went on to make my dreams come true. None of it was easy, but I am proof that it can be done, and if you learn nothing else from this writing, I hope that no matter where you may find yourself, you will be inspired to know that nothing can stop you from finding self-love. My dreams were small, and I have gained much more than I dared ever dream. I encourage you to never stop reaching and to learn to find your own happiness: You will because you can. Never listen to the evil. If evil is splattered on you, and I assure you it will be, transform it into goodness; from my experience, this is a no-fail recipe.

One of my favorite words is "persistence." It means to stand fast, be firm: *persistir.* Those who persist in their endeavors against all odds arrive at something far beyond any worldly dream. It is my most unquestionable belief that we arrive at our very own force, power, essence, seed, origin, the spirit of our very own being: God. When you arrive at your true self, you are home. I know this from my own experience in this life-form. I have not achieved what I thought I was aiming for, but I have met, without a shadow of a doubt, the God in me. And this is priceless. In Ms. Lee's sentiments, not for all the gold in the world would I have missed the disguised gifts! Duchess, Black Beauty's mom, gave a universal message that was instilled in me from the womb: "I hope you will grow up gentle and good and never learn bad ways." I may not always have lived up to Duchess's words, but I have persisted and given it a darn good try—and I trust I will continue to do so for all eternity.

Slowly, very slowly, I learned how to read. No one, absolutely no one, knew about my love for words and for books. In my childhood,

I would find order forms for book clubs and encyclopedias in magazines. *Time* magazine even issued a western series that fit me perfectly since I love the open plains. In this series, I eventually learned about the plight of the American Indians, the courage of Geronimo, and the vanity in the rush for gold. There were Bible series that taught me about Solomon and his wisdom as well as slavery and the evils of empires. I ordered them all! It was then that I was truly a delinquent! "*Pero este nino es un delicuente. Mira como ordena libros sin pregunater, y total no sabe ni leer!*" Oh, my dear Abuela, how your words hurt me then, but how I have learned to forgive you for what you did not know: "This kid is a delinquent. He orders books without asking, and he does this without knowing how to read!"

The truth is that my grandmother was illiterate all her life, not even knowing how to sign her name. It was an embarrassment for her, and perhaps this was why she could never drive and why bitterness consumed her. Perhaps this was why she couldn't understand the need for books and perhaps why she did not realize the pain her words caused. Words had little meaning for her. Not unlike the illiterate ancients, an X signaled her name. I can't help but feel sorrow for this truth. Books must have been an alien and scary idea for her. I, on the other hand, had books and books, and every day, I understood more and more. I did not know how to add numbers or structure a sentence! Most importantly, I kept the secret of my literacy from all I knew, including the gardeners, for it was obscurity that meant the most to me.

I was shuffled around from my grandmothers to my aunts to some weekends with my mom, but I always carried a book with me. The adults thought I was pretender, never really recognizing the knowledge I had gained in the mail-order books that made me a delinquent! I have read *Black Beauty* as many times as I have watched *Out of Africa*, more than one hundred times! *Out of Africa*, with Meryl Streep and Robert Redford, is one of my all-time favorite films. Even as a kid, I loved movies.

Weekends with my mom were cryptic, uncertain, dubious, sad, horrendous, happy, exciting, enigmatic, and wonderful, and I wish I could remember more of them. Sometimes I learned on a Friday that Mami would pick me up the next day, and sometimes they didn't tell me until she was honking outside. When I knew she was picking me up, I could barely sleep that Friday night. I would pack all my favorite toys, which usually included a couple of Mattel cars and a couple of books. I would wait on Saturday for a vehicle to drive up with the most beautiful woman in the world, my mom. Some Saturdays, I waited longer and longer till it was dusk, but I never gave up my optimism—I couldn't. Some Saturdays, after sunset, the phone would ring to let my grandmother know that she would not be able to make it, and that empty feeling of the dark clouds hovering and enveloping me came over, disallowing any luminous sign of hope. She had forgotten me again; life had interfered again.

When my mother picked me up on Saturdays, I was brought back on Sunday. It must have been gut-wrenching for my mother to leave me in such a frantic crying state, but she did. My grandmother would start at me as soon as my mother dropped me off. "*Que le pasa al mariconcito llorrando como una ninita? Este nino va hacer maricon. No llores mas cono que los hombres no lloran.*" I barely heard her words, but I felt her disgust: "What's wrong with the little faggot, crying like a little girl? I think this kid is going to be a faggot."

The weekends I was shuffled to my Aunt Daniela's house was another arroz con mango, or wild mix! My aunt, my uncle, my cousin Marlon in his late teens, and my cousin Josefina and her husband were all alcoholics living under one roof. The beasts started drinking on Friday after work and did not stop all weekend long. Often, it was fun because I had no bullying from the beasts when they were passed out! Frequently, there were ruthless brawls that included the police and arrests for domestic violence—or just a nuisance to the whole of Hialeah. There were times I did not eat for days except what I could grab from the half-empty refrigerator: rotten fruit or rice and beans with mold growing on it. My favorite was always the leftover pizza—with mold and all. Eating was a triviality that interrupted the really important things, like drinking alcohol.

These formative years were so full of contradictions that I can barely summarize the few memories I have been able to retain. By now, I was "a maricon," "lazy," and a "delinquent," and I was damned in every way a person could be damned. Amid all the chaos, there was Jesus Christ, the Catholic Church, my First Communion, and hell, which I learned unequivocally was to be my destination. My beloved therapist always called me a miracle to have survived the environment from which I came, and most importantly, I did not become like them. I was not always free of bitterness and anger, but I persisted against it because I knew what it did to the beasts. This was their gift in disguise, they showed me without a doubt what I did not want to be under any circumstance.

I was learning, without a shadow of a doubt, that I did not want to be like the people surrounding me. I was a keen observer and a listener, and I was graced with the knowledge that I had to be the opposite of what the world was showing me. I knew the opposite existed because I saw it on TV, and now, well, now I had books! I read a book by Temple Grandin called *Animals in Translation.* It is a pivotal book for animal lovers and those I believe who have that extra DNA. In it, she writes about how some people seem to see everything. What I have learned from my own life experience, my therapy, and the little research I have dabbled in is this: Some of us have been called hypervigilant, and some of us have been called highly intuitive, creative, and/or even highly spiritual beings. Some of us believe we can talk to animals like Dr. Doolittle. None of the labels or findings surprise me because there must be exceptional traits that are developed to survive the seemingly unsurvivable. Reading and colors were the mediums that God used to save my life.

Our free will, our conscience, is a gift, a tool for our lessons in this world. I believe that part of the measuring staff to enter the kingdom of heaven is our conscience and, most importantly, our hearts. Be careful with injustice. Be careful even witnessing it and remaining silent. God's eyes see our hearts, our intentions, and our actions. Ms. Anna Sewell saw those injustices in her world and set out to write for the adults who mistreated these animals. Ms. Sewell never intended for her book to be for children; she wanted to cure the world of a frightening evil. Using the gift of her creative DNA, Ms. Sewell wrote about what it was like to live a day in a horse's world. Her book was written in many voices but mainly in the voice of the horses, especially Black Beauty.

What force set Osvaldito's heart into motion to desire Ms. Sewell's book that day at the Grand Union? Some may call this coincidence, fate, or free will, and the most cynical will call it good advertising. I call it the spirit of God calling out to a child who was an orphan under the dreariest circumstances. It was this book that opened the world of literature to Osvaldito. All it takes is a mustard seed and the innocence of a child, and you have the keys to paradise. I have forgiven everyone, and I am grateful to God Almighty that I did not become like them.

My entrance exam to college surprised the counselor administering the exam. In her words: "I have never seen such a disproportion between reading comprehension and all your other subject scores. Your reading comprehension is at the genius level, while all the others are extremely low." Then she said with wide-eyed amazement, "I would like to know how this is possible."

I smiled and replied with five words: "*Black Beauty* by Anna Sewell."

"He who fights with monsters should look to it that he himself does not become a monster."

—Friedrich Nietzsche, *Beyond Good and Evil*

CHAPTER 6

Before getting to my mother's house, I would always think of her on the porch or even on the street, sweeping. She had a light way of sweeping, as if removing the dirt were not as important as moving the broom over the ground. Her way of sweeping was symbolic; so airy, so fragile, with a broom she tried to sweep away all the horrors, all the loneliness, all the misery that had accompanied her all her life.

—Reinaldo Arenas, *Before Night Falls*

From the moment I entered my mother's womb, much had been decided about the man I would become. In an instant in time and space, a seemingly random act occurred. The seed of what would become this writer entered the fertile womb of a woman who would continue to give life to the man I call *self* beyond the miracle of my birth. My mother's womb carries a rich memory that is embedded in every cell of my being. That same matrix continues to nourish my soul and will continue to be a main source of light in my life.

What I have missed the most in my life, without a doubt, is having more time with my mother. Regardless of our trials and tribulations, and there were many, our love was the most genuine I have ever known. God has been kind, for most of my dreadful childhood memories have eroded, faded, and remain unattainable, buried deep within an unreachable, sealed coffin. Those that remain are softly worn, distorted enough to dull their sting. The good memories are treasured and sprinkled with a romanticism known only to poets and the innocence of children. My mother is a watercolor, a Georgia O'Keeffe orchid watercolor painting from a bygone era, a fragile and elusive figure with an omnipotent voice within my psyche. Her darkness was acute, bitter, and thieving. All is bittersweet, but all is mine to choose. The more I reconcile with my demons, the more the goddess transmutes into a mere mortal, and all is forgiven.

One of the masters of Impressionism had blurred vision, but it was his vision and his alone to choose. Claude Monet chose to keep what was his rather than ameliorate his vision, risking what he chose to see. He had glaucoma and refused to have an operation. He created beauty with his vision, and he used what could have been the death of an artist to create for the world. We see what we choose to see, what we want to see, and what it's best for us to see. We can use manure to create a garden or to bury us alive; it's all in our attitude with a pinch of faith. In Calixto's paintings, dark versus light unites to create the original, true spirit that lies beneath the forms of appearances. You were right, Mami. I have learned much with my art. There is no light without darkness and no darkness without light; this is my mother, a yin and yang painting, a monochromatic kaleidoscope, Pablo Picasso's very own Blue Period.

My mother was always in a hurry. I remember her in her young years as a beautiful creature who was a magnet for the males of our species. I did not understand it then, but she attracted many women into her circle as well. She moved in and out of artist circles, and fluidity was a staple in our lives. As a child, I perceived her as a goddess; she was bigger than life itself. She was the Rita Hayworth of the Cuban hood, the Marilyn Monroe of my father, and the Joan Crawford of my bittersweet memories. There was never a more beautiful woman for a son than Marta Virginia Amador Alvarez. I idolized the goddess whose swagger put Marilyn's walk to shame.

The woman was the queen of femininity with the courage of kings. She moved deliberately, with a mission, through winding roads leading nowhere. She was in a hurry, preoccupied with survival. She kept moving so as not to think; she fled so as not to find her truth. She missed out on my first everything: my first birthday, my first day at school, my First Communion, and all my important firsts in life except my birth. She had little time to be in one place; she was to be everywhere and nowhere simultaneously. She was a goddess for Osvaldito and for those who admired her jovial spirit in the beautiful shell provided by Mother Nature.

I can remember the good times well, for no one knew how to fashion a good time better than my mother. It seemed to me that she brought the good times wherever she went. It was her spirit or my vision, but the combination of her spirit and my vision made for some unforgettable, rich times that I treasure. I enjoyed watching the seas parting when we approached a Cuban café stand for Mami to buy a *café Cubano.* There is no denying my sense of pride in observing the power of my mother's allure. Mami never paid for *café Cubanos* or *pastelitos de guayaba* for me, and I always ended up with a nickel from some passing stranger who admired Mami and hoped to gain even a second of her attention, but since Mami was always in a hurry, no one got more than a *gracias.*

Leaving the café, swaggering her hips from east to west, she left traces of salivating men magnetized by her delicate strength. This was an ordinary scene no matter where we landed. Mami was blessed by a deluge of womanhood, and she carried it with a power that exuded mastery in the art of seduction. It was not so much in the surface of her looks—or even in her authentic charisma—it was in the God-given gift of having been born a full-fledged woman with a capital W. The island of Cuba came abroad with my mother; it was in her curvature, her shiny black hair, plump lips, hips made of merengue, and in the aroma of Varadero's beach spreading warmth and cool palm breezes simultaneously. Like the best-tasting ice cream from La Habana's Coppelia, creamy in texture, and soft and cool to the soul, once glanced at, she would never let you forget that power comes in many forms. She was all of her ancestry combined in one eminence, from the Canary Islands to the mightiest river in Cuba: the Toa. She left Cuba, but Cuba came flowing in the figure of a "Maja," the very goddess of all springs.

The few times my mother went to my school and was seen by all, I hated it with all my heart and soul. Oh, why couldn't Mami look like all the other moms? No, it was the seventies, and Mami wore tube tops, tight polyester pants with huge bell-bottoms, her signature six-inch platform heels, and her big round earrings like those on *Soul Train*. She had a seventies Farrah Fawcett hairdo with waves that moved in the exact motion of her swagger. A melody followed her wherever she went, which alienated some of the females of the species and made baboons of the males, young and old alike. Like Mrs. Johnson in *Harper Valley PTA*, a Barbara Eden with her Charlie perfume and full, red Angelina Jolie lips. She wore imitation Jackie Kennedy sunglasses bought at the local five-and-dime store. She would have made a great Madame Bovary—except she was not given the relatively good fortune to choose.

There she was, walking into the cafeteria in the middle of lunchtime rush hour, and the whole commissary, teachers not excluded, had their wide eyes bulging out of their sockets toward the sashaying, voluptuous Cuban goddess bringing me a lunch bag. I wanted to die there and then; it would have been preferable at the time if the earth had swallowed me whole. I was not ashamed of my mother's beauty. It was the magnetic attention she received everywhere her heels hit the ground that overwhelmed me. I wanted invisibility, and Mami could never be invisible. It's ridiculous to see eight-year-old boys drooling over your mom. But, worse, this was the only time I got the slightest positive attention from any member of elementary academia. "Is that your mom? Wow, she is hot! How did you get a mom like that?"

"*Coje, Osvaldito, se te olvido el amuerzo. Comete lo todo. Te quiero mucho.*" "Here, Osvaldito, you left your lunch. Eat it all. I love you."

My white skin became flushed and rosy with a big mark of lipstick right in the middle of my chunky cheek. As she sashayed in, she would sashay out. Henry M. Flagler Elementary would never be the same again. The decibels in the school cafeteria rose with her entrance and exit. It was a Super Bowl wave in the audible world that day at H. M. Flagler, the school named after the railroad entrepreneur who brought salvation to commerce and tourism in Florida.

The weekends with Mami consisted of spending Saturdays under the care of Teresa or accompanying Mami to her new career when she graduated with honors from beauty school. Who else but the Cuban hood diva herself could transform a plain Jane into a ravishing Barbarella? Mami, of course! The beauty salon was glamour, a backstage at a Broadway theater with costumes and set decorators all combined under a two-thousand-square-foot plush New York Studio 54–style hair salon. Mami worked at the salon that catered to the Mercedes-Benzes and Rolls-Royces of the time. Her fellow actors adored Osvaldito, and, well, what else can Osvaldito do than adore them back? It was Donna Summers in the background, silk tapestries, glitter disco balls, hair spray, and overbooked frenzies that made for tempestuous artistry. Everywhere I looked, there were mirrored walls of Cinderellas in the making. The Saturday crowd was always adrenalized as they got ready for their evening passions.

The beauty salon was a world of its own, and it was not just the obvious glamour that intrigued me. It was the drama. Every woman had a story, a plain Jane, a Bardot, or even a Julia Roberts in *Pretty Woman* being transformed by new wealth. They all had a particular demeanor, a scent, and I knew without a shadow of a doubt who the influential powerful patrons were. These commanding devotees of the Warren Beatty look-alike hairstylist in the film *Shampoo* freely expose half their breasts in the pink satin robes provided by the backstage crew. Their skin was fluorescent regardless of the color. Their ice-cube-sized diamonds were carried loosely, freely, without a concern for the other half of the population, which their iceberg diamond could had fed. Their toes and nails had the appearance of always being freshly done—with a wet gloss that could pierce someone's eyes. They gave the appearance of shallowness and aloofness, but I knew that underneath the lustrous nail polish and gorgeous skin, a tiger had crawled on bare knees through the Amazon jungle to park her Jaguar at the very front of the red-carpet entrance.

It was exciting to be part of this crowd—well, the observer of the crowd anyway. Every childhood place I journeyed through had its unique quality; it was as if time and space had an individual characteristic that was condensed in my senses. The aesthetic salon was always a joyride for Osvaldito because he got to see, hear, smell, and learn the stories that would fill his imagination with significant leverage in the gloomy times. It was good to know that there was another world far away from the ordinary madness of the beasts. Yes, indeed, perhaps there was some madness in the climactic profusion of characters in the salon, but it was an artistic madness full of vibrant colors and explosive personalities amid the grasp of creation and not destruction.

Most of these women were strong and unashamed of their multiple personalities. One minute, a roaring laughter, and the next, a sorrowful cry—all in the name of love. "How could he? How could he do this to me? Tell me, Angelou. I do everything for that man!" One tear rolled ever so slowly down her pancaked makeup cheeks. The next moment, before the tear got to her glossy red lips, she would be roaring with laughter at Angelou's suggestion to let him go without! "Yes, Angelou! I will let him go without until next week—that will teach him!"

There were of course the magicians, the main stars in the crowd, and these were the beautiful gay men who could create a coiffure, a beehive, for any occasion. They had the fanatics, the Anne Bancrofts—you know, Mrs. Robinson trying to seduce the wild, youthful, muscular gay hairstylist in tight jeans. These men were adored, hugged, kissed, given lavish gifts, and told the deepest secrets that filled the heads under pounds of Paul Mitchell hair spray. Unlike the strong women at the salon, these men had dramatics that could fill an opera house and bring the place to a standing ovation. I pretended to read, and I often was able to read a few sentences in between the more intriguing scenarios in front of me. It was difficult to focus on the Wild West stories in my book when the wild Miami real stories of the rich and famous were in living color on stage—and I had front row seats. A side note, but an extremely important one, not one of the gay men that Osvaldito got to know as a child treated him inappropriately.

On Sundays, Mami would take me to McDonald's, and then we would go to San Juan Bosco, the Catholic church named after the priest who had a special mission with children, orphans, and the underprivileged. The church was located on Flagler Street and was dimly lit, and Mami told me that it was God's house and that I had to be very respectful while in there. I felt his presence as a child; he was watching me. I had to sit correctly and stand up straight, and I could not be bored even if I had to fight the stubborn yawns with all my might. When the others closed their eyes to pray, I peeked, wondering if God could see me peeking. I don't think he minded very much, for no lightning hit San Juan Bosco while we were there—and the building never crumbled on us because of my deviant peeking.

After church, there were times I got to go to the Tamiami Trail, or Calle Ocho, and ride ponies that went around in circles. I even got to pet the ponies and feed them. Often, Mami took us to the beach, Crandon Park in Key Biscayne, and I got to play, building sandcastles under the watchful eye of the person I loved the most in this entire world. My mother loved music, and on some auspicious occasions, I got to see live, in-person concerts with some of the most outstanding Spanish singers of the time: Raphael, Olga Guillot, Julio Iglesias, La Lupe, Celia Cruz, and The Miami Sound Machine before it was even a band! I became exposed to the kind of music I can appreciate today and danced to as a child.

There is a funny story my mother liked to talk about the day we went to see Olga Guillot in concert. Olga Guillot was a Cuban singer who had left Cuba, opposing the Communist regime, and became known worldwide for her beautiful ballads. She was a beautiful, strong, and prideful Black woman who made no efforts to hide her dislike toward the Castro regime. On a concert tour in Europe, she learned that one of Castro's men was in the audience, and she refused to come onstage until he was removed.

That same beautiful and proud woman called me onto her stage. Yes, she would discard the oppressors and invite the innocent onto her stage. My mother owned every one of her LPs, and we sang along to Raphael's songs and Olga's songs. I knew the words to all the music she could afford to buy. I barely remember the day, but I remember dancing onstage with Olga Guillot. The story goes that we went to the concert, and we were very close to the stage, and when Olga Guillot noticed me dancing and singing to her music, she signaled me to come up onto the stage. To my mother's surprise, I went up very willingly and started dancing next to my idol from the covers of the LPs!

My mother had a passion for the universal language of music. If a singer came to town, she would sacrifice her meager factory pay to take me. She could play the piano by ear, and she wrote songs. She had an angelic voice. She was a true artist, and she created her own world and survived on her imagination—like mother, like son.

My mother tried relentlessly to make the best of the new world and forget the world she had left so far behind. She could not afford feelings and memories. My father's last words at the crossing echoed: "*No mires hacia atras.*" Don't look back. The memories of my father's guayaberas, her last Cuban coffee in her mother's humble kitchen, the streets of La Habana Vieja, *El Malecón* with its crashing waves where she spent so much of her youth with silly girl's dreams, her roots, her father whom she adored, her siblings, her heart, her firstborn, and her very own Campina were best left buried deep in the catacombs of forgetfulness.

My mother left Cuba believing she would return. As with most Cubans who left in the early days of the revolution, everyone believed the malady would be temporary—and they would all be back where they belonged. José Martí's verses would not be silenced by the grotesque scream of Communism. The fortress of El Malecón, built by America, would withstand any temporary tides of a distorted revolution. The Cuban people's dreams, hopes, and passions were more potent than a wall made of sea. My mother left Cuba in 1966, and she never returned. As I write this, the wall that separates the Cuban people from freedom remains. The wall that silences its people is as strong today as it was in 1966. There are now new generations that know nothing else other than a dictatorship and Communism.

The Cuban youth have been brought up to believe that the United States is their enemy. Democracy is their biggest foe, and capitalism and a free market are to blame for their human indignities. They have been taught without internet or access to the world's leading thoughts and ideas, and they have been given a potion for the masses of which Karl Marx would have called an opium to haze their vision. The Castro regime and its inheritors have full bellies, but the ordinary citizens can't walk into any market to find fresh bread or milk. I am not certain the Cuban people living on the island support their regime, but I am also not certain that they have a choice. Their enemy is next door, in their own homes, and in their own backyards, listening to any sign of dissidence.

She was so poor as a child that her mother often gave her water with sugar in a tin can. "*Osvaldito, que rica nos sabia esa agua, mi hijo!*" "Osvaldito," she would tell me, "That water with sugar tasted so good to me!" I come from a long line of resilience made in Cuba. It was not until I was older that I realized we were poor. The fact that my mother was a garbage collector did not give me a clue. Marta was the best trash collector, and one man's trash is another's treasure. My mother never had real extra savings, and when she took me on those excursions, I realize now how strenuous it must have been for her. She used to tell me that being poor is only for the weak in imagination. "*Yo me tomaba esa agua con azucar y me parecia que era un helado de los mejores de la Habana, de los que sirven en Coppelia.*" "I used to drink that water with sugar, and I used to think it was the best ice cream in all of Habana, like the ones they served at Coppelia."

Mimi was a cable network decorator, a Martha Stewart, and a QVC queen before any of these were remotely familiar. What I mean is this: She would be driving (she eventually learned how to drive because she was going places), the brakes would be hit abruptly, and my sister and I would slide down or sideways on the huge vinyl back seat of the old Dodge. We wore no seatbelts back then—if the old baby-blue Dodge even had any. My sister and I would brace ourselves because we knew what was coming. We knew immediately what a sudden stop entailed; it meant work! My mother had spotted a garbage pile, and like a hawk, she could spot her treasured prey in a pile of rubbish from miles away.

It could have been anything—a chair, a wooden box, an old doll, an old frame. Anything that could be revamped, restyled à la Marta, would rapidly be placed in the walk-in trunk of the old Dodge. The trunk of the Dodge was a hidden treasure in itself. Mami had many different pairs of shoes for all spontaneous occasions in it. There were purses, blouses, skirts, and makeup with huge aerosol spray bottles. She understood that a festivity could happen from one minute to another, and a wardrobe change would be required. The old Dodge trunk was a replica of Mami's bottomless purse. When Mami had to dig into her bigger-than-life seventies duffel bag, a.k.a. purse, to find her infamous lipstick, the lights would go off in Georgia before she reached her desired wallet or specific lipstick shade. Her closets, her cars, and her purse had all one thing in common: too much baggage full of nothing to fill her emptiness.

Some of the fondest memories I have of Teresa and me are those times we spent rebuilding some old chest Mami just had to have from a pile of garbage. Mami always had the best efficiency in the hood. Her friends loved how she could transform a three-hundred-square-foot run-down hole in the middle of the Miami Cuban diaspora to look like a mini-Versailles. I know her gay friends—the Warren Beatty's of the opera spraying gel on Saturday afternoons—had a lot of input in the fairy dust her places received abundantly. I am grateful that part of my grandmother's prediction came true: I did become a garbage collector. Not unlike my mother, I love treasure hunting and thrift stores. I am like a pig in mud! I learned early to value things that most people take for granted and don't value. The most meaningful things in life are free, including others' garbage.

There were the rides to downtown Miami to buy "*retazos*," which are remnant pieces of fabrics that Mami could afford at bottom-dollar prices. I can't tell you how many Saturday nights my sister and I spent helping Mami sew, strip, stain, paint, and create curtains à la Marta. It is amazing how much you can do with a three-hundred-square-foot dump. In *An American in Paris*, the film with Gene Kelly, his character's apartment is not surprising: that was Marta's style. When I first saw the film as a young adult, I realized the ingenuity in art, and perhaps that was another spark toward my love for the French culture. Even the word "*merde*" sounds exotic, and it literally means shit.

Unfortunately, I let go of my sewing talents and regret it because it would have been very handy to sew some pieces together that remained torn for too long. What's worse, I threw away parts that could have been mended and sewn to create a beautiful patchwork, a granny's quilt I so adore, but at the time, I did not have the tools or mind to understand I could integrate it all. We abandon so many things on this journey called life—only to learn later how seemingly meaningless most things are and how truly meaningful seemingly meaningless things truly are.

We made cushions, curtains, placemats, and napkins—and often in a Cuban minute. This is one of the world's greatest wonders: Everything takes only a minute for my mom and most Cubans. "*Estas cortinas las hacemos en un minuto, tu veras!*" "It will take a minute to make these curtains, you'll see." *Yeah, right!* My sister and I would glance at each other with rolling eyes. Cubans have my mother's sense of timing—or is it the other way around? No matter, time is nonexistent in the throes of pure creation. For the Cubans I know, there is nothing that can't be done in a minute; I believe this can be called optimism.

CHAPTER 6

Every space I have lived in has my mother's touch; those early days of treasure hunting and fabric buying created a ritual that manifested itself in every corner of my safe place. She would say a home is what you make of it, and she would create Cinderella's castle out of a cardboard box over and over throughout her gypsy years.

Mami had a great line of male admirers, but I believe she never trusted any man after my father. She knew well what men wanted from her. There were rich men, married men, young men, and old men who were always offering castles in the sky. I met many from the ridiculous mob of admirers, and too often, Mami had red roses delivered by a fox with his tail between his legs. After the delivery, I could hear her chatting with her girlfriends, comparing the hopeful suitors to dirty, squeaky rats.

The line of admirers was longer than the line at El Refugio. Laughing boisterously, she would speak into the phone that she would rather remain poor than give any of these bastards the time of day. My mother gathered her street smarts fast, for she had no choice. She knew well that any transaction between a beautiful, poor, single woman from the hood and a sexual predator would never be a fair one. It had not been only me who had heard the stories at the beauty salon; Mami eventually learned the unfair plight of women, especially beautiful poor women. Some did get lucky, but they paid the price of a soul, which my mother was reluctant to do. She was mostly content with her female friends and her gay male friends who were her entourage. These so-called misfits she could always trust, even if they were like Sappho and Oscar Wilde.

My grandmother felt repulsed by my mother's friends. This distaste my Herculean grandmother had—and the effort she made to inculcate the same hatred in me—failed miserably.

Mami moved a lot and made friends quickly. My mother had a knack for speaking with anyone. She was a talker, but she taught me never to gossip. No matter where she moved, inevitably the neighbors could always be counted on for a cup of sugar. "*Pidele a Yolanda un poco de azucar, Osvaldito.*" "Ask Yolanda for a cup of sugar, Osvaldito." And there I would go skipping, for skipping was natural when I was in my mother's hemisphere. Somehow, these transactions were all too normal in the Cuban hood, and no one gave it a second thought when asked for sugar, coffee, or a cup of rice. It was a natural market of goods, a Cuban Wall Street of rice and beans. Everyone agreed to the exchanges without the slightest contract or hesitation.

If Yolanda had to go out for a while and couldn't take her two daughters, Hilda and Maria, she would bring them and tell Mami, "*Cuidamelas un rato. Vengo ensequida.*" "Take care of them for a bit. I'll be right back." That was all that was needed. Mami would take care of Hilda and Maria, no questions asked, and our routine was never altered. Somehow, Hilda and Maria became part of the pack. If we hit it off, Hilda, Maria, Teresa, and me—and when we all got too loud, we were sent outside to play. The outside was usually a huge parking lot, or it could have been an open hallway; it mattered little to us. It might as well have been Disney World because we did not know of anything else. The outdoors inevitably held the familiar smells of Cuban cigars; black beans in pressure cookers, steaming and whistling; and Cuban coffee brewing, which meant we were in our territory and safe.

The neighborhoods my mom moved into were always open and had a sense of familiarity; one place did not differ from the other. Except for the interior space that changed, all the neighborhoods smelled and sounded the same. All the windows of the small, cramped quarters were wide open, and I could see inside, which created a sort of trance in me, a hypnotic, intoxicating rapture of familiarity. These were my people; I could walk through their doors, and they would ask me if I had eaten. I would be served a glass of milk with Quik powdered chocolate and *arroz con frijoles negro* (black beans and rice).

Poverty in the Cuban hood never meant going hungry; it just meant you did without the luxuries you were clueless about anyway. Food was always available, regardless of its point of origin. The Cuban *cazuelas* (pots and pans) were unique and had their own character, which transmitted the essence of all Cuban abuelas. They were big pots, often stained black from the excess usage. No one cooked in little pots; that was unknown in the Cuban hood. Somehow, guests were expected; if not, there were always those who needed the food, and it was transported without Uber. These tiny apartments often had two generations in them. Somehow, to little Osvaldito, they seemed to hold the families—and the community—together. One apartment connected to the other, and it did not matter if they were across the street; all could be communicated and understood without using Wi-Fi.

I was always fascinated by the number of activities inside the cramped spaces that often spilled into the outdoors. There was little need for gossip; after all, everyone knew everyone's business. I felt entertained by these surroundings. Mami's world was a traveling Cuban circus that only an Almodóvar film on steroids could recreate. We were the clowns, the women with rollers on, with Olga Guillot's or La Lupe's music playing from afar. All the grandfathers in guayaberas, which opened at the protruding belly, sat outside on benches, smoking Cuban cigars, some on half-broken wooden stools and others in old rocking chairs, but they were all talking about El Diablo. Grandmothers would show up at the right intermission with a fresh colada of Cuban coffee, and the beat went on, missing nothing. It was an Alicia Alonso choreography to the rhythm of the Cuban diaspora. Kids would wind in and out through the abuelos' wooden stools with their only toys consisting of imagination and little legs to run after each other. A Cuban *Nutcracker* ballet was improvised every evening with costumes and artifacts we could gather from the periphery of our mini enchanted forest. It was good to be around kids who spoke my language in every way possible, not just in the spoken word.

On occasion, a well-deserved reprimand by the guayabera-clad holy men whose political discourse had been interrupted by the *Nutcracker* ballet would burst into the air like an exploding water balloon. They made sure we understood that they were solving the world's problems, especially Cuba's problem, and our intertwining Alicia Alonso's choreography was an unwelcome espionage. If the interruption was grave enough, we had to stand at attention like army soldiers, and we were forced to hear their reasoning as to why our playing was an imminent danger to their plan to revolt against Castro. We heard the dangers of Communism in no uncertain terms, and we had to pretend to understand that our games were a menace in their scheme to save the world from this malady, even if few of us cared or understood. In the end, going back to our game was as important as their discussion, so we behaved accordingly because it was essential that our show went on!

Laundry was an everyday chore that required lugging plastic baskets endlessly back and forth from the laundromats that were part of the stomping grounds of the community. The local barbershops and bodegas (Cuban mom-and-pop convenience stores) and the hot and humid laundry mart were the community's clubhouses, where you went to hear any news from the motherland. These early entrepreneurial Cuban markets were the news predecessors of *El Nuevo Herald*. But in those days, when the Cuban world in Miami was brand-new, the *Nuevo Herald* was fashioned in these commercial places that everyone frequented for a necessity—or just to have a Cuban coffee and learn about the really important news.

You didn't need to buy beans or get a haircut or have laundry to wash to participate in any of these unofficial borough board meetings that took place every evening; you just needed the extra five minutes between chores to stop and stomp your feet, emphasizing your point of view. It was the stomping that mattered—or was it the loudest voice? It was a challenge to be heard when everyone was speaking at the same time. Somehow, at intervals, one voice was heard above all, and this was the winning point of view for the evening. It often lasted a couple of nights until someone had a better stomp or a better view for the small crowd that gathered around this nightly ritual. This folkloric festival was my early language, and I understood it well. I was made to understand without any doubt that the devil was a dirty, bearded, old "*hijo de puta*" (son of a bitch) dressed in green camouflage called Fidel Castro.

Mami was the only woman in the hood who drove, and on Sundays, the old Dodge could have as many as six kids and four adults inside of it, sitting on top of each other, arguing jovially. In the Cuban hood, one must learn early that excitement and arguing can be easily blurred. It was the old Cuban *chancleta* (rubber flip-flop) that was the decisive factor for us kids. A gesture with a Cuban chancleta was all that was needed to know you had to run for your life.

Sundays were often an extensive combination of events, and the logistics planning could perplex the finest NASA engineers. The Sunday expedition's strategic planning started on Saturday night. It could have been six or seven in the evening, and the compound, which resembled an ant farm full of Cuban-ness, would already be buzzing. The kids usually wanted the beach and no church. The mothers struggled with the effort it took to go to church and the beach. There was the potato salad, and who was going to make it? How many could go? The Dodge was not the wagon from *Chitty Chitty Bang Bang* or even a minivan; it was a dilapidated Good Samaritan disguised in a metal carcass that could only crunch in so much Styrofoam and flip-flops.

If guilt won, church was in, and we were to change in the church parking lot or at the Grand Union once we stopped to get ice for our watered-down Kool-Aid. From ties to tank tops, skirts to shorts, and church to the holy waters of Crandon Park in Key Biscayne, everybody seemed to be going to the beach on the same day. We became the traffic on the bridge that merges the mainland to the key; we were the amusement park sideshow. As with the windows in the hood, all the windows of the Dodge would be wide open, and every passenger vehicle that accompanied us had a story of its own. All the other metal Good Samaritans were packed full, with sweaty, young, and happy skin half hanging outside the windows.

Frequently, traffic was so slow that friends were made with total strangers from other vehicles stuck in the same fiesta of internal combustion engines. Most Cubans have never met a stranger; it is usually the stranger who does not want to mingle with a Cuban that denies themselves a friend. Most Cubans will be willing to speak with a wall even if the wall has an opposing point of view. Truth be told, a wall's opposing view is fuel for an animated conversation for Cubans. God forbid that the bridge that merged the mainland to the key would be up, letting one of Miami's infamous cruise ships pass by; then it was literally dancing in the streets! Some people would get out of their cars and start dancing or passing Cuban bread with *lechon asado* around (Cuban bread with roasted pig meat).

Those days with Mami were some of my happiest childhood memories. There was no time, and I felt life inside me. I felt free from the bullies, including the beasts at Abuela's. However, the gut-wrenching pain always surfaced in my solar plexus when my return to Abuela became imminent. It was then that the gift of my imagination granted me a tool that has been available to me from my very first sunrise and will remain until my very last sunset. As much as I tried to envision that time was nonexistent, it has a way of making its point. I ventured into the sphere of my surroundings and allowed my imagination to dance freely to the sound of the distant Cuban salsa, whose rhythm emanated from the AM radio waves.

The universal language of music soothed my soul because the pain of returning to my abuela's was too severe. I indulged in the illusory, transient dream of becoming a part of the world of every family that passed my vision. I heard their stories in my mind's eye. I listened to a little boy saying "Papi" and wondered what that meant. I envisioned them returning from the beach to a *Leave It to Beaver* cottage with a white picket fence. I believed they were my family and entered their world, a world with no separation and no Mother Teresa/Satan. My favorite vision was the jungle, more precisely, *The Jungle Book* by Rudyard Kipling. I loved Mowgli's world. Living in the jungle with the animals was one of my favorite fantasies. Baloo the bear, who cared only for the "bare necessities of life," was a hero in my world because he taught Mowgli how to live relaxed in his own backyard. Bagheera saved Mowgli and was the word of reason. To this day, I dream of living in a tree house, with Wi-Fi of course.

"*Osvaldito, despierta, mi hijito. Que ya llegamos a casa de tu abuela.*" I must have fallen asleep between the beach and the drive back to my grandmother's because the next thing I heard was my mother's voice saying: "Osvaldito, wake up, my son. We have arrived at your grandmother's house." Like a tsunami, the pain gushed into my little body, and the tears would flow with the desperation of being ripped from the very core of my being. I could never say goodbye to my mother. It was a fallacy to believe that Osvaldito could ever say goodbye to the woman he idolized. God was good to both of us because, in her last days on this earth, we were unable to say goodbye to each other.

Osvaldito never understood why he had to separate from Mami at all. Even as an older man, I used to have nightmares of calling out for my mother. It was not until her recent death that those nightmares have ended. She was the one lifesaver I needed and begged for night after night. During my early years, Mami worked in a factory, went to beauty school, lived in small crevices she could afford, and made the best of her remaining dreams and hopes. She was born in a home with dirt floors by a vast river surrounded by wilderness in "*el campo*," the countryside. She was a shoeless child with a second-grade education, a half-breed delivered out of wedlock.

My mother became a white swan with an angelic voice who melted the pavement she walked on. She had three children and married three times. Marlon Brando would have considered her a great contender, a Cuban Raquel Welch with the courage of Joan of Arc. She navigated a cold, unknown world alone. Few were those who extended a helping hand, and when they did, they expected payback. Half her heart was left in Cuba: her first daughter and the love of her life, my father. She bore her sacrifices with grace and laughter, dismissing all bitterness. She was Osvaldito's mom, and not unlike Mami, Osvaldito did not understand the world he had been cast into.

After my grandmother's death, when I was around twelve years old, I got to live full-time with my mother, and these memories feel like they were with an entirely different woman. Most of my childhood consisted of the ever-too-brief visits with Mami. This first stage of my childhood was the Polaroid snapshot of the Crandon Park beach, Olga Guillot concerts, and the presence of the goddess herself. The second stage was my coming-out-of-the-closet stage, feeling like I had let her down. The final stage was the best: We became the best of friends due to the power of our love. Her last few years in this world were wretched.

What I know for sure is that my mother loved me with all her heart and soul. She gave me the best of what she had to give—even when she had little left for herself. I know she missed me all those years I missed her. We were the result of a dice game, and in this land, we lost so much. I hear her voice, and I feel her eyes; she is my goddess in tube tops and bell-bottoms. She is upstairs sitting next to Mary Magdalene and the rest of the gang. She never cared for labels; she cared only for hearts. My heart rests in hers, and her heart rests in mine. We were the luckiest ones of them all. My mother and I knew without a shadow of a doubt that our love would transcend this life and that the power of our love would enrich our spirits long after our bodies ceased to exist.

She was a beautiful woman in her prime. She literally stopped traffic with her swagger and her near-perfect feminine figure. Her last days on this earth were cruel and undignified. My mother was ninety at the time of her death, and about her death, I know very little. If one can die of a broken heart, I am certain this was the cause of my mother's demise. On the Friday prior to my mother's death, I lit a candle with a French vanilla scent that soothed me. There was a calm and a neatness in my world that was pleasantly surprising.

I learned about my mother's death the following day, a Saturday, with that notorious clear, crisp, baby-blue Miami sky. On Saturday, March 20, 2021, I awoke pleasantly serene with a calm heart. My most urgent engagement was to hurriedly open my back door for my precious furry kids. I had by then lost five of them almost consecutively, and the grieving was ongoing. My usual routine is to feed the furry angels as fast as I can because, well, they won't have it any other way. After they are fed, Daddy has his breakfast, which usually consists of a quick version of something appetizing and resembling nutrition: a protein shake or a protein bar. If I'm feeling glamorous, I will have fresh fruit. Food and I have a lot of issues to work on. Along with my glamorous morning meal comes *una tacita de café Cubano*, a cup of Cuban coffee. After my children are fed, and Daddy gets some fuel in him, I feed the wild birds and the squirrels, and I am most certain there are some other critters who shall remain nameless that grab a good meal from my morning offerings.

Once all the little animals in Ozzie's world are belly content, it is time to thank my creator and set my intentions for the blessings of the day to come. Long ago, I learned that prayer and meditation are not optional in my life. Truth be told, I would not be able to witness this thing called life without a power greater than myself and acquiescing to his will with every sunrise. As I walked back into my room to read some spiritual literature based on love, I had a deep sense of serenity and belonging. I read, I prayed, and I wrote to God. My prayer is a simple prayer of gratitude and direction for the coming day. Every morning, as every night, I always feel I am in the best possible world when I have entrusted my life over to the care of the divine mother who tends lovingly to all. It was indeed a beautiful Saturday morning.

Every morning is the same routine. Once I am done with my morning priorities, I pick up my cell phone and answer all the beautiful good morning blessings that I am graced to receive. As I picked up my phone, I saw two unusual texts, both from my nephews. One text simply read: "She will be missed." I knew she was gone. After taking a deep breath, I sat down on my bed. I was silent, and my body had become unusually tranquil, as still as the beautiful, clear sky. There were no moving clouds, just clear blue that stretched beyond eternity. That day had begun like any other day, with my usual morning routine. Gently, my soul swayed my thoughts to my morning prayer: "Thy will be done, not mine."

This was the day I learned about my mother's passing. I am grateful for the silence that God brought to my realm that morning. Suddenly, just as a gushing storm hits unpredictably, so did my torrents of tears. I confess they were fewer droplets than I could possibly have predicted, as I confess that the strength that kept me from falling apart felt unreal. I knew instantly that I would never again experience the kind of love my mother gave me for as long as I lived. I also knew that God stood with me, holding me up and keeping me in the palm of her hand. Kika and Blackie were my faithful companions that morning, and I could not have asked for better solace.

The woman I called Mami was no more. Her death, her slow, undignified decay, was over, and part of me was so very glad. Osvaldito had known many stories of painful goodbyes, separations, abandonments, suffering, betrayal, and abuse, but this one was to end the physical root of the matrix of my light.

The most valuable legacy Mami left me is the power of forgiveness, the power of faith, the power of love, and the power to know that anything is possible with a loving God. I am lucky to have absorbed this nectar from Osvaldito's goddess. I had witnessed her struggles to exist, to survive in a world where few good souls survive, and those who do often remain broken and embittered by life. "*Hay que perdonar, Osvaldito. Dios nos pide que perdonemos a todos los que nos hacen dano.*" I can hear her voice in my head over and over again, always prompting me to forgive because it was what God asked of us. How could she? There were so many times in my youth that I found her ludicrous and weak. In my rebellious years, I could not fathom forgiveness. I could not bow to a God that I thought had abandoned us. Somehow, she always had faith. And somehow, she was always able to transmit that faith to those who paid attention.

I wrote this on September 5, 2021, and tomorrow will be my birthday. Of all the things my mother would forget, she never forgot my birthday. Even in her last years, having suffered from the onset of dementia and multiple episodes of severe physical and emotional abusive traumas, she never forgot. The indignities of her lifetime, of her death, went beyond the decaying degradation that often accompanies poverty and old age. My mother suffered much. I remain certain her gentle voice sings among the angels. If I listen closely, I can hear her celestial hymns. Some of us on earth are privy to the melodies from the empyrean. Our guardian angels enable us the courage of lions, the innocence of lambs, and the melody of the celestial mockingbirds. There is no doubt that my mother's spirit is among the heavenly chorus that transcends space and time.

On this day, I missed my mother and grieved for her loneliness in her old age. I suddenly felt myself a decaying man, a man of bone and flesh without a spirit, broken, with mere dust remaining. The only relevant umbilical cord that kept me interested in the world had been severed. The baby-blue Miami sky opened, and my third eye was privy to that hymn, that celestial calling from the love of a mother: "*Escribi, Osvaldito, no tengas miedo.*" "Write, Osvaldito, do not be afraid." And so, I did.

To write about one's life can be considered an impossibility, an arrogant attempt at justification, obviously an unobjective form of regression into a make-believe land. It has been a gift to be able to reconcile and find the courage to express what has been hidden for too long. Any true artist will tell you that the results of any artistic endeavor are never the main focus of the everyday trials of bringing to life a new form. It is the journey, the love behind the scenes, and the need to extract a growth that cries to be freed from the deepest core of our soul that has helped me maintain this task of writing, of putting my voice on paper. It is my mother's courage—her plea for our love to be counted—that energized my strength and valor.

I understand what you told me in a lifetime, Mami: Your legacy was your life, all of it. "You will learn much with your art, Osvaldito." How did you know, Mami? How much did you keep silent? How much inside of you yearned to be heard? How did you bear it all with such grace and gratitude? How did you remain alive in spirit after so much loss? How did you keep from crumbling? Whose arms did you yearn for? How many dreams did you let die? Why do I get to write, paint, read, and live in a world where you no longer exist? To

God, I tell the truth: I know nothing at all. I know nothing, but with your love, I am able to remain.

Your spirit gives rise to my strength, to remain in a world where you no longer exist. Although I cannot feel your embrace, I know that you are here with me. So powerful is the love of a mother for a child that it transcends corporeal death. Who am I not to forgive? Jesus himself forgave those who crucified him: "Forgive them, for they know not what they do." I was reborn through the death of my mother. I write to save my life; I write because I have risen from the darkness. I write because I am the son of a true artist; my creator, my heart is filled with joy and love, amazing grace. May this spring be the torch that dethrones your shadows. Your hurry has ceased, and mine has diminished. Together we shall always remain—Mami and Osvaldito forever.

Montecristi, March 25, 1895
Madre Mia,

Today, March 25, on the eve of a long journey, I am thinking of you. I think of you ceaselessly. In the wrath of your love, you are pained by the sacrifice of my life, but then why was I born from you with a life that loves sacrifice? Words I cannot understand. The duty of a man lies where he is most useful, but in my growing and necessary agony, the memory of my mother is with me always.

Embrace my sisters and your friends. Might I one day see them all around me, contended with me, and then I will take care of you with tenderness and with pride. Now give me your blessing and believe that no work that is not charitable and pure will ever emerge from my heart blessings.

I have good reason to set off more contented and certain

than you can imagine. Truth and tenderness are not useless. Do not suffer.

Yours,
José Martí

CHAPTER 7

You can never know how much of me such a young child can take away. A few weeks ago, I accounted myself a very rich man, and now the poorest of all.

—Ralph Waldo Emerson

The words "papi," "papa," "dad," "padre," and "father" were total enigmas to me. By the time I was fifteen years old, I had given up any hope of ever getting to know my father. He was a story told by a drunken tribe that forever toyed with a young child's need for his dad. My mother's voice was the only conscious tone that spoke about my father's kindness and courage. I am among the lucky ones who got to know—if ever so briefly—the loving embrace of a father.

He was a late-night, static-filled phone call from the Communist country called Cuba, whose leader was El Diablo, whose proximity might as well have been the planet Mars. The man's image was in a faded little black-and-white photograph of a caricature with a stark white ironed shirt. The most concrete evidence of my father's existence was the cardboard birthday card he made in prison that my mother gave me. As a young boy, I did get to hear my father's voice on more than one occasion. Exactly how many times I heard my father's voice is uncertain, but if I had to guess, I would say that by the time I was fifteen, it was probably fewer than five times.

If I were to add the actual minutes, it was, well, maybe twenty or thirty minutes in total in all those years. In those days, calls from Cuba were few and far between. The request for a call had to be placed from the States, and Cuban authorities allowed the appeal at their whim, if ever. When the call did happen, it could be at any time, say midnight Miami time or two o'clock in the morning. Truth be told, no one truly knew if the call would ever be actualized. The family on both ends who wished to speak had moments of a static line interrupted by beeps and undeniable espionage that made the communication cryptic.

Not knowing what it is like to have a father spared me certain foreboding. My father, Osvaldo Amador, knew well what it was like to hold his son in his arms. He also knew what it was like to let go of his son without knowing if he would ever see him again. I have learned of many courageous deeds, and letting go of a loved one prematurely by a resolutely self-made decision is one of the noblest and most heroic decisions a man is called to make. My father offered his life for our lives in freedom. "*No mires hacia atras.*" "Don't look back," he told my mother as she crossed the invisible line that would separate them forever. Somehow, my father knew that looking back would be too much to bear for both of them. He never went back to our home, to his home, and he never got his family back. Not unlike my mother, his spirit never died; he remains my hero in a Cuban guayabera.

Working in a factory and attending beauty school at night allowed my mother a small allowance, which she paid the brave souls willing to undertake the perilous journey to bring Cubans incognito to the land of the free and the home of the brave. Every escape attempt bought and paid for to rescue my father from *isla bonita* failed, leaving my mother's purse as empty as her hopes. In his clandestine attempt to leave the island, he was captured by the Cuban authorities and imprisoned. Writing about his experience in a Cuban prison, Armando Valladares does much more justice than any words I could ever write about what it is like to have been in a Cuban prison. In his book *Against All Hope*, he chronicles the inhumane torture that was given to all, regardless of the crime. Armando Valladares was a political prisoner, and he lived the injustices—and he lived to write about them. Like Nelson Mandela, he lived to tell his story because of his spirit, which was the kind of spirit my father possessed.

My father's only crime had been trying to escape an island submerged under a dictatorship. Castro's revolution robbed the Cuban people of any form of free thought. Its oppression and tyrannical brute force pitted brother against brother and separated fathers from sons and mothers from daughters—all under the guise of equality for the masses. Later in my life, as both an undergraduate student in history and a graduate student in sociology, I read Karl Marx and *The Communist Manifesto*. I became enthralled by all the theories written about political ideologies that dispossessed me from my roots. With God as my witness, the dichotomy between reality and the written word has never been more of a stubborn conundrum—with the exception of human nature, to which I have finally acquiesced.

He was given electric shocks for not accepting the ideals of the revolution. The torture was subtle and brazen, but my father did not cave in. The inhumanity in Castro's prison was notorious to those inside and outside the island. It was screamed, it was whispered, and it was pleaded. The inhumanities in the prisons of countries like Cuba do not listen to reason or distinguish between crimes. You are treated inhumanely if you murder a man at leisure or do not believe in the prevalent ideology. Seeing Pope Francis visit Cuba and being received by Castro's brother Raúl, I couldn't help but want to be a fly on the wall during their human rights discourse.

The immensity of pain human beings inflict on one another in the name of religion and political ideologies is something that my simple mind will never truly be able to grasp. I belong to the same species, and I do not feel immune to the propensities that I find so abhorrent, which has led to an incessant clash of forces within my soul. Consciousness makes a fool of us all because awareness should make us a better animal, yet this is an inevitable question for anyone who is even half awake: Are we better? I find that humanity has evolved, and we are better than we have ever been. I also find that we have a long road ahead to truly revolutionize the word "God." To simple minds like mine, God is love, and the striving toward that love is my purpose in this incarnation. Obviously, this is too simple, and those who profess this simplicity are ridiculed and called dreamers.

> *"God is dead. God remains dead. And we have killed him. How shall we comfort ourselves, the murderers of all murderers? What was holiest and mightiest of all that the world has yet owned has bled to death under our knives: Who will wipe this blood off us? What water is there for us to clean ourselves? What festivals of atonement, what sacred games shall we have to invent? Is not the greatness of this deed too great for us? Must we ourselves not become gods simply to appear worthy of it?"*
>
> —**Friedrich Nietzsche**, *The Joyous Science*

CHAPTER 7

In my child's mind, I created a hero of the man they called my father. I did not realize then that, in fact, my father *was* a hero. When other boys spoke of their dads, I made up stories of mine being a descendant of kings, a fearless warrior like Geronimo. He was a samurai warrior who I worshipped at his altar; I had a goddess for a mom and a god as a father, both enshrined in my imaginary sixth sense. He was a millionaire in a foreign land made of gold and rubies, pumping diamonds out of the ground at his leisure. These were my child's images of a hero. The truth seemed shameful and empty. Our story, Osvaldo and Osvaldito's, is full of the kind of courage and heroism that I have learned to respect and admire in the history of humankind. The years have not gone in vain, and my idea of a hero has grown in proportion to the disappearance of my childhood dreams. The strong line of heroism lived unyielding and robust in both my parents.

We were not allowed what many take for granted: to exist together in the world as a complete family. A roll of the dice separated us; we were given little time to know each other, and our embrace was short. Despite the ocean that separated us, a more similar son and father would be hard to find. We both fought an oppressor, and our resilience and courage won us a freedom that weaker men can only dream of. We are carved out of the same stone—my father and me—and we personify the fundamental virtues that enhance our species rather than destroy it. My father was one of the most unselfish and courageous men I have ever met. I cannot imagine living the sacrifice he made for his family. Osvaldito fought his oppressors with the courage inherited in the seed of the man I was gifted to call Papi. Because of my father's courage, I have been able to taste the nectar of democracy.

My father was able to leave the island through the grand exodus called the Mariel boatlift. This is how, at the age of fifteen, I met my father for the first time. Full of hopes, anxiety, pimples, and raging hormones, I was rushed to the old, abandoned baseball stadium in Miami. The stadium was part of a holding station for the influx of refugees arriving from El Mariel, the port in Cuba that Castro had allowed as a point of exit from the island, which Jimmy Carter's policies made welcome on our shores. At fifteen years of age—knowing full well I was a "maricon," a sissy, a faggot—I was told the man I had dreamed about meeting all my life had arrived. Would he like me? No one seemed to like the "maricon," the boy who couldn't do the most basic of arithmetic, the boy my grandmother belittled and called "*un basurero*," a trash collector. Would all these labels be carved on my forehead for the man to see?

All the clan was in an ecstatic uproar, eager to go to the old baseball stadium. I…well, I was terrified. I had no idea what to expect. Would I be able to recognize him if I saw him in the streets? Nope. I was about to face the man who gave up his life for the sissy I had become. Being fifteen is not easy for the best among us, and for me, it was cataclysmic. I had come out to my mother and, in turn, Teresa. I was an abomination whose mere sight brought nausea to the people who raised me.

My mother, who had many gay friends, had not taken my coming out well. Years later, I understood it better when I saw an interview with the iconic diva Cher. Speaking about her child, Cher was as sincere as sincerity can be. This was her child, it meant little that she was accustomed to that artistic world of fluid genders. Chastity was her baby, and it was OK for her to have a hard time with her child's desire to transition from female to male. Cher reminded me of my mother in more ways than I can write herein. I perceived her public admission of her difficulty in acceptance as courageous and authenticity personified. Because of learning about her difficulties with her daughter, I understood my mother better. We never know how our words and deeds impact the lives of others; it's like a ripple that can reach far and wide. How could my mom, who hung out with Sappho's and Oscar Wilde's doubles, react so harshly? My mother's disappointment was new, and I had yet to learn to navigate this impasse.

I had heard it said over and over again by my father's clan: "*Preferio un hijo muerto que maricon.*" "I would rather have a dead son than a faggot." If I knew anything at all, I knew that I had not chosen to be a "maricon." However, no explanation suffices for the repulsion felt for roaches and maricons; they are despised. Although both creatures have been around since the beginning of human history, aversion remains. I am going out on a limb here, for only God knows about these things, but I am confident that the crawly creature that creeps in sewers would never have chosen to become one of the most despised insects in the history of the world.

As for me, I question all, including the innate repugnance for the roach. There is no speculating when I write, as I live and breathe, I never chose who I was born to be. In my family, I had become a roach, a maricon, a good-for-nothing nonbreeder who brought shame on the shameless. To kill a maricon could be comparable to killing a cockroach; this was the sentiment I heard and felt and had come to believe. To kill a cockroach is easy for most, but I have a new view and a new attitude about this trend. I don't have to like a roach, I don't have to live with a roach, but I do not hate a roach. I do not despise the animal, and I often look at it with empathy for the creature born creepy by no fault of their own. Perhaps I have gained some of that radical empathy that Harper Lee and Anna Sewell wrote about, and to my surprise, I have applied it to the creature that I have been repulsed by all my life.

If there was one thing I knew, it was that no one had told my dad that I was gay; no one dared speak the unspeakable to the man who had given up his life for his firstborn son. The day I met the man for the first time is one of those memories that no amount of suppression has ever erased from my mental archives. *Time* magazine was one of the many news outlets covering different angles of the Mariel boatlift. Local, national, and worldwide news organizations had their eyes and cameras open and ready for that seductive, tragic, loving instant that brought family members together again for the first time in decades.

We waited outside the stadium: my grandmother, aunt, uncle, and cousins. My mother did not go. It was a painful choice she made. It had been almost fifteen years since she had last seen the love of her life, and his last words to her, "*No mires hacia atras*," don't look back, may have resurfaced as a reminder that we can never go back, even if we want to with all our heart and soul. My parents had remarried, unhappily, and there was no consolation for their lost love. Perhaps she feared that the handsome, courageous man she had left under a falling Cuban sky would reject her, or, worse, not recognize the once beautiful silhouette of the woman he gave his life for.

As I stood under the blazing Miami sun with sweat running down my well-orchestrated wardrobe, I heard my grandmother's voice as never before. Her voice was a faint whisper, a breathless, hopeless sound that was uncanny for the vociferous matriarch. "*Es ese Osvaldo?*" she asked as if thinking to herself out loud. "Is that Osvaldo?" Chaos broke out instantaneously, commotion ruled, photographers ran to us, and there were cries, screams, an uproar, the kind I had only witnessed once, at my grandfather Tata's funeral. Without warning, I started crying as I heard my grandmother scream, "*Mi hijo, mi hijo!*" "My son, my son!"

The love of a mother toward her child is one of the most divine demonstrations of the existence of God's love for his creation, for it instantly transformed Satan into a helpless, loving Virgin Mary. I had never witnessed the softness I saw in my grandmother that day, and it gave me a whole new outlook on the woman I had so often seen as a wicked witch. There is good and bad in everyone, and we must learn to reconcile that in ourselves—and accept it in others. I, on the other hand, have always remained calm in the middle of a storm. It is usually when the storm passes that I tend to fall apart. Yet, no matter how much I tried to keep a semblance of composure, my soul would have none of it. It was indeed him. Although he was still far away, walking with a group of three or four other refugees, my grandmother had recognized him.

My grandmother had her first embrace with her son, and *Time* magazine used that picture because, in this case, a picture was worth a thousand words. Seeing my grandmother embracing my father allowed me to see kindness in her for perhaps the first time in my life. She repeated a mantra: "*Gracias, Dios mio, por dejarme ver a mi hijo otra vez.*" "Thank you, God, for allowing me to see my son again." Her grip on my father was tight, and my anxiety had been raised to maximum capacity.

My father had not seen me as I waited on the periphery of the madness. Immediately his voiced asked, "*Donde esta Osvaldito?*" "Where is Osvaldito?"

"*Aqui, Papi. Yo soy Osvaldito,*" I said in my cracking teenage voice. "Here, Papi. I am Osvaldito." My voice couldn't have sounded more vulnerable had I been a lamb that could speak. It was the first time I had addressed a man as "Papi," and it was both strange and comforting.

My father's eyes and mine met for the first time, and all we could do was reach out and hug each other tightly while the storm of my tears and his splattered randomly in all directions. The man who had let go of his nine-month-old child had his son in his arms after more than a decade of lost hope. I felt our hearts pumping in each other's chests, and time stood still. What will always stick out about this embrace with my father is that it was the very first time in my life that I recognized what it is like to feel secure.

Have you ever had one of those deep breaths that surprises you and frees something deep inside that felt acutely clogged? The kind of exhalation that removes a heaviness from deep within your soul? That is what I felt in my father's arms. I have never felt it again no matter how I have searched. I predict I will die searching for it, for there was nothing that made more sense than that feeling of belonging and sacred security. For the first time in my life, I felt I was complete, and I finally had strong shoulders to cry on. How amazing it must be to grow up with a strong sense of security. How amazing to be able to run to a parent and feel comfort knowing the parent stands on a solid foundation. Every child deserves this security, for we all grow up too soon and must navigate in a world where the only assurance is contradictions. A bond with both parents—or at the very least a strong loving bond with a caring adult—is something that every child should have. Nothing could feel more natural.

He broke our embrace, and with both of his dry, calloused hands, he firmly held my face, locking our eyes together as he said, "*Pensastes que nunca ibas a conocer a tu viejo? Hasta la muerte, nunca me iba a rendir.*" "Did you think you would never meet your old man? I would die trying, and I would never give up."

I did not utter a single word. I couldn't stop crying, but my sweaty palms held onto his. I couldn't let go. I was afraid he would be taken away, and so I held onto the man I had just met as the last lifesaver available to me. I have never felt so complete in my life, and words cannot describe how meeting my father for the first time filled my emptiness so profoundly. Cubans have a saying: "*La sangre llama.*" "Blood calls out." I understand this because I instantly loved the man as if I had known him all my life. I now had a real father and a mother: *Mami y Papi*. Osvaldito felt whole, if only for this ephemeral moment in time.

The motorcade began, en route to my aunt's home in Hialeah, and

CHAPTER 7

I sat in the limo next to Papi. The limo was a brand-new mint-green Dodge Charger with a dark green half-vinyl top. It did not matter; it could have been Herbie the dilapidated Volkswagen Beetle. All that mattered was that I had a father—and I sat next to him. Every cell of my body radiated with pride and love. Papi had his arm around me, and when our eyes met, it was the strangest, the most wonderful feeling of love from a man I have ever experienced. Every boy should experience this love from a father, even if just once.

There was a big celebration waiting at my aunt's house. The banquet for the king had been prepared with the usual Cuban spread. His Majesty was treated to a Cuban dinner on steroids with the power of ten in exponential terms. On the table that had now overtaken all of the living room and parts of the Florida room in the Hialeah house were proudly showcased a roasted pig, black beans, yuca, *pastelitos*, flan, *arroz con leche, platanos maduros y verde*, and, of course, *colada* after *colada* of Cuban coffee. That night, no one slept. The Cuban cigars, Cuban coffee, and mojitos kept flowing in all directions—as did the stories of the good old days in the old country that was now in ruins. It was a celebration like none I had ever witnessed. Even the beasts were on their best behavior.

Something was missing in this celebration. No, it was someone, not something, and that someone was my mother. I stepped away from the celebration and called my mother on the phone. "*Mami, Papi esta aqui.*" "Dad is here."

Stillness followed on her side of the phone. After a long silence, her voice cracked and broke the quietness between the two of us. "*Estas contento, mi hijo?*" "Are you happy, my son?"

I responded, "Mami, I love him as much, as much as I love you. I can't believe this."

My mother was happy for me; this I knew. If I felt any silence, I am confident it had to do with her place in the world at that very moment. The only man she had truly loved was now minutes away from her, so close and yet so far. My mother had resigned herself to her destiny and her new world, and her world was very different from my father's. I hung up the phone and returned to my father's side, feeling at home.

In the weeks that followed, I spent most of my time with my dad as he was reunited with long-lost friends and distant relatives. One reunion was preeminent and overrode all the others, and this was the reunion between my father and my mother. This get-together was the scene that no one wanted to miss, and no one did. It was arranged and would take place at center stage in my aunt's home. Hialeah was the center of my world in those days; everyplace else was foreign land. My mother arrived at the gathering, and everyone froze, like soldiers in a military training camp standing to attention. Not a move was evident. Voices were hushed, and my father and mother exchanged glances. There was a sudden eerie feeling in the room, and even the huge Florida flies stood at attention.

If my memory serves me correctly, they each said a faint hello to each other, and the other people in the room failed to conceal their intense focus on the Shakespearean play in front of them. The frozen atmosphere heightened to the extent that someone should have broken the massive iceberg about to clash into the Hialeah living room, but there was a strange, deviant desire to allow the main characters to ad-lib freely, to roam the stage without direction, and the silence seemed eternal. I felt terribly sick to my stomach. I knew my mother was not taking this as I had expected, but I really did not know what to expect. What I did know was that the uninterrupted moment seemed to be as intolerable to my mother as it was for me. I was becoming physically ill, seeing my mother's cheeks become paler by the second.

My mother was sick inside; I could feel this even if no one else in the room could detect it. The man I now knew as Papi became solemn, and I suddenly woke up to the fact that my parents had a life outside my world, about which I was clueless. The thread that unites a child with his parents may be invisible to others, but it felt like a gravitational pull from the center of the universe, and it was pulling me right down the rabbit hole quickly. The discomfort was real and palpable for me. It was my mother's pain I felt the most. I had not anticipated this. What was I thinking would happen? What was anyone thinking?

The afternoon moved slowly, dragging and heavy. The fiesta had ended, and a new reality was setting in. The room became alive with an ever-so-slow trivial conversation irrelevant to any reality confronting the audience of willing spectators. Like a wheel without motion, the room slowly but surely became alive again, the wheel slowly started to turn, and all the spectators chose a much-needed intermission to exhale. A lion and the tigress had been set free onstage, checking each other's scent for any subtle aroma of familiarity or discord. The ringmaster began to feel the peace of mind that follows when a good performance that could have gone abominably wrong is survived without any fatal wounds. The sound of music was heard, and the mojitos were flowing again, but the main act was over, and no one knew what to make of it. One critic would have called it "a painful, lethargic suspense, a foreboding romantic tragedy with a sequel in the creator's mind." Another would have called the whole scene "an empty tale of two lovers, devoid of life, trying to recapture their stolen youth."

As dusk approached, the pair was found alone in a remote corner of the wooded garden, sitting under a flowering royal poinciana tree that majestically formed a covering in all the right angles. Its feath-erily leaves drooped to create shadows and highlights on the once lovers who had lost their chance at life. The old Florida sunset had a stained color to its usual burnt orange. The golden hues peeking through the light fluffy clouds resembled a forgotten era that draped the world we inhabited. Nature conspired to gift this moment a tender touch with its routine breezes.

Far in the distance, you could hear the faint song of the mockingbirds proclaiming their territory. How the overture occurred remains a mystery. The once beloved found themselves a piece of the world to secretly give voice to this anomalous episode in their lives. A sigh of relief entered Osvaldito's body, for he saw his parents united, expressing harmony toward each other for the first time in his life, the miracle of miracles, and what an odd and marvelous moment in the history of my family's life. I am happy to note that this was only the beginning of many more banquets of words spoken between my parents, for they remained friends until my father's death a few years later.

I was deliriously happy. For the next few months, the little family that had been separated by no fault of their own came together instinctively and shared the familial bond God had intended. I remember one prodigious event when Papi slept over at Mami's with me in my room! Papi and I had gone to dinner, and upon returning to my mom's, we stayed up late just talking, like I had always seen done on TV: a mom, a dad, and a son talking trivialities just for the fun of it! This rare event was so new to Osvaldito but so agreeable that time ceased to exist. Soon it was past midnight, and Mami suggested that my dad spend the night with me in my room. Yes!

My dad slept in my bed, and I slept on the floor, watching some old black-and-white western that served as background light to the makeshift father-and-son campground. As we went to sleep, we had one of the most important nonsensical conversations about absolutely everything and nothing at all. I had never had a friend, much less a father, to converse with. Our chat strikes me as one of the most congenial and important communal events I have ever experienced.

CHAPTER 7

There was a moment when Ozzie was so immersed in this newfound relationship that he had forgotten that this was the first time he felt camaraderie with security—and the selfless companionship of another man. Having never had this, it was the greatest gift I have ever received from a man whose name was my own.

The following day, I had the best breakfast I have ever had in my life. Mami made café con leche, pancakes, and Cuban tostadas. I could feel the love these two human beings once shared. Although the passion was tempered, at least to my perception, the inevitable fondness that these two souls felt for each other was detectable by any sentient being. There was love in every movement they made, every sound they gave, and every particle of air in the room where the once Romeo and Juliet now stood was a particle bursting with love. The seed of their passionate romance was faithful even in their endearing silence. It was unmistakable, palatable, and assuring. I was born out of love, and in front of me was the untainted evidence.

My father was the kind of man who walked slow; he was not a man of many words, and he was a careful listener. Osvaldo Amador Sr. had a perceptible sense of humor to those who understand that having a good sense of humor means seeing and telling the truth. He had a quiet grin that made others stop and think about their laughter. Unlike my mother, he was never in a hurry. He spoke with the clarity and wisdom of having lost much but having reconciled with God. He spoke words of wisdom to Osvaldito, and he did it subtly, without the arrogance of a preacher. "*El valor esta en el comportamineto y no tanto en las plabaras, Osvaldito. Nunca hables de mas. Acuérdate que el hablar es común y el hecho es poco común.*" He told me that the real value is in our behavior and not so much in words, never to overtalk, and to remember that speaking is common and doing is uncommon. "*Observando y escuchando aprendes, Osvaldito.*" "Observing and listening, you will learn more, Osvaldito."

Much of what was coming out of the master's mouth I had already incorporated into my life because of his family. At this point in my life, I could not articulate my belief, but his lessons resonated with me. I learned what I did not want to be by observing and listening to his family. I believe he had done much the same in his earlier life. There was a part of my father that was very loyal to his clan. On the other hand, there was an apparent distaste for his own kin that I recognized. It was my father's inner strength that allowed him to be loyal and allergic to the beasts without causing injury, especially to his mother, my grandmother. There is no doubt in my mind that my father knew well the unfavorable qualities of my grandmother. Still, his gift of strong character enabled him to stay apart from the chaos and remain compassionate.

It was not long before I saw the dismay in my father's eyes. I understood too well the loneliness that was inching in, even if he put up a good front. He was now living in my aunt's house, where pandemonium was the order of the day. My mother and father became close friends, but I am confident that there was a sense of lost time. "*No mires hacia atras.*" "Don't look back." But the next part of that sentence I will add is this: "You can't go back." He found himself in a new country as an older man with a fragmented family. What was left for him to do? He worked night and day. Like his son, my father always loved cars. Unlike his son, my father could rebuild a car from scratch.

It did not take long for my father to have his own auto body shop to restore old gems. He took me to his body shop and taught me much about repairing a car's body, which was a poor investment. Osvaldito loved cars, but he did not learn well any aspect of rebuilding them. My father gained ground in many areas of his life, but he also knew there were areas he would never be able to win. For example, he would never regain his Juliet, the true love of his life. He would never regain watching his children grow, and he would certainly never regain his youth. He now had a semblance of freedom with a lot of emptiness to fill in his older years. He did not give up. He remained steadfast—as all of us who have remained have learned to do.

I was fifteen, and for the first time in my life, I had my first boyfriend. A mature man of twenty-one, Luis was one of the most beautiful men I have ever seen. I met him while walking home from school, and he pulled up in his beautiful brown and gold Trans Am with that black spread eagle on the hood. As it turned out, Luis lived around the block, but our paths had never crossed before. I had admired the Trans Am many times before; how could I, a car lover, have missed it? However, I had never seen the Adonis who drove the Trans Am. How could I have missed him?

The rest is history. It was puppy love between Luis and me. I had two men I loved in my life—one was puppy love, and the other was the love of a father that I never knew I needed until I had it. Although Luis was twenty-one, he looked seventeen. Our difference in age was not a matter of concern for either of us. I thought he was the coolest guy in the universe, and I felt most alive when I was with him. My life was changing, and the changes were visible and invisible. For one thing, I was growing up physically, and I was to learn that I was not the ugly duckling I had been told I was. Spiritually, I was learning about all different kinds of love, and this was where self-love planted its seed.

My father knew about Luis, as did my mom, and they spoke extensively while trying to hide their disapproval. The truth is that the word "maricon," or "gay," "faggot," "sissy," or any other negative connotation pointing to my sexuality, never came out of my parents' mouths. My father and I spoke about my gay "lifestyle" (most straight people thought, and think, being gay was and is a lifestyle, a choice) in circular ways or avoided the big elephant in the room, but we never completely opened up about Osvaldito being gay. Don't ask, don't tell was not an invention of the Clinton administration; it was the Cuban way of dealing with gay kids for generations.

In my family alone, I know of at least one gay man before me. Everyone knew he was gay and accepted it—with conditions—and it was never spoken about. If it was talked about, it was spoken about much like how Osvaldito and Osvaldo spoke about it, like walking on eggshells or burning coal. I know my father loved me, but he hated what he thought was my choice. My father never overtly criticized or negated me, but there were many uncomfortable silent moments. I believe that my mother had a more difficult time with me being gay than my father did. I do not want to get ahead of my story, but suffice it to say that my mother was not silent about her disapproval, which left me like a deer facing an eighteen-wheeler head-on.

"*La familia, Osvaldito, es todo, los hijos, los nietos, eso es todo en la vida. Sin eso el hombre que es?*" Was that a question, Papi? He would tell me that family is everything, kids, grandkids, that without that, what is a man? I understood his words, and how I wish the manufacturer would have encoded me differently. I love kids, and I would have loved to have kids and grandkids, but there is just one problem. I did not choose to be gay, any more than a roach decides to be a roach. In Lady Gaga's words, I was born this way. Perhaps he was questioning his own life and what had become of his kids, his grandkids, and the woman he had loved with such fervor.

Was Osvaldito just another great disappointment in a history of mounting disappointments? I will never know what it is like to be a father; I barely know what it is like to have a father. Søren Kierkegaard said, "Life can only be understood backward, but it must be lived forward." Life throws dice at us, and we often feel ill-equipped for the winding roads that we have to travel, but forward, and certainly not straight forward, (pun meant!) is the only place to go. We can never change the past. I believe, somewhere in his soul, my father thought I would have turned out heterosexual if he had raised me. This is, of course, a huge fallacy. Straight parents have gay kids, and gay parents have straight kids.

There is so much I understand today about the people and events in my life, but none of us can go back; we must move forward with open hearts. Being a gay man does not exclude me from surmising that being a parent must be one of the most gratifying and demanding callings a living being can ever encounter. I also have a hunch that a good parent wants all the better things in the world for their child; this is elementary and not hard to understand. I am a proud gay man, but it took many trials and tribulations because of the world I was catapulted into. It would be insanity to wish my journey on anyone, much less a child of my own. Forty-five years later, I unconditionally send my father part of my heart. We are all on borrowed time, and our time together was not enough. The feeling of that first embrace I had with him was the only time in my life I felt totally secure. Both my father and mother are in heaven today, and I know I am loved unconditionally.

On this terrestrial plane, we saw less and less of each other. I was a teenager with a severe case of puppy love, and he was a man trying to stop time and create a little life for himself. We started to slip away too soon, and I began to feel his absence. My father achieved a little piece of the American dream through hard work. He was an excellent craftsman, and he was trustworthy. One of his subtle pieces of advice to me was that a man must try always being true to his word: "*En los tiempos jóvenes, mi Osvaldito, grandes negocios se hacían basado en la palabra entre dos; no se necesitaba más.*" In the good ol' days, he told me, some of the greatest businesses were made based on the words of two people to each other; nothing else was needed.

He never made it rich, and I am almost sure that he lived paycheck to paycheck, but he was able to be his own man with freedom and dignity. Despite the heaviness, a little triumph made his eyes shine. I can remember one of those times when his whole face lit up with pride, a day I was at his body shop trying to learn to fix a dent on a Fiat Spider he was refurbishing. A few of my father's old buddies showed up at the body shop to smoke Cuban cigars and talk about the old country, and I was trying desperately to fix the dent without much success.

When my father introduced me as Osvaldito, the most gregarious and vociferous of his friends said, "*Pero este es hijo tuyo? Pero este muchacho no es para estar en un taller arreglando carro. Ademas a quien salio tan buen tipo?*" His friend was doing what Cubans do best, poking fun and trying to have a good laugh. "Is this your kid? This kid is not meant to be in a body shop. Besides, how did he get his good looks?"

Well, I became red, pink, and probably one hundred shades of orange because I was not used to being flattered in a fraternal way. On the other hand, my father beamed with pride. He had a beautiful smile with perfect white teeth. I have had only two cavities all my life, which I owe to my father's genetics.

With his bright smile and a handsome grin, he responded, "*Salio a la madre.*" "He took after his mother."

Yes, I look like the Alvarez, but I also look like Osvaldo Amador. My father was not handsome in the usual, customary way of Hollywood icons, but he had his own charm, and looks never stopped women from flocking around him. He was a man of small stature, but he was big on charisma. He had a beautiful smile that lit up the whole room, and he used it wisely and accordingly.

From my mother's stories of their youth, my mother stopped vehicle traffic, and my father stopped the lady pedestrians. He had a kindness that was evident on his face without words. The allure of the man I got to know was his intensity, wisdom, and humility—

with the right amount of sense of humor. He was a man you knew immediately you could trust, a man of rare sensibility in his generation. His charm was in his low, strong, masculine voice, which seldom was raised above anyone else's. He never felt he had to; he was a man who knew his world and had adjusted to its rhythm, and this was enticing to all he allowed in. Like father, like son. He was a loner; he enjoyed company of quality, but never overextended visitors that, like fish, smelled after three days.

His world expanded to his own place and his own music. Leaving his sister's house was certainly something he had looked forward to doing. Both my parents were music lovers, and I inherited my father's love for classical music. He was never a connoisseur of classical music, but he told me all I had to do was listen to it, and I would love it or not, no need to know more. Art, like love, is in our hearts, and no explanation is needed. When I attend any symphony, opera, or ballet, I can't help but think of my father. *Madama Butterfly* was my father's favorite score, and he did not even know about the little boy who waited for his father's return from across the oceans in Puccini's tragic opera. Whenever I hear *Madama Butterfly*, tears for my father's love slowly emerge from the windows of my soul. In my father's favorite aria, the soprano sings, "One fine day, we'll see." Indeed, Papi, we will.

The first time I saw *Madama Butterfly* was in Rome in my twenties, and it was hell trying to hold back the tears in that intimidating grand opera house. The little boy's scene waiting for his father to come from another world, across the vast sea, threw me into a convulsion of emotions I had never expected. I remained composed like the best of aristocrats, but the collar of my shirt was soaked in tears by the end of Puccini's score. I was that little boy on stage waiting for his father from across the big body of water. I was that little boy on stage who yearned to know what his father looked like. I was that little boy on stage holding his mother's hands as his only savior. It was an unexpected opera—it was also my first time at the opera—and it began my love for opera because I suddenly understood its pain and joys. Art imitates life, or is it life that imitates art? On stage was part of my life in a perfect Puccini score.

My world was exploding. I was learning a world I never knew existed. Sparks of love and hope were emanating from all universes. I was not the center of my father's world, for there was his daughter, Teresa, and his grandkids, not to mention the beasts. He was not the center of my world; I had Luis, raging hormones, new friends, new music, and newfound freedom. He was living a newfound second chance, and I was starting to venture out to a world utterly different from his. How did it happen? How did we become distant? Was it because I was gay? Did he lose his child twice? Was I moving further away as I learned that love existed in many forms? After all, I was learning that there were others like me, other "maricones" who lived happily and made their own world regardless of the scraps society handed them.

Soon, it seemed that the new distance between my father and me was much further than the island of Cuba. A part of me felt his struggle to accept the new world with a "maricon" as a son. A part of me started feeling rejected. That old empty feeling of abandonment was lurking, ready to devour me again. I can't sugarcoat this. The second and last time I saw *Madama Butterfly* was at the Metropolitan Opera House in New York, and I had grown more mature. I had seen this before, and still, to my surprise, I completely lost it. A torrent of tears came gushing through in that endless moment when the child looks over the sea, waiting forever for a father he would lose many times over. I cried silently but passionately, for I was encumbered by an audience that was witnessing a memory of my very own childhood. It was too late for my father and me—I had lost him to the inevitable eternal sleep that took him in one ordinary night. This time, he would never return from across the big body of water. I won't ever see it again; my father is dead—and so is *Madama Butterfly*.

"*Mami, hace dias que Papi no me llama. Le deje un recado y no me ha contestado. Creo que no me acepta y no sabe que decirme.*" I told my mom that I had left my father a message, and it had been several days, and he had not returned the call. I was sure it was because he was avoiding my gayness because he just did not know how to reject me, and this was an example of his teachings: actions speak louder than words.

"*Sientate, mi hijito. Mira tu papa se murio.*" My mother told me to sit, and very calmly began to tell me that my father had passed away.

I did not understand. I was stoic, like a marble statue, a sea of sand under a blazing heat wave. I was in a stupor of disbelief. It was as surreal as an ocean of dry emptiness. We had so much to talk about; we had an engagement, he and I, and it couldn't end this way. God was a sadist, and I hated him. Such a wasteful time to bring my father from the forgotten island only to lose him. My father lost his child, and I lost my father. It was never meant to be, he and I. We were strangers who loved each other in a hurry. We were victims of a political game played by automatons. The world had been mad for ages, and this madness hit the Amador family where it truly hurts.

I can still remember him smoking Cuban cigars in his guayaberas. In those early days, upon his arrival to the promised land, he gave me all he had. I did not know he had little left to give, but I do know he gave me everything he felt a father should give a son. He gave me freedom and love, and he showed me what real security felt like. I had been prepared to absorb all of my father's words. I was so proud of him, and I regret never having the chance to tell him. I did tell him I loved him, and I remember his grin and his embrace like it was yesterday. He gave me so much wisdom in his silence. He showed me his dreams—without words—and he taught me what courage and sacrifice look like. Being a man is growing with good character against all odds.

Neither of my parents showed any bitterness for the cards they were given. They loved music, laughter, and life. I am so proud to come from such stock. I was not reared by either of my parents entirely, yet I feel them so alive in my skin. Every word, gesture, and song remind me that I am my mother and father's son. I was bred from love, and that love remains my unshakable foundation, the matrix.

I learned to accept the world with all its stings and joy. I learned I was but a small piece of a mosaic in the grand gallery of the ultimate artist. I fit in, and I was a part of it. Regardless of the seeming chaos in the works of the master, only the artist knows.

CHAPTER 8

I celebrate myself, and sing myself.

—Walt Whitman, "Song of Myself"

I was born old and had to fight, crawl, and slay the demons on my way back to my erased youth. I have learned to be a child again. I was called "el viejito," the old man, in my youth. I was a sensitive, shy, introverted child with an innate receptivity to my surroundings. My childhood was spent dodging an oppressor that preyed on my innocence. I was a caterpillar imprisoned by a hostile environment of cold mortar. I had a master's in survivorship with a doctorate in courage. I was assigned labels, but, without exception, Osvaldito understood none of them.

My journey toward a God of my understanding has been a bittersweet one. I was taught early that God, both loved me and hated me. I became tired on this pilgrimage toward self-love because I didn't understand God's abomination for his own creation. It was a lonely battle to fight. I often became dispirited and hopeless, for without God, nothing made sense. I had no voice of my own, and I could not hear God's voice—much less have a song in my heart. I was a full-fledged maricon before I knew it, for it was told to me by the world that hated me before I had a chance to know who I was. I dare say that much of the gay population of my generation grew up with some sense of not fitting in. The worse part was not the nonacceptance; it was the hatred and condemnation my generation heard from all sides of the pulpit.

I remember the moment I realized I liked boys and not girls. I was eight or nine years old—who can remember exact times anyway? We were in a line in school, and we were going somewhere, perhaps to my favorite subject: lunch. At the teacher's request, the line stopped, and in front of me stood a male classmate. My classmate Willy turned to talk to me about whatever boys are compelled to talk about. It really did not matter what he had to say. What mattered was that the world had flipped upside down on its axis, giving me a lightheaded, swirling, airy, gay (pun totally intended) feeling like I had never felt before.

Until then, I had never understood why everyone thought I was different, but at least now I had a clue. Willy was the shining star that illuminated my path, or at least made it possible for me to understand why I was hated. It would take decades to understand that God never hated me; in fact, she loved me. It was the men, the institutions that proclaimed to speak for God that hated who I was; it was never God. God is love, and that was all I ever needed to hear.

Willy was not only the cutest boy I had ever seen; he was also kind to me. I do not believe he was on the same planet as me—you know, with the axis going out of control. Nevertheless, he did not mind me, which was more than enough. To this day, it is kindness that attracts me the most. A good-hearted man can sweep me off my feet as easily as a particle of air is lifted by the most tender breeze. Kindness is a magnet for me, regardless of how it is disguised.

This feeling for Willy was electrifying and, at the same time, terrifying. I became resolute about prayer because if I prayed hard enough, God would remove this newfound curse. The shining star lit the path, but now I had to find my way home, my way to self-love. I was raised Catholic, and the Catholic Church has always held a sacred meaning and space for my belief in God. Although the same church condemned me—and told me every Sunday that I was a sinner and was going straight to hell—I still loved it. Fortunately, at the time, I lived within walking distance of a Franciscan Catholic church.

This church had a small chapel attached to the bigger sanctuary. I believe the communication connection was best in the small chapel because there were fewer electromagnetic interruptions. It was there that I felt God would listen to me without the static experienced in the Cuban phone calls from the Communist island. The small chapel had a better direct line to God. Years later, I would create many paintings resembling stained glass. My memories of my time at church are always coupled with the beautiful, warm colors of stained glass. The filtering outdoor light that echoes its colors inside a chapel is mystical and spiritual, and I felt it inside all my pores. I never paid attention to the images on the stained glass, for they looked like ordinary people trying to be saints. I was always inspired most by the feelings that came through it.

In so many occasions in my life, my feelings have betrayed me, and I suspect this can be true at any moment. On the other hand, feelings have always carried more truth than any word or image I have ever heard or seen. The feeling I got from the warmth of the combination of the light, color, and texture in the windows remains a grand inspiration for many paintings. My avoidance of images in my paintings is because I feel my paintings and images make me think.

Abstraction will always be my lover in the art world. I will never say never, but I will write it: I will never paint an image that does not result spontaneously from abstraction itself. I am not interested in the image of; I am propelled by the feelings of.

I cried a lot. I felt devastated, confused, angry, excited, and shameful. I begged Christ on the altar, in my mind's eye, to please remove these feelings—and I would do whatever he asked of me. Mostly, I would be a saint because I thought this was what he wanted of all of us. This is a heavy burden for any kid. I was already carrying a heavy load, and the thought of suicide was becoming very attractive. It's hard to believe that I was contemplating taking my life as a child. But, you see, my load was heavy, and now I knew for sure I would roast in a burning inferno with *el diablo*.

The suicide rate among gay youth is among the highest of all groups nationwide. *Madama Butterfly*'s aria: One beautiful day, we will see! Indeed, we will see the atrocities we have inflicted on our very own species. The thought of my young gay brothers and sisters committing suicide because of hatred sends chills up my spine and anger to my blood. When the heavens and earth become one, we will see, and we will know. I had faith that I just had to work hard on it. After school, every day, I went to this chapel, knelt, cried, and begged not to be a "maricon." I begged Christ on the cross to take the "faggotry" out of me. I begged Christ to show me a better way out than suicide; suicide would kill me, and it would certainly kill Mami.

As usual, my life was a dyad. I was still severely bullied at school, and the beasts never missed an opportunity to humiliate me. I was a sinner in my dreams and a penitent at the same time. But, alas, there was William, the dirty-blond nine-year-old who tolerated me. Whatever pleasant feelings I allowed myself to experience in my mind, the forces of hell kept their intrusive thoughts, interrupting any temporary relief with a punch of shame and guilt. Shame sat down inside me indefinitely. To this day, I feel its residue. Willy was clueless, of course, and I never dared risk telling him or showing any sign of my adoration. But seeing Willy brought butterflies to my stomach, the good kind, the kind I got every time I fell in love later in life. I love butterflies, but I do not like the patience of the incubation period as a caterpillar. I want to feel the butterflies and not the struggles; this, of course, is an impossibility.

Osvaldito learned he was captured in a whirlwind of demons with no escape. He now understood why the world despised him; the diagnosis was evident. The cure? There were only two ways out of this disturbance: prayer or death. The first I did ardently; the second was obscure but tempting. The deal I made with Christ on the altar was that I would kill myself if he could not cure me of this angel of darkness that had possessed me. The pain was unbearable, and the "viejito" (the little old man) in me was getting tired and more tiresome every second of each hour. I had no one I could confide in, and even if I did, the outcome would have been potentially worse than the vortex consuming me.

"*Me gustaria que hablaramos, si quisieras?*" From behind—no, next to me—no, from above, a voice said: "I would like it if we spoke. Would you?"

"Yes, Father," I heard my sobbing, fractured voice respond.

I followed the priest, whom I had never seen before, although I frequented this church, to an office behind the chapel. I sat down in a dimly lit room with a young priest, and I was ready for the flagellation coming my way.

"*Porque siempre lloras? Dios te ama.*" He murmured in a low tone that God loved me.

God what? To my surprise, I responded, "No, he hates me, and I hate myself, and I hate him!" I am glad they were saving electricity that day and that the room was dim, for I did not, could not, see him eye to eye.

"*Dios nos ama a todo; somos sus hijos.*" "God loves us all; we are his children."

His words did not make me feel cleaner, and it was a monsoon of tears that followed, denying me the ability to speak further.

He stood up and said he would be right back.

I began to shake, for I knew he was going to get Christ to come down from the altar to escort me to hell that very moment. I was preparing myself for the journey; I was ready. Christ had done all he could with the sissy in his chapel. It was time travel that was needed, the type that would instantly beam me up to hell. So what if hell awaited me now? Hadn't I already experienced hell on earth? I had seen the pyres in the old black-and-white films of Joan of Arc, so I wondered if hell was a momentary fire that would eat me up like a twig or a straw or was a slow, painstaking flame that would continuously carve me like the pain I had known. I was ready either way: Let the fire begin. I had no bags or pending goodbyes. My only thought went to my mother, and surely my journey toward hell was preferable to telling her I was a maricon. I was ready to be escorted, passing purgatory, for I would plead guilty before the Almighty.

Christ came in the form of a glass of water rather than the admission to perdition. Drink some water and try to breathe. I drank the water as if this was a potion, a serum, a tranquilizer from the holy water stoup itself. I remember blurting out, "*Me gustan los barones, Padre!*" "I like boys, Father!"

The priest settled back in his chair, getting ready to instruct me on all the rules sent down with those heavy stone tablets in Cecil B. DeMille's film *The Ten Commandments*. Moses himself was staring at me from beyond the young priest's good looks—or my idea of Moses, who looked like Charleston Heston. Oh, yes, making the occasion more conspicuous, the priest was an Adonis with no right to be celibate. He looked at me and asked, "*Tu escojiste el color de tus ojos?*" "Did you choose the color of your eyes?"

His question stunned me. "No, I did not."

"Did you choose the color of your hair?"

"No, I did not."

"Did you choose to like boys?"

"No, I did not."

"*Dios te ama exactamente como tu eres.*" "God loves you exactly how you are."

Suddenly, I felt my breath again and a light at the end of the long, dark tunnel. Willy's shining star appeared in neon lights with a gracious smile. What this angel sent by God told me that dreary day behind the wall where Christ himself was hanging saved my life.

"*Dios es amor—nada mas.*" "God is love—that is all." How simple is that?

This was the first time Osvaldito absorbed those words with every cell of his body. What this beautiful young angel dressed as a Franciscan Catholic priest said next, I have kept close to my heart all my life. He told me that I was too young to have any type of intimate relationship, but the day would come when I would have one. He looked me straight in the eyes and told me that when that day came to always remember that any relationship based on true love is a gift from God. I tell you here and now, his words saved Osvaldito's life—and they also saved Ozzie, Osvaldo, and all the men I would ever become. God is love, simplicity at its most profound bestowal.

My mother was defeated by the news. The woman who had survived some of the most oppressive commands life had imposed was crushed by my proclamation. I am glad I came out to her at fifteen years of age, for I had the audacity and courage of youth. I am not certain I would have been as courageous years later. I came out because I had met Luis, because I was in love, and because love gave me the courage to do so. It was rainy; it was an overcast day with a dark heaviness that could obliterate optimism in the top-notch hopeful among us. The day blended with my mood, for I had felt increasingly alienated from the woman I had idolized as a child. But how do you tell the woman who gave birth to a perfect little boy that he would not be the man she had hoped for? Mami, you will have no daughter-in-law and no grandchildren from me. I will be the conversation you avoid for the rest of your life. When my name is mentioned, your stomach will churn in disappointment. Some will be kind and help redirect the tête-à-tête at social events, yet others will stab the knife deeper and nudge it in to feed their false sense of moral superiority.

I had been living with my mother for quite some time by then, and I knew she accepted all her mixed bag of friends because they came and went with joy and laughter from our little imitation Versailles. I had hoped that she would accept me as she accepted her coworkers from "*la peluqueria*," the beauty salon. The storm outside was relentless, as was the one inside me. Something, someone, had to give—or I would explode. I needed to escape the burden of carrying the weight of so much shame. I had never told her about the molestation or the bullies. I had never told her about the attacks from the beasts. But, somehow, I couldn't keep Humpty Dumpty together anymore: He was falling expeditiously, and I wanted desperately to keep the pieces from splattering all over, never to be gathered into one piece again. I thought if I told my mother I was gay, I would find some relief from the heaviness that was weighing me down.

I did not know it then, but telling my mother I was gay—truly hearing with my soul what the priest in the dark little chapel had told me, that God was love—this was the beginning of a huge endeavor, a huge step toward learning to love myself and respect the creation God intended me to be. The fifteen-year-old teenager thought it was about being honest with the person I loved the most in my life, my mother, but I now know it was about letting go of the shame that was crippling me and burying me alive.

CHAPTER 8

I was embarking on a spiritual journey that was equivalent to crossing the Sahara Desert on foot with a tiny water bottle; it's a good thing I did not know this because it would have paralyzed me. Courage was always in me. It is always in all of us. We hardly recognize how beautiful we are, but we are in multidimensional ways. The things we do for the love of others, for love of self, these are enough to obliterate all the pain, and that's the power of true love. We are beautiful, and it is a pity we are not taught this earlier on, especially from the sacred institutions, for billions follow their doctrine. Imagine the change, the power to ameliorate the lives of all, if the only message was as simple as: God is love. Period.

It was an early Sunday evening when I asked my mother if we could talk. It is strange how often we know without knowing. My mother's eyes profoundly looked at me as if to say: *I know—let's get it over with.* For me, it was like sitting in a doctor's office waiting for a test result that could end my life as I had come to know it. Every glance my mother had, every gesture, I scrutinized it all in order to read my soul's destination.

My mother started the conversation, and I remember her words: "*Lo que sea, Osvaldito, tu eres mi hijo, y nada cambia el amor de una madre hacia un hijo, nada.*" "Whatever it is that you will tell me, Osvaldito, I am your mother, and my love for you will never change." This was a mirage, a hopeful shine without truth.

Then I said what I thought I could never hear my voice say out loud to my mother: "*Mami, yo soy gay.*" "I am gay, Mami."

Her look was penetrating, as if searching for the real meaning behind my words. This blow was too harsh to assimilate quickly. Her face became lifeless. A marionette appeared in my mother's absence. She manically searched for a way to integrate this revelation into the new reality that had just abducted her life. Nothing would ever be the same again. The wires had crossed, leaving the wood figurine lifeless. An electric circuit had occurred, and the crackling fire inside her brain tried to discern all that my words entailed. If smoke could have come out of her head, the Mauna Loa itself would have erupted from the electricity my mother's circuits were experiencing.

"I will never be a happy woman again," her disheartened voice muttered.

My mother's words pierced my soul, for I was the guilty thespian in this tragic act. I knew she would be hurt, but I never expected her piercing words, which punched me right where Toto lay so often with her unconditional love.

She regained all her consciousness, and the puppet strings devised a plan. "A psychiatrist would help us, Osvaldito."

"OK, Mami, if you think it will help you, help me, help us, I'll do whatever you say."

It was an introduction to the Freudian world of penis envy and hysteria. Doctors and more doctors circled around me to find a cure for my malady. I was no homosexual, according to the goddess on six-inch heels. There was no immediate relief for me, and certainly, I had introduced my mother to a new kind of grieving. Her words and her look on that bitter rainy Sunday will always be one of those memories I would gladly give up.

Someone died that Sunday for my mother: the son she thought she knew. There was a death in the Amador family; a child of fifteen was buried under historical and sociological shame. Would I ever be alive again to my mother, or would the death of me remain encased in a burdensome casket forever? What followed was a long procession of silent cries and woes and the extinction of what she thought I was. I had ceased to exist for my mother, and she did not know how to find me. She was lost in her deep wounds; she had made this about her and her failing dreams.

CHAPTER 8

Where does love go when it dies? I wondered. It is fragile like life itself—one moment here and the next gone. A living death removes the sufferer from the face of the love and the loved one. The heart of a lost love gains more pain by its presence. I know what it is like to feel alone in a room full of eyes. If no bridge exists between people, others' eyes become piercing reminders of one's lonely existence. My mother's eyes strayed from mine, and to look at me was to remember my death.

There were many silent days, weeks, and months ahead for both of us. I was used to silence, but feeling alone gained a new meaning. Her friends stop coming, and the hall of mirrors at our mini-Versailles stopped all reflections of the sun outside. I had more confusion added to my already overburdened conscience. There were days that I never saw her, nights I waited in the dark, hoping to hear the handle of the door turn, and nights that I fell asleep waiting and hoping she would return to who we were. But, no, we were not those people anymore. I was now *el maricon*; somehow, her child was more a maricon than her child. One second, one word, one shift in perception, and she forgot who we really were.

If she couldn't love me for who I truly was, did she really love me at all? *I am still Osvaldito!* I screamed inwardly, but no one heard me. I was the same to myself but not to the woman who gave birth to me. Her expectations and societal expectations were battling against her motherly love. She struggled on whose behalf? I wondered. Not mine. I needed nothing but her love. Was it God who gave her shame, or had society become her god? God needs no justification for his creation; he is the creator of all life-forms, even the cockroach. Was it vanity? Was it another lost hope? What on earth could turn her away with such disregard for my pain? Did she forget her little boy who loved ties, who sang in perfect harmony with her, who admired her parting of the seas, and who kept vigil for her return to Abuela's house? Was her pain bigger than mine? Had she forgotten my heart, my suffering, my own flagellation? She had lost herself, she had lost me, and we were both lost in this fog that blocked our eyes from meeting.

I wondered if all of Freud's colleagues were going to bring us back entirely. Were they going to use Krazy Glue to put Humpty Dumpty's pieces together again? Or was this the land of lost hopes? God's screenplays were sadistic, and I became angry at the entourage of this tragicomedy that kept streaming in uninvited. Round and round went my head with abandonment, fear, and shameful tantrums that stole my earliest memories of my teenage years and my sleep. How could I tear this phantom from me? I was now in a sea of scientific investigation by a discombobulated team from *Doctor Who*. The vestments inherited from the gods did not go well with this incarnation, and I knew little of the lessons to be transcended. I was the giant creepy insect creature in Kafka's *Metamorphosis*. The child turned into an abomination overnight.

Sometimes, God is out to lunch, and then there is television. The old wood-framed Magnavox sitting in our empty living room became the nourishment for my soul's vacuum and my surrogate family. Old black-and-white films kept me from falling apart. I heard words of wisdom from Bette Davis, Orson Welles, and Catherine Deneuve, the latter of whom is partly responsible for my love of the French language. Ingmar Bergman taught me about the meaninglessness I was experiencing through these pixels that became my source of light.

Luis's eyes were the only eyes available that did not look away in repulsion. I felt Luis understood as perhaps few others could. It truly did not matter if Luis understood what was going on under my embalming. I was alone, and he granted the only semblance of humanity to the fifteen-year-old Osvaldito. Once again, youth allowed me the strength to dream, grasp onto any tiny hope, endure, and remain openhearted. Or was it God? Or was it me? What was this little light inside me that enabled me to stand and face the troubles that were piling into a mountain of grief?

I have heard that time can heal many wounds, but some scars are never truly erased, and I am grateful my light has not been canceled altogether. I went to the psychiatrist every week, but they were not providing the desired answers. I was tired. I had learned to live in an exaggerated carnival house of mirrors where the images of my world remained greatly distorted. God had abandoned love, I searched in vain, and Mami had forgotten it. I had little faith or recourse. Salvation came disguised as sissies, the reprehensible, and the Mary Magdalenes of the modern world. By now, my overworked imagination was on full throttle, denying the prejudice against the man I would become. But the pain was real, and no overdose of my artistry could stop the hurt.

Time went on as time usually does; we had bad days, good weeks, and worse months. I became comfortable with being uncomfortable. Our relationship was a turbulent one. We went to several psychiatrists and counselors, and when none gave my mother the good news, which would have been that I was born wrong and that they would fix me, she turned to the mystical side for my exorcism.

The African spiritual Santería religion would transform me into the straight, child-producing, right-wing, zealous Christian, corporate, proletariat man my mother would rather I be. Santería in Cuba was, is, a religion of African descent brought over to the island from West Africa. The *Santero*, for masculine, is the priest, the healer, the voodoo god who performs rituals that the mainstream Catholic saints are too busy for or refuse to grant. Perhaps the saints' appointment books were full, and Mami had no patience. The Santero's appointment book was open—for the right price—and the performance, the ritual of an embodied spirit that possesses the Santero, was the final exploratory surgical incision procedure for me. A few thousand dollars to the Santero gifted by my mother for this uninsured procedure would set me straight.

The Santero drank and spat out a heavy alcoholic beverage called *aguardiente* while simultaneously smoking a Cuban cigar in my face. This ritual, which I had no choice but to attend, was meant to expel the demon of homosexuality out of me; the Dark Ages were alive and well in Little Havana. The combination of the smoke and heavy African drums was enough to intimidate anyone. Osvaldito respected the ritual, but he needed an escape route once more. He pretended he was in the Tamiami youth fair, walking through the distorted castle of mirrors, except this time there were profusions of drums, Cuban cigar smoke, and the smell of a mix of cheap colognes entangled with the heavy stench of that alcoholic aguardiente syrup. Flying petals of white roses, blemished with blood from the sacrificial cock, were smashed against my body, the same way Keena's uncle had smashed his belt against Keena's tiny, skinny legs. I have been intoxicated once or twice in my whole lifetime, but that was the worst type of drunkenness I have ever experienced.

Nothing that was ever done has stopped the creation God has made. Toward the end of her life, Mami and I had become the best of friends. It was a long and winding road, and one I would have rather left untraveled. I was barely over my teens, the exorcism, and the loneliness of having lost Mami's loving eyes when my first beautiful friend died. Andre was a beautiful twenty-three-year-old blond Cuban-born man with supreme joie de vivre like few I had ever known. Andre was only the beginning; eventually, I would lose twenty-three friends to AIDS.

By the time I was in my mid-twenties, I was attending a funeral every month. God hated homosexuals I had been told repeatedly since my first memory, and we would be punished like Sodom and Gomorrah. It was a punishment, all right; it punished us all. I was as sad as I was frustrated at the lack of response from the world. The White House had little to say about it until Rock Hudson, a friend of the Reagans (Ronald Reagan was US president at the time), came down with the "gay cancer." I can't help but wonder: If the world had responded sooner, how many of my beautiful young friends would still be alive today?

> *"We must take sides. Neutrality helps the oppressor, never the victim. Silence encourages the tormentor, never the tormented. Sometimes we must interfere. When human lives are endangered, when human dignity is in jeopardy, national borders and sensitivities become irrelevant. Wherever men and women are persecuted because of their race, religion, or political views, that place must—at that moment—become the center of the universe."*
>
> —**Elie Wiesel**, *The Night Trilogy: Night, Dawn, The Accident*

In my wildest dreams, I never could have imagined same-sex marriage. In my wildest dreams, I never could have imagined a Black president (two terms) in America. Sadly, but truly, never in my dreams would I have imagined a female vice president in America. God has his way of showing up. I have lived through many uncertain times, not the least an attack on democracy in America like I would have never dared predict. Life has shown me that miracles exist, and it has also propelled me to be on the right side of history. It would be arrogant to declare that I trust my moral compass, for it has not always been undoubtful. I am not a saint, nor do I have the makings of a saint or a martyr, but I have that funny little thing called a conscience. Conscience has made a fool of me on more than a thousand occasions, but who's counting?

While I was carrying Toto into Campina, I was surprised by a huge Florida flying roach. It was between me and that sacred place I now called home, and there was no way around it. It appeared that the cockroach had always been there without interrupting my sphere of reality. It was enjoying the stars and the light of the full moon as I had been doing. She had not harmed me, Toto, or my abode. Here is the thing with conscience: It can hit a man any time without warning. Beware when it does because it has brought the strongest to their knees.

That night, I had a flash of awareness, just like when I heard Gregory Peck's character in *To Kill a Mockingbird*. I knew for sure that all of life is sacred, even blue jays, and this presented me with the roach conundrum. I am still dumbfounded as to why Harper Lee said it was acceptable to kill a blue jay and all kinds of birds. I am dumbfounded as to why it is OK to kill at all. What was I to do with this roach whose only offense was to have been born a cockroach? Had not my offense been the same as this roach that stood in my path? Who was I to blame for being a maricon? If I killed this roach, wasn't I the oppressor to a species whose only perversion was to have been born from my same creator but in the fragile, creepy vestments of a roach? My conscience alerted me to a riddle; it asked the impossible questions and left me to find the answers—the questions that much greater minds than mine have asked only to come up short.

To kill or not to kill; this was my question. Oh, God in heaven, why on earth am I cursed with this mind that can think and create this jocose thing called a conscience? As if dodging the demons inherent in our existence were not tasking enough, I now had to contend with a question to which I may never find an answer. Roaches repulse me. Is this repulsion the same as what my mother was feeling? Was it not enough that on my twenty-first birthday, I decided never to eat meat again so as to eat lower on the food chain and cleanse my body and soul from heavy carnal karma? Cervantes's Don Quixote read too many books and fought windmills; this was the result of too much reading and thinking. Had I become Don Quixote? Should I be satisfied with the famous soliloquy of Shakespeare's Hamlet: "There are more things in heaven and earth, Horatio, than are dreamed of in your philosophy." No matter how I pondered, the roach was still between me and my womb.

I remember Mami always telling me that if you don't know whether doing something is wrong, God may forgive you, but be warned that if you are consciously aware that your action is bad and still do it, this may be written down by St. Peter in your permanent archives. Loving animals the way I do, it became more difficult to eat meat, and I eventually got very sick. I was not eating sufficient nutrients to support my energy output. It became imperative that I learn the correct way to be a vegetarian; otherwise, I would have to resort to eating meat again. Becoming a vegetarian was not about nutrition for me; it was about not being able to eat an animal whose eyes I could see. This night, I swore I saw the eyes on the Florida roach.

It is so strange this species of mine, for it is the only species that keeps as a pet the same kind of animal it consumes. This killing, or not killing, became relevant early for me. When I speak about killing, I am not talking about going out to kill people as in a war—that brings up layers upon layers of perplexity for me. It became challenging for me to exterminate rats in my attic when I moved into Campina. And now? Well, now I was conscious of the roach, and its eyes were becoming more and more distinct as the conundrum became louder. Sometimes I hate eyes, including my own, because they reveal too much without the carrier's permission.

One of my earlier studies was to delve into religion, the philosophy of religion, and mythology. I read ferociously about the meaning or lack of meaning in life. These readings allowed me to make up my world as best I could. My religion is love and a smorgasbord of theories and philosophies I have had to weave together—bad sewing and all—in order to temper my thirsty intellect. For instance, the *Bhagavad Gita* is a narrative story between Arjuna and his godhead, Krishna. In this story, Arjuna must go to war for a just cause. However, Arjuna finds the idea of killing unacceptable. He confesses in no uncertain terms to his guide (Krishna) that he does not understand the world he is living in. In this battle that Arjuna was called to fight, some of his opponents were his relations, family, and friends, so he asked Krishna how on earth he was to fight against these men. I can't help but wonder if Arjuna would have felt the same way about roaches. Or have roaches always been the exception to every rule?

The Spirit Is Eternal, Body Is Transitory

The invisible Spirit (Atman) is eternal, and the visible physical body, is transitory.
The reality of these two is indeed certainly seen by the seers of truth.

The Spirit by whom this entire universe is pervaded is indestructible. No one can destroy the imperishable Spirit.

The physical bodies of the eternal, immutable, and incomprehensible Spirit are perishable.
Therefore fight, O Arjuna.

CHAPTER 8

The one who thinks that the Spirit is a slayer, and the one who thinks the Spirit is slain, both are ignorant. Because the Spirit neither slays nor is slain.

—*Bhagavad Gita*

How do I kill a cockroach? I do it as fast as possible, knowing that "the spirit neither slays nor is slain." If I found any courage in allowing myself to kill this roach that had not caused me any harm, it was because I had let my conscience enter a debate that had begun with Anna Sewell's *Black Beauty*. I am not saying it's right—I am not even saying I understand any of this—but what I am writing is about awareness of my own repulsions, my own hatred, and my own humanness.

I am in the same merry-go-round as the rest of creation, no better and no worse. Acceptance of my humanity has allowed me a relief that I could have never found had I not ventured into these questions, regardless of their answers. If this is read, the reader may comprehend the algorithm that has enabled me to exist in a world of contradictions. I shamefully admit here that, at one point, my life had little value to me. I had no one, and no one had me. I became adamantly aware that I could not carry the life I had been given, and I did my best to dispose of it. It was not meant to be that I should end my life, although I tried consciously and unconsciously to end myself. The man who could not kill a cockroach would not think twice about taking his own life. This was the point of no return for this writer.

In my darkest hour, I had to fight against all odds to live: God would not have it any other way. I was stuck in this world with many dragons to confront and no energy. I would have chosen death many times over if it were left up to me. This would have been my will; it was not God's will. This is when the light gradually introduced itself to my darkness. I began to understand what I thought I knew: All life is sacred, including mine.

Since I was a child, I have known the sacredness of all of nature, yet I never felt the same sanctity about my greatest gift: my own life. I always felt defective, unimportant, and even unloved. Perhaps it was all the hatred that I had received, the words I heard, and the fear of ending in a burning hell, which religion insisted was my soul's destiny. Perhaps it was the years of experiencing the contradictions in my world or the fact that no one accepted me exactly as I was. The truth is that I never had self-worth, and this has been a lifetime struggle to mend. True clarity came at that moment when I recognized that I was a part of creation, just like the roach. I was no lesser than, no more significant than, but I was as unique as my very own fingerprints. It took me a lifetime to realize that the oppressors could not slay my spirit—only I could. I had been the roach for many, and many like me had died in flesh but certainly not in spirit.

I killed that roach that quiet evening at Campina, but I did it quickly. I did not want that roach to suffer a slow death like I had known. I forgave myself for being human and killing one of God's creations. The best I could do was done because the creator gave me a repulsion for the creature. I often wonder if my conscience is a blessing or curse. My best thinking told me that if I killed it fast, it would not suffer. There is no comparison between a roach and a human life—if the need for comparison is to be contemplated—yet I often think humans pay little mind to what we do to one another, as if hurting or killing each other requires no more effort than killing a roach.

As a history major in my undergraduate years, I found the material extremely depressing because we do not realize as a species that we make the same horrors with much more conscience. The key word is "conscience." If we have evolved, why do we continue to suffer from the symptoms of hatred? I do not have the answers to such lofty questions, and I abhor my questions. Why am I given a conscience when my conscience is not good enough to satisfy what part of me feels should be foundational in our human endeavors? A famous quote attributed to Gandhi reads: "I can only be the change that I want to see in this world." The only lesson that I learned, which I could never oppose, is to learn to accept and love myself with all the fallibility inherent in my very own species.

I am a spiritual warrior, a gay, maricon, homosexual, faggot, sissy spiritual soldier who is now learning to do what Atticus taught Scout: walk inside my own skin. I found a home in the most fertile ground: myself. In the end, an essential ingredient in the algorithm is to believe in me, which is to believe in my sacredness, in an omnipotent, benevolent creator I choose to call God. The synthesis of all the good and bad that has happened to me has found a more perfect harmony. The equanimity was compiled like Lego bricks, a jigsaw puzzle from the five-and-dime in Little Havana; every piece has its own purpose and fits in with its tribe. Every event in my life was chosen in a time and place unknown to my material self to fulfill a universal meaning. I am not equipped to answer the real important thing in this life, and I caution those who believe they have found any answers at all. I have found some self-love that is in constant evolution, as is all my world. Truth evolves, and I am not privy to its preview.

The Buddha taught that the way to enlightenment is the middle path, no extremes, no negation. Bring it all in, *arroz con mango* (rice with mango), all of it, and incorporate all the pieces into the whole, finding placidity with the dissimilitude. I am called to forgive the unforgivable and to love the seemingly unlovable, and it all had to start with forgiving myself and loving myself. No one could do this for me, even for all the money in the world. And it does not end here for all I know; the beat most definitely goes on.

Shedding the years of trauma and victimization did not happen overnight. There were periods of severe depression and total incapacity. Coming out to my mother was just another episode in the days of my life. I had always understood depression, but what I had never understood was true joy, serenity, and the security found within myself. This was the hardest lesson to learn. I had to start by surrendering it all and accepting it all. I was in the rudimentary stages of self-love and acceptance. In the process, the virtues that served me best were courage, discipline, and relentless persistence like I had never known before. I tried not to be embittered, to rejoice in gratitude, but being a maricon disenfranchised me from the core of humanity, and this was bitterness itself.

While amid a severe clinical depression, it is difficult to see anything at all, much less a loving God. I spent much of my life wasting away in isolation, scared, lying in a queen-size coffin with the shades drawn. Amid my most severe depression, I had no energy to walk a few steps to the bathroom. I had lost everything that constituted being a man, and I detested my image. I felt betrayed and abandoned by a God that played dice with life. Loneliness is gut-wrenching when you feel abandoned by your own kin, your mother, and God.

The blue jays pecked at my bedroom window, and the blue jays often got me out of bed to feed the settlement that honored me with their daily visits. I lost the desire for everything: body perfect, mind gone haywire. I couldn't read. No films, no focus, no interest—it was total apathy—but the blue jays gave colors to my darkness. Perhaps their shade of blue was the first thing that came to the forefront of my mind when I heard the words about killing all the blue jays; they had a sacred place in my heart. Perhaps, for some reading this, the roach is that sacred entity since I have learned that there are those who find them beautiful and as complex as all of creation. I must admit that I no longer feel the same way I did about the roach after learning from a little research.

I climbed out of the depths of a vile degradation forced upon the innocence of my inner child by letting go completely. No human power could have excavated my decaying spirit from the bowels of hell. I had hoped that anger remained, but it, too, was consumed by the vast emptiness. My childhood was taken away, society and religion thought me a heinous homosexual, my mother remained at my funeral indefinitely, AIDS was killing all my friends, and I was certain it was coming after me next. I was abandoned with the trauma of a lifetime by a God I was learning to despise. I had to learn how to crawl because I could barely walk. There was a time I kept a bucket by my bed to urinate because I did not have the energy to walk the ten steps into the bathroom. On the good days, I was able to shower, and on the great days, I was able to shower and brush my teeth. I could not eat; I had no appetite. The smallest task was burdensome. I was in the prime of my life when the devil kept me hostage with his sharp, clinging tentacles.

The Hero with a Thousand Faces by Joseph Campbell is perhaps some of the best writing I found that allowed me to understand the ancient cross-cultural and archetypal historical journey toward the light. We are the heroes, the beings whose mission on this earth is to transgress from the depths of darkness to our inner light. I had to find my way out of the mound of garbage dumped on me by an environment fueled by generations of abysmal hatred. The freedom at the end of the tunnel never promised me a new world; the world, as nature, has its cycles and its routine, and it would continue to be the world. What I found was a new me. I found a new lens, a new attitude, a new kind of people, and, most importantly, a new God. It was imperative I leave my belief in the God of my childhood behind. He never was a loving God; he was an invention of hatred, for prejudice, for the society that gained from twisting love into hatred. All this took courage and guidance, and somehow it was given. My new God was simple: love. My new life starting to become simple: self-love.

My journey toward self-love required that I repudiate all that I had learned, all that I had been told, and all that I had believed. My human software needed deletion, and an entirely new operating system had to be installed into the mind that had been misguided. I had to stand back from humanity to become truly human. I had to become self-absorbed to be able to give honestly. I had to become a full-fledged maricon to be a real man. I had to give everything up to gain it all. This was the secret I had read in ancient texts but had only been able to intellectualize, unable to fuse it with my heart and soul. It was when I died to myself that I was genuinely reborn anew.

"El viejito" was now all ages. Time became slightly relevant, and chronology became a matter of practicality and not the essence of any reality. The idea of the Christian resurrection, rebirth, found true meaning. I was not contained by dogmas, although I could pompously recite them. My understanding of emptiness, in the Buddhist sense, got a new twist. The emptiness is to be filled with what I choose is most important. I choose love. Some may choose Prada shoes or golf—it's all good—but we are our own keepers.

From the ashes, like the phoenix, I rose to face the morning and care for the little boy who dared to endure to make me a man. I shower him with blessings, the ones every child deserves regardless of his nature, for it is love that heals the contradictions that make us human, and it is our compassion that glorifies the creator and her creation. It took many lifetimes to shed the weight that was not serving the Godhead, my world, and the man called Osvaldo Calixto Amador.

I decided to show the world my paintings, writings, and true face. The heaviness of shame that I had inherited disintegrated into the unity of my new being. I have incorporated the feminine with the masculine and both my parents' wisdoms. Osvaldito will no longer be bullied, and neither will Ozzie. Osvaldo Calixto Amador is a man on his own terms, not restricted by any societal norms. Yes,

Whitman, I found my own tune, my own song. I found the love I had been seeking all my life, and it was all there across the dry desert. I am forever in a spring of blooms, seeing each sunrise through the eyes of a child. I know the spirits of my forebears are here, never gone. To myself, I sing in perfect harmony with the beautiful child I have come to know. He has the courage of a lion, the wisdom of all our ancestors, and the heart of a god.

"Our Lord has written the promise of resurrection, not in books alone, but in every leaf in springtime."

—Martin Luther

CHAPTER 9

The hidden harmony is better than the obvious.

—Pablo Picasso

I have always painted ever since I can remember. I have loved colors, shapes, textures, and the intense contrast between light and dark. Van Gogh used colors, and spoke about colors, as the enthusiasm life needs to live. I have a congenital reverence for harmony in contradictions, especially in dark versus light and the hues that unite them. Perhaps it's because I find that life is a contradiction where I have been poised to find acceptance with the seeming incongruity of it all.

In my childhood, I spent hours alone putting colors together to make what in Osvaldito's world was his masterpiece. Later in life, at the university, I would take drawing and painting classes, which I passed with academia's perfect scores. Osvaldito is still very much alive within me, and he prefers to paint as his heart desires. He paints totally outside all the lines that pertain to restrictive boundaries in the art world. Pablo Picasso said that it takes a lifetime to paint like a child, but I never lost that part of me; I have been blessed to always paint like a child.

Part of the world I grew up in felt antiseptic and barren. But for the times I spent with Mami, I had little or no exposure to art. The most incredible artist I have ever known was my mother. My mother taught me that true art has no rules that your soul does not already know and can traverse. "*El artista nunca es pobre, porque crea de la nada. Yo jugaba con munecas hechos de palitos, de papel, y de carton tejidos juntos con hilo que Mama me dejaba usar. Nadie me enseno hacer eso, nadie tenia el tiempo; eso vino desde mis adentro, de mi alma.*" "Artists are never poor," my mother would recite over and over throughout my life, "because an artist creates from nothing. I used wooden sticks found outdoors, cardboard pieces, and paper, stitching them together with thread Mama used to give me. No one had the time to teach me; that came from inside of me, from my soul." Like a seemingly chaotic bird nest, mother and son built their fortress from the weeds of nature, for nature is abundant with all of its creation. Sensitive souls learn the tools of the master through grace; "...consider the lilies , how they grow; they toil not...", said Jesus to those who paid attention.

The tools I used to survive the chaos became my art. I never showed my art to anyone. Around the age of seven, I conversed with my mother, and we both recollected the conversation many decades later when I was to have my first art exhibit. It was Osvaldito who somehow prophesized he would someday be called a painter. "*Mami, yo voy hacer pintor, y desde ahora voy a firmar mis pinturas como Calixto porque los Americanos no saben decir Osvaldo.*" I told my mother that I was going to be a painter and that I was going to sign my paintings as Calixto, my middle name, because Americans did not know how to pronounce Osvaldo. Mrs. Brush's words remained, and Osvaldito used the fertilizer. In retrospect, this does not make much sense at all since Calixto is not exactly an easy name to grasp. Looking back, Osvaldito may have been made to feel ashamed of his own name, but this did not stop him.

Every artwork I have created since, I have signed as Calixto, in honor of that little kid Mami called Osvaldito. There have been exceptions where Osvaldo has come into the signature, and when I get to heaven, if I make it through the pearly gates, I will make sure to add this to the list of questions I have for Mr. and Mrs. God. Never in my wildest dreams did I think someone would pay good money for any painting of mine. Yet, Osvaldito knew something, and I predict he knows much he has yet to unravel for me. Of my childhood paintings, only a couple remain, and they are priceless to me. Much like my father's cardboard birthday card, they materialized from the indisputable spirit of love.

Art has been my savior: It is my refuge, all of it. I believe that all of life is art. Everything I have ever done, everything I do, and everything I'll ever do can be viewed through the lens of art, knowing well, that for me, art is love, and love is art. One interpretation of the meaning or origin of the word "art" is to craft, make, and fabricate, among others. For this writer, art began in my mind using the enticing, elusive imagination of a little boy escaping his dark world. Imagination is the ability of the mind to be creative or resourceful, and while Osvaldito was growing up, his survival instincts plunged him into the world of imagination in more ways than I could possibly consciously uncover. I have found it propitious that Osvaldito was shielded from the darkness without, more importantly, as Nietzsche said, not becoming a monster while fighting them. If you can dream it, well, you can dream, and if you can dream, you are not dead. Dream away.

I believe it was art, especially painting, that God used to save me from falling into the depths of human depravity. I was amazed at my first exhibit, which I called *Resurrection*. I was surprised that my art was enjoyed, admired, and even respected. My paintings were always a part of me, a second skin if you will, and to be honest, apart from the brief moments of a child's dream, never did it occur to me that my paintings straight from my imagination would be hung in any exhibition. Having an exhibit felt oddly strange yet familiar.

Writing is a different story altogether. To write has been to try to penetrate that glacial mass that has taken a lifetime to expose to light. As much as my paintings can reveal my inner world, writing is the nudist camp of the soul. I can slightly, not altogether for the third eye, camouflage my inner world in my paintings. Writing reveals the marrow of the man. The first painting I ever sold I named *Hope*. I painted *Hope* with a total absentmindedness that enabled me to tap into a mystical source that has always been the root of all creation.

I had a complete and utter confrontation with God. I needed an answer to a question born many lifetimes ago, and during a severe depression, I decided to paint, allowing my inner forces to take over everything I considered human. Without a vision, plan, or expectation, I let go of myself completely. This was not unusual, for this has been my mode of painting since I can remember; even as a child, it was my escape. This continues to be the only formula that works for me. When I am painting, it is the only space where I forget myself, time and space become one, and I am less than human while divinity intermingles with my skin. Painting grants me a gentle touch of divinity's hem.

The difference with *Hope* was that I was getting ready to die. I did not know how or when, but I was exiting life, and I had prayed for months for God to relieve me of this torment that did not cease, day or night. The result was *Hope*. I have admitted this to only two people in my life, but I offer it here for anyone who reads this: When

Hope was done, I lay on the floor for hours, half naked, exhausted, and overwhelmed. I lay on the cold, hard ceramic tiles and cried because God had revealed herself through this profound experience, letting me know my time in this incarnation was not done. I had entrusted the blank canvas to this force that goes by many names with all my faith. The canvas came alive without my conscious awareness. A painting resulted out of the seemingly nothing at all. The beating of my heart was present, but my mind had left—and *Hope* had manifested in the absence of the man.

Every painting I have ever done has been an act of faith. I love abstraction because when I am in front of a blank canvas, I entrust that canvas to my higher being and let go. Some paintings happen effortlessly without the clashes of my inner worlds. Other paintings take years of confrontations, and I mean years because the feelings do not reveal themselves clearly. I am a painter of feelings, not subjects, and the cost is years of nothingness. Like God, paintings play hide-and-seek; they reveal themselves in their time, not mine. I have put paintings away for eons.

As I write this, I am in the process of a series of paintings I started ten years ago that have not manifested themselves, and perhaps they never will. With each painting, I am more faithful to the Almighty. With each painting, a part of me grows wiser and more faithful. While in the process, there is the pain of labor and the exhilaration of manifestation. Every abstract act is a tug-of-war between ego, humility, God, and all my selves, which reside in spirit in and around my chaotic unity.

With each act of creation, I struggle; it is a life-form with its own spatial time and universe. It is a long labor without epidural anesthesia. It is the clash of all the creative powers converging in one man's body. This magnetism of opposites, this battle of the gods, takes its medium to unknown territories, which can give madness a new definition. Without the faith of a true paladin, Freud himself would have to be called in for immediate resuscitation of the mental capacities.

Art, like life, is a learning process in which we must choose our guiding star, our compass, our terra firma, and without it, we can become indisposed. Art is a surrendering and an opening of our total humanity, including the otherworldliness part of our being. Like resurrection itself, it is losing it all and allowing it to be on its own. I am just the medium, impatiently waiting with tiresome patience. Sometimes, after years of nothingness, a huge harvest of creation rises from the energies that have been incubating to manifest a new birth from the gods. It is that awaited birth, the fruits of my reliance on the spirit of truth, that make me feel most alive; it is love itself.

There was interest in buying *Hope*, and this was my trial by fire. *Hope* was hung in my bedroom, and I kept it dimly lit every night to remind me of the revelation that had shown its message during some of my darkest hours: Have hope—for there is always more than you will ever know.

Enters Mami.

"*Osvaldito, tus pinturas son un don que Dios te ha Regalado. No son tuyas; son para compartir con el mundo.*" As usual, my mother's wisdom proved to be the potion I needed. With the wisdom of all ages, she said: "Osvaldito, your art is a gift that God gave you. Your paintings are not yours; they are meant to share with the world."

Therein was the answer to my endless questioning. Osvaldito was right. I was a painter, and it was a gift to be shared. Art was my love, my lover, my second skin, my passion, my god. No love can stay if it is not given away, for what good is love without the other to reflect its beauty? It is not ours; it is our greatest gift, it is the gift of life, to live, to receive, to integrate it all. That is art; that is love. Love is free and unconditional; otherwise, it is other than.

I do not profess to know much about humanity, but I believe that our humanity is meant to be shared, the good, the bad, and the ugly. Only when we accept it all, lose it all, can we understand that we are one. We are love, I am love, and I am, you are, the passing of the light, the torch to create or destroy. I choose to always create. Sharing my world, I share my vulnerabilities, my strength, my pains, and my glory. Ultimately, I am really sharing my own humanity. The lessons from art have been my guardian angel. Now I know love, and now I know what Mami meant. With a heart, I can battle the Trojan War. I am not alone; I never was.

Picasso said, "The hidden harmony is better than the obvious." It is one of my favorite quotes from him. In my life, the hidden has been more relevant than what the naked eye can see. In my paintings, I strive for a harmony that only the third eye can sense. The unceremonious may touch the light without sight. The spirit in everything is in the unseen, grasped by the sensibilities of the sensitive. Plato's theory of forms reminds me that the physical world is not as accurate or true as the timeless, absolute, and unchangeable ideas inherent in the unseen; the seen is only the shadow of any real truth. What our naked eye sees is just a mere shadow of the real beauty.

I know nothing of art, which is precisely how I like it. Scholars of art study the craft and creation. Knowing only what pleases my senses is more than enough. Art can't be truly explained: What I feel is real. Glancing at a sunset in Key West, Florida, gives me a knowing that permeates all the cells of my being without the need for stirring the intellect. What I know is that I feel, and what I feel is natural and requires no dissertation.

Every onlooker is correct in their interpretation of an art piece. It's simple for the likes of me; they either like it or don't. We may not always know how to express in words why we like or don't like an object, but all of us have a knowing. All of us have the prerogative to change our minds. At first sight, something that was not appealing may become a beloved object once we open ourselves to see it from a different perspective. A love affair may happen at first glance, or it may slowly grow; at least, this has been my experience in the world of art and love. I have fallen in love with artists because of their spirit, life, and intentions rather than their art. I have fallen in love with the art of some artist and disliked the artist; it's a mystical formula, much like life itself.

I don't have a magical creation formula, although I wish for it unreservedly. If I have learned anything from my creation process, it is that the muse can be as random and as certain as all of life can be. My first exhibit, *Resurrection*, was held in the historic Tower Theater on Calle Ocho under the auspices of Miami Dade Community College and the City of Miami. How on earth did that exhibit ever take place? If you ask me, it was nothing short of a miracle. Creating, publicly showing, and selling your art are very different. I could not handle a public viewing of any size of my artwork. This was certainly an unknown territory for me and a dangerously scary one. The muse nudged, stirred, and prompted the first baby steps toward an exhibit. I knew no one in the art world of consequence, but God did.

This is how *Resurrection* came to be. One day, out of the blue, I decided I would get into my car and go out and allow myself to be driven by that uncompromising holy spirit that has always guided me. I wanted to feel the places that moved me, to dare ask if my artwork could be shown in their sphere. I entered many places that turned me down, and I somehow got the impression they were also insulted I had dared to ask. Later, some of these same places would pursue me vigorously to show my artwork. It did not matter how disappointed I was; I had a calling and would do this on several occasions. I know when something is meant to be because I do not give up on it, regardless of the disappointments. Anyone who has had the burning urge, the calling from the realm of spirit, will understand that we go on regardless. We are guided, and the doors are opened.

There was one place I was particularly drawn to, and it was the historic Tower Theater. It was a place Osvaldito recognized, for he had been to this same theater with his Mami many times as a child. I walked in, and coincidence or not, the curator was in the house. I told him I had been a student at Miami Dade Community College and wished to show my art. In retrospect, this kind man must have thought I was crazy, but it takes a bit of craziness to do something like this. Call unto me? What was I thinking!

The truth—and the best part of it—is that I was not thinking. He was kind and gave me the time of day. "*Traeme un portfolio de tu arte.*" "Bring me a portfolio of your artwork." A portfolio? Yes! Of course! A portfolio like a real artist! I was carrying nothing but courage and a knowing with me; the thought of a portfolio had never entered my mind! With these words, he gently opened the window of opportunity.

As I write about the events that took place, it all seems rather planned, on schedule, a divine hand was at play—and no one could be more surprised at the interventions at this juncture in my life than me. I am amazed at the courage and willingness that showed up at this crossroads. For one thing, I was coming out of a deep depression. Secondly, I have never been one to be comfortable at any big social gatherings. I had no experience whatsoever in what it took to bring about an exhibit.

No matter what, the beat went on, and one baby step in front of the other kept the pulse moving forward. There was a fuel in me that was not of this world. I was being guided, and for all the doors that closed behind me, many more were opened. I needed carte blanche for the exhibit, meaning I had to be the curator of my work. What an audacity! It was given when needed! How on earth does anyone know better than I how or where my work should come together? I was blessed, and I do not trust my art to be curated—no matter how many degrees in art the curator may have. This is not arrogance; it's the love of the creator for its creation. And if I missed it, and it is arrogance, so be it; I bore the labor pains.

The day came when the doors of the Tower were opened in preparation for the exhibit by Calixto Amador, and Osvaldito was a very happy little boy. What had I done? I was given the OK to exhibit, the miracles of miracles. Enter my therapist, who, for a little under a year while I was preparing for the exhibit, had prepared me for the inner revolution that was taking place within Osvaldito, Ozzie, Calixto, and Osvaldo. And it was a revolution for the hurt parts of me. I was scared, petrified, and even guilty of believing I deserved such an opportunity. Day after day turned into week after week and, eventually, month after month, and I prepared like a marathon runner.

My therapist knew me like few people have ever known me in this world. I never kept anything from her. Angelina was the person I have trusted most in this world, after my mom. She believed in me like few people have ever believed in me. More than a decade later, a month after my mother's death, she suffered a brain hemorrhage, and I felt like I had lost two moms in a row. She supported me through the creative process and assured me I was worth it. I grabbed onto her words like a drowning man amidst a severe storm in the middle of the Gulf of Mexico.

I was very focused and trusting with the creative process. Although I hoped for a favorable outcome, part of me was oblivious to the results. The only way I can explain this duality of hopeful, but ambivalent feelings is by confessing that this was not about Calixto; it was about all my parts coming together to honor the God I knew without a doubt was the creator of the artwork and my world. There is freedom in faith and letting go and letting God take charge. The creative process is not so much about the outcome as it is about the wonderful journey it takes me on.

On the exhibit day, I knelt before the altar that had saved me so many years earlier. My mother would always say, "*A Dios no le puedes mentir.*" "You can never lie to God." On my knees that day, in front of the altar that had saved me so many decades before, I confessed to God. God knew what I was confessing before I confessed it. I did this in gratitude for resurrecting my spirit time and time again. "I did this for you," I prayed. I did this for Osvaldito, for that little orphaned child who colored outside the lines. I did this without knowing why I was being drawn to paint. I thanked him for the opportunity to wrestle with courage, the demons of a lifetime. God does not need anything from me, and I need him desperately. But like the story of the prodigal son, I come home again and again, and he smiles.

When I pray and meditate, it is not to ask or tell God anything he does not already know; he is omniscient. I pray and meditate in order to align my ego and bow to the Godhead in my humble human frailties. *Resurrection* was an exhibit that I will forever treasure in my memory. Success is relative. As for me, there can be no greater success than feeling the presence of the Almighty that night among his creations hanging on the wall of the historic Tower Theater. The painting in the poster of that exhibit went to Bacardi, and it was surreal to see my painting hung among creators that had negotiated with the same life I was living, the life of an artist.

It has been through my art that I have been able to temporarily put aside the social ineptitudes that I have struggled with all my life. Most people do not know that I am hard of hearing in addition to having social fears, but I have known this since I was a teenager. Being in a group of people with background noise, be it music or the conversation of others, is taxing for me on many levels. I have always avoided gatherings, partly because I am, despite appearances to the contrary, very shy and introverted. I try very hard to mask this shyness. Therefore, few people who meet me would ever define me as an introvert. On the contrary, they would probably say that I am among the most sociable and extroverted people they've met. This is due to the amount of rigorous work I put into not being discovered. I also enjoy people and enjoy having people feel comfortable around me. Nevertheless, for me, the perfect exhibit scenario would be if I could hang my artwork and remain as a fly on the wall—or perhaps not even remain. This is a toss-up, like butter or mayonnaise on Abuela's big Cuban crackers. The reality is that my feelings were binary during the opening night of *Resurrection*, as usual.

The joy was evident, for I was in a state of enchantment, gratitude, and intense satisfaction. On the other hand, for parts of me, it was torture to talk about my art, about me, and anything to do with life. Period. Inside the strong outward demeanor lies a scared little kid who feels awkward in social situations. Inside resides that little boy with hand-me-down clothes who never got picked to play on any team. That night, the Tower Theater was packed, it radiated wall to wall with shimmering lights of hope, and the full moon lit the way to the opening night of Calixto's first art exhibit.

When I left Campina, toward the exhibit, I looked up and saw one of the most beautiful full moons I have ever seen—and I knew all would be well. I drove alone even though a few friends had offered to go with me. I wanted to savor every moment with God, and solitude was required. I knew well it could have failed and failed miserably. It did not matter because I had peace, the peace that only a loving God can provide. I had done what I felt in my heart God had wanted me to do: I had to let go of the ego that asked for anything else. I do not know how to explain the serenity I felt, but I have felt that serenity in very important moments in my life, including the death of my mother. It is what I call faith, for lack of a better word; there are no words to explain it. A faith that come what may, I am loved, and nothing added or subtracted can ever change this.

The festivity was palpable; love was in the air. Mojitos were being had, and laughter resonated throughout the whole of Calle Ocho, for it was not only the historic Tower having Calixto's exhibit; it was also a block party celebrating Latin art heritage in all the surrounding galleries. I was amazed at the crowd that showed up, and I was amazed at the positive reception of my artwork by some artists who, by chance, just happened to drop by. Not! Nothing is by chance in life, that much I am certain of. One of those artists was a man who became a friend, Josevelio Rodriguez Abreu, and he gifted me a poem I treasure about my artwork that night. I could not have been more honored:

"Nacer en una isla no es solo una precisión geográfica.
Es ser la espuma traslucida de las marea, con el talento
del cuerpo para tejer la melodía de los conquistadores
del milagro. Así es la pintura de Calixto. ¿Quién
puede resistirse a la amistad de un isleño, que su
apellido es Amador? Sí, en sus lienzos asistimos,
a la ceremonia de las pasiones, los ciclones, y el
sosiego etéreo de los lotos que flotan, para conservar
los recuerdos, los agravios y la esperanza. Acuden
las mariposas a la ventana de su estudio a dar fe y
reconocerse en la fragilidad de lo hermoso. Nadie como
el artista; puede dar lo que no tiene, y así a través
de sus visiones adueñarse de los sueños, los ajenos
y los propios, en la quebrada del arroyuelo. En otra
serie de lienzos mas recientes, Calixto Amador nos
propone resolver el crucigrama de la soledad urbana,
en el laberinto de la existencia. Perturbadoras
divisiones del destino, con trazos verticales de la
espiritualidad, y horizontales cuadrículas pequeñas
para el reposo. Lienzos ajedrezados; donde poner cada

ilusión en su lugar. A veces en estancias de profundos negros y azules, un hilo de luz para escapar: ¿O será la diminuta puerta angélica de un talismán? Por siempre está Cristo en la cruz para protegernos y guiarnos por el camino, de la concordia y la tolerancia. La obra de Amador es un privilegio visual, tan inefable como tocar el cielo con las pupilas."

—Josevelio Rodríguez-Abreu, June 2010

"Being born on an island is not just a geographical precision. It is to be the translucent foam of the tides, with the talent of the body to weave the melody of the conquerors of the miracle. This is Calixto's painting. Who can resist the friendship of an islander whose last name is Amador? Yes, in his canvases, we attend the ceremony of the passions, the cyclones, and the ethereal calm of the floating lotuses, to preserve memories, grievances, and hope. Butterflies come to the window of his studio to attest and recognize themselves in the fragility of beauty. Nobody like the artist can give what he does not have, and thus through his visions take possession of dreams, those of others and his own, in the ravine of the stream. In another series of more recent canvases, Calixto Amador proposes us to solve the crossword puzzle of urban solitude, in the labyrinth of existence. Disturbing divisions of destiny, with vertical lines of spirituality, and small horizontal grids for rest, checkered canvases, where to put each illusion in its place. Sometimes in rooms of deep black and blue, a thread of light to

escape: Or is it the tiny angelic door of a talisman? Christ is forever on the cross to protect us and guide us along the path of harmony and tolerance. Amador's work is a visual privilege, as ineffable as touching the sky with your eyes."

—Josevelio Rodríguez-Abreu, June 2010

Credo, one of the major highlights of my painting career, was held at a Catholic church in the Chapel of La Merced in Miami's art district zone. La Merced is joined in the same property as Corpus Christi in Midtown Miami, and I have never worked so hard or been more fulfilled in any kind of work than with that exhibit. To have been able to exhibit my work in what Mami taught me was God's house, well, this goes beyond elucidation of any kind. I literally worked day and night with very little, if any, sleep for days. So much is spoken about coincidences, destiny, self-will, and the power of the individual to be master of his own fate. The former and latter have their origin in the history of language, trying to symbolize the human experience. To try to explain the birth of *Credo* would necessitate a new language of its own. This opportunity came to be through those celestial powers I will never be able to explain.

I will backtrack many years to give this time in my life the merit it deserves. My college years were divided between Miami Dade Community College, where I earned an associate degree in arts in secondary teaching, and Florida International University, where I took the painting and drawing class and graduated with a bachelor's in history. Finally, there was Nova Southeastern University, where I earned a master's in sociology. I was accepted into a doctoral program in psychology, but life and I chose differently, and I did not pursue this course. In between degrees, I took graduate courses in psychology, philosophy of religion, theology, anthropology, and philosophy. Abuela was wrong because it took a lot of work to learn how to do the most basic of math, the most basic of grammar, and to learn from scratch all the academics I had missed. By the way, Abuela, I passed all my classes with above-average grades. I am a basurero (trash collector); in that you were right, for I still love thrift stores!

I have always painted and loved abstraction, but it was a secret love affair. Few, if anyone, knew I painted. I was never interested in taking art classes, and it was only when I entered MDCC that I had to take my first class on the history of art as a requirement. I dreaded taking the course, for it meant I had to intellectualize what I felt, which went against every grain in my body. The truth is, I had decided never to take painting classes as a young man and had chosen to visit very few, if any, museums. I wanted to paint from the inside out and not from the outside in. Perhaps the inside and outside find their harmony and converge in a Jungian or Daliesque sense. I have reconciled this lack of interest in museums, but it was torture to do so. It may have been artistic arrogance, for I felt that museums were for the bourgeoisie, in both the creative talent and patronage. Or it may have been fear. Today, I know it was a bit of both.

My inspiration for art is life itself. Everywhere I look, I see it. The ultimate inspiration for this man is his own rarity, his own lens, his own way of perceiving and understanding his world. I can only paint from my truth; I have no choice. The observer in both Harper Lee and Anna Sewell was more than enough for their magnum opuses. The observer in Osvaldito was more than enough for his creations. As a very young man, I was resentful of the middle classes, the rich, and those they patronized. Somehow, I associated the most esteemed art with the patronage of the elite in society, and I wanted nothing to do with them. I had been raised poor, and I was loyal to poverty. When I heard the intellectuals speaking about the established artists of our time and those of the past, I felt they did them an injustice. Some critics can make art more complicated than it truly is, and other critics make a sham out of the complexities in art and the artist.

None of it was for the younger me. I had my rebellious period, and I wanted nothing to do with the upper echelons of my world. This, of course, was based in prejudice, envy, and the feeling that I did not belong. The truth is that art belongs to every class of society, but patronage is highly necessary for those who aspire to eat bread *and* make their voices heard. Indeed, fear can be the root of prejudice, and I am a better man for having learned this lesson early. So many wasted opportunities as a young man, for when I visited one of my favorite cities in the world, Paris, I entered the Louvre and exited it rather quickly. I wanted to see only those artists who had been rebels like me, like my favorite, Van Gogh.

> *"They are so damn "intellectual" and rotten that I can't stand them anymore [...] I would rather sit on the floor in the market of Toluca and sell tortillas than have anything to do with those "artistic" bitches of Paris. "*
>
> —Frida Kahlo

On the first day of art history class at MDCC, I sat far enough back to be invisible. I do not know what I was expecting, but this was not it. My other classes were filled with button-down plaid shirts and khaki pants and Ivy League wannabe professors. Here, in my first art history class, entered a Napoleon-sized Cuban with long hair. The professor was wearing faded jeans, wooden clogs, and a Cuban guayabera. He boasted savoir faire and a flirtatious swagger like none other I had seen. His heavy Cuban accent resounded vividly with a rich, dramatic baritone that bounced off the walls of the acoustic auditorium classroom setting. Undoubtedly, he was well caffeinated with the obvious Cuban drug, for which the street name is "café Cubano."

This man took me on a joyride for the whole semester. With every class, he was able to pull me in closer to his exposition. For me, his style was a spirited, buoyant exposition of truth. I love passion; life can get stale without it. His passion for art, especially for abstraction, was mouthwatering. The projector in front of the almost empty auditorium provided vivid, towering images of works from Jackson Pollock, Mondrian, De Kooning, Kandinsky, and Rothko, just to name a few. With the towering images came the delicious contralto Cuban accent daring us to give voice to our thoughts and feelings about the bigger-than-life screen images in front of us.

I dared not speak, but I was afraid my heart palpitations would be heard. My passion burned deep inside me, for never had I seen the explosion of such wildness come together in an unexplainable equilibrium that defied all logic. This was it! This was what Osvaldito had been trying to show me all his life. Ozzie was learning that Osvaldito had an inner wisdom that is encoded in our species, and there were words of respect attached to these seemingly obscure visions.

More than teaching a class in art history, Dr. Napoleon Cuban Café Art Genius awoke my senses to a dimension I had been trying to reach since my earliest childhood. This man was made of the stuff good teachers are made of: a passion for his subject matter and respect for the uniqueness of his pupils. I never spoke in class, but I could not help myself from seeking him out in the isolation of the auditorium once all the other inconveniences were out of the way, mainly the other students. Here, in the intimacy between apprentice and master, I heard the sacred words the master imparted to his young disciple: "*El abstracto es la forma mas alta de arte.*" "Abstraction is the highest form of art." Jesus, Joseph, and Mary, did I hear him correctly? I did. It was the shortest semester, the shortest class, and one of the most memorable classes I have ever taken in all my academic career. Dr. NCCAG was a vehicle that allowed me to be resolute in my journey toward abstraction.

Almost thirty years later, I ran into him at a café in Miami where he was being interviewed for a book he had just published. He still had that savoir faire demeanor, yet the old master had toned it down a notch. Perhaps it was because he was being interviewed for a piece of art literature, not trying to inspire students, or maybe it was the inevitable mellowing that comes to some folks of a certain age. It did not matter to this fan; I was in awe of the master and felt privileged to observe his gestures, so typical of him, as he maneuvered brilliantly through his interview.

I observed his undying love for art from my table, deliberately chosen way back, almost invisible like in the good old days in the auditorium. That was the last I saw of him. I later learned he had to use a wheelchair and had lost everything material, so much so that a collection was taken up for his support among his peers and former students. He will never know that I was among his supporters.

Dr. Jose A. Martinez passed away—but not before inspiring and giving from his heart. I loved this man; he gave me so much, and I know he gave all his students everything they would need—and more—to inspire the love of art. I hold so much love in my heart for him for all he taught me, and he remains a part of me. What a difference a good teacher makes. He is always near, and during *Credo*, his voice resonated through the cathedral as the master of all masters in art. Thank you, Dr. M., you helped make me a better artist, but more importantly, you helped make that young man at the back of your class a better human being. I love you.

When I was allowed to exhibit in la casa de Dios, in God's house, I remembered him, and I remembered all that he had taught me while working on *Credo*. Among the many mysteries disclosed from master to disciple was that only I can determine what art is for me—to thine own self be true. Freedom! You see, up until that point, I thought Osvaldito had made up abstraction, which brings me to my next art professor, Dr. Jane Doe at Florida International University.

Dr. Doe was the antithesis of Dr. Napoleon Cuban Café Art Genius; she was an intellectual on steroids, and she taught the rules of art. I hated the two classes I took with Dr. Doe—every second, minute, hour, and day. It was two very long, drooling semesters! I did not hate Dr. Doe; she was pleasant enough. In retrospect, she was a much-needed ingredient in my rice with mango, or chaos, really. In fact, she was very accommodating to my conscious, unconscious, and subconscious rebellion. I was a rebel with a cause. I set out to dismantle all the rules of art, and I wanted Dr. Doe to know it in no uncertain terms.

I was a young stud in my twenties, and I had more courage than a man has a right to have. I took two classes with Dr. Doe: painting and drawing. I was already nauseated by the idea that I foresaw myself drawing vases with flowers, shapes of ludicrous Styrofoam still life with atrocious sheets swaying to challenge the art student to learn about light, shadows, and blah, blah, blah. So why did I take the class? Part of me must have been a masochist in those days, but the real reason was that I wanted to prove that I could paint. I could have chosen a better venue where I could be incognito and it was not necessary to complete the class and pass it with a grade, but I can be ballsy, and this was one of those occasions. Ah, the arrogance of youth. *Bienaventurados sean la juventud!* Blessed be thy youth!

The class began with the academics, the theories, the rules, and the Magna Carta of the art world, and I yawned through it all, pretending to be above such mediocrity. If eyes could be rolled inside oneself, I was rolling three of them. Plainly speaking, I was a prickly prick, but I had to pay attention because I needed those grades to earn my bachelor's degree. Why I chose to torture my already tormented self is forever an enigma, but it felt like Abuela's enemas. There have been times I have made life harder than it needed to be.

I walked in late to almost every one of her classes. OK, it was at the north campus of FIU, which required a much longer drive during rush-hour traffic, but the rebel prick did not want to be on time for the lecture on traditions, laws, and the blah, blah, blah of academia. I was above and beyond these topics. Fear is often disguised as arrogance, for beneath my bravado there has always been a terminal case of fear. At the root of all my fears lies that incessant nauseating stench of not being good enough. The projects were lengthy: drawing a skeleton, a musculature dummy, pipes, and the proverbial still life with plastic flowers and fruits. The drawing class was painful, and the painting class was unbearable. Nothing is more unnatural than telling an artsy inner child what to draw and/or paint.

There was to be one final grade in each class at the end of the semester: one grade for the drawing class and one grade for the painting class. We were not to have any other clue of how we were measuring up. As for me, all I got were distant looks from Dr. Doe. If I had any clue about measuring up in these classes, they were slight disapprovals. Dr. Doe believed I could always do better. She quickly picked up on my lack of interest—or at least my display of lack of interest.

Some of my display was true boredom, for I could not imagine ever being interested in drawing what I could see; for that, I had Annie Leibovitz, Bruce Weber, and Ansel Adams. The creative part of me always wants to paint what I feel and not what I see. Seeing is about techniques, and painting feelings is about revelation. Osvaldito likes to paint outside the lines and create joy with the surprises emanating from his purposeful mistakes. Perhaps this is Osvaldito's mischievous angle, which he had hidden. Like the *Mona Lisa*'s smile, only the knower knows.

At the end of the courses, Dr. Doe called me into her private office at the corner of the enormous warehouse art studio at the north campus of Florida International University. She was a solemn woman, a no-nonsense kind of gal; she was Barbara Stanwyck in *The Big Valley*, and I was certain the matriarch would be telling me I was failing for lack of enthusiasm. Suddenly, my bravado wimped out, deflated, and I became the vulnerable little kid whose true essence was timidity and insecurity.

I was curious to know if I had passed or failed, but there was no turning back. In a few minutes, with a few words, Barbara Stanwyck said more to me than she had said in the two long and tedious classes. Sitting at her desk on one side, she motioned for me to take a seat. I was ready, for I had fought a good fight with drawing and painting.

Barbara Stanwyck kept writing with her head fixated on the paper that seemed to be swallowing all her real attention, or so I thought. "Your grade may come as a surprise. You know, Ozzie, to break the rules, you must first know them." She said this with a steady tone, never deviating from her task, and she wrote as she spoke: slow, focused, and with intention.

I started to say I was sorry. I wanted to let her know it was nothing against her personally and that I was a fearful jerk, but she stopped me before I could make a total fool of myself.

"I wish you well, Ozzie." With that, just as she motioned me to sit, she motioned me to exit.

I cried all the way back to my car, which seemed parked at the outer edges of the universe. I failed, and I failed miserably.

Is ego an essential element for an artist? Indeed, it takes courage, drive, and a certain amount of ego to desire to create. Is humility more crucial for an artist? If a gift is given, one should never take credit for it, or at least not the total credit, and most definitely never take it for granted. What is that balance? What is that "hidden harmony" that Picasso talked about? Why had I committed myself to all my history classes, sociology, and philosophy? I mean, I was a dedicated and committed student, and some of those classes where extremely difficult! Those classes required at a minimum complicated literary research, theses, and good old-fashioned academic sweat. Especially for me, coming from my inadequate educational background, I had to put in the extra hours in all my classes, and I did so earnestly and with passion, except in Barbara Stanwyck's classes.

I was afraid that when it came to art, I was not good enough for the world of academia. It could not have been more obvious. Barbara Stanwyck had seen through my facade and called me on it. I received a perfect score of 100 in each class—two perfect A's in Dr. Doe's classes. I was bewildered when I received the grade via the old-fashioned mail. In those days, I had to wait to receive my grades, which was hell! I had thought I failed her classes, and my whole undergraduate GPA and graduation would have been altered by these classes.

The following semester, I sought out Dr. Doe, and she seemed softer and more open to listening to what I had to say. Or was it the other way around? Was it I who had changed, now copacetic and less intimidated? All I had to say was, "What happened?" I thought I had failed. She responded, "I have never seen a student love art so much in all my years of teaching. You tried so hard to sabotage yourself, but in the end, you have more respect for art than you do for yourself and your gift." Huh?

She saw right through me! She understood what I had yet to totally recognize! I loved art more than I loved myself! Art was my savior, and I was afraid I was not good enough to be saved! A lightning bolt cracked my hard head wide open, and I allowed that to sink in. "You have more respect for art than you do for yourself." I learned that I felt I was not good enough, especially not good enough to be saved, and that lesson was not in the syllabus. I had not even signed up for it. It was a revelation from my grandmother's neon God hanging in the dark Hialeah apartment, teaching me lessons through splashes of paint. Osvaldito smiled his Mona Lisa smile because I had accepted his gift: to paint like a child! I was blessed among the curses. The hidden was revealed. Art is my passion, my love, and my god. God is love, art, and passion. Now, I am good enough, now I am strong enough to accept imperfection, now I am a full-fledged human being, faults and all. God, I love art!

I thought long and hard about *Credo* and what I wanted to feel through my paintings, which would be exhibited in God's house. When my ego decides, it all becomes dung, and the struggle ensues. Without the ego, desire is passionless, and an uninterested result creeps in inadvertently. Hence, I wrote about the passion of Dr. Napoleon Cuban Café Art Genius versus the balancing element of Barbara Stanwyck. For me, art, like life, is a balancing act. Mami was right: "You will learn much through your art." *Credo* will always be Mount Everest for this painter. I was the medium for which the creator's energy manifested itself. It was a high-wire balancing act like none I had dared undertake.

During the creation of the exhibit *Credo*, there were days that I thought I was literally going to die. My energy left me on many occasions. The church walls were massive, and my task was to fill them with my paintings. At the very least, I was to make the paintings worthy of such a space. I was given carte blanche, and I was as happy as a pig in mud. Yes, it was incredibly challenging, but doing this in "la casa de Dios," in God's house, gave me all the life force I needed. For the months that I prepared, the universe conspired in multidimensional ways. People, places, and things showed up when needed, as if by magic. Ozzie in Wonderland is not a fictitious characterization but a working phenomenon. I read somewhere that Einstein believed that imagination is everything. It is the preview of life's coming attractions. Imagination is more important than knowledge, and Osvaldito's imagination had brought him and his paintings to God's house.

The night before the opening of the *Credo* exhibit, Father Juaquin Mora John Doe De La Cruz Jr. walked into the church as quietly as a field mouse. It was approximately one o'clock in the morning, and no one but me and a trusted assistant, Juan, remained. I was putting some finishing touches on details that only God herself would have noticed, and I knew it was enough. From the corner of my eye, I saw him walk in, and with his hands behind his back, he strolled, stopping in front of each painting. Eventually, our paths met inside the cathedral, and he said, "I believe you are making history, Calixto. I do not know of any other living artist that has exhibited inside a Catholic church." I was humbled and pleased by his words. I do not know if this is a fact, but it does not matter. The most important history of that exhibit was that Osvaldito, the little boy who had been traumatized by a life full of violence and neglect, was so very happy that God allowed him to hang his paintings in his house. I have not done another exhibit since.

Credo was passion with equilibrium. I had to find a way to unite these two forces in this body in order to allow the creation that took place to manifest itself. I also understood that my life was in peril, for I did not eat well, did not sleep well, and was exhausted beyond words. I had stretched my body, my soul, and my imagination to the outer limits, and I felt it in every nucleus of every atom. My body and soul had been to the mountaintop, and like Moses, I came back much grayer than my vanity would have liked.

CHAPTER 9

I can't even begin to imagine what Michelangelo must have gone through panting the Sistine Chapel, but I believe his life was in imminent danger—and this is a fact in my mental archives. When I first visited the Sistine Chapel, I felt I was in the DeLorean vehicle in *Back to the Future.* I was in a time travel machine that left me speechless. I could not speak, and I could barely breathe. I could sense Michelangelo's energy, his passion, his love for art, and his death. I will never risk my life again; I know I love art, but I also love myself.

I will always paint, but I do not know if I will ever exhibit again. *Credo* took every ounce of my being, giving me the highest satisfaction I have ever received. I feel like I am yet to discover the ramifications of what I am about to write: Somewhere deep inside, a beginning and an ending transpired with *Credo.* I do not know what began or what ended, or if any of the two have any truth in it. My art was always meant for me, and God took me to places only Osvaldito could have dreamed of. Osvaldito, Ozzie, and Calixto have not died inside the man I call self, but they remain much alive and full of hopes and dreams. To paraphrase Borges, the idea of rebirth rises, and it's an unstoppable force whose origin flees my sensibilities.

The word "artist" is full of images and definitions; some of which may fit me, and others remain alien. I am not interested in labels—never have been. It does not matter what you call me; what matters is that I feel my life and live it through all my broken pieces. I have an insatiable curiosity and a congenital fascination with creating. If some call me an artist, so be it. If not, I have my own world with my own definitions, and these are the ones that truly matter. It is not ingratitude; it is bowing to the greatest gift a human being can ever receive self-love. Living authentically with myself is my holy grail. I never dared to dream big dreams; I only dared to dream to be loved, and that dream has sat down inside me.

At this stage in my life, what became important was to write in order to make sense of a seemingly nonsensical life. To make sense in words of what I have been trying to convey in paintings. The child, Osvaldito, grew up. He is never gone, but he has gifted the man a new life, a new world, a new art form to explore, no margins, no indentations, just words and more words to aid the man who was once lost. My reason for painting came from a time immemorial, as perhaps is my ardor to write. Dostoevsky wrote, "For a woman, all resurrection, all salvation [...] lies in love."

I know this is true because through the love of creating, I feel reborn anew time and time again. I am a woman and a man, or pieces of us all, another label unrequired. It is in the hidden harmony of myself that freedom lies. There, deep within the seat of my soul, all the pain and joy graciously converge to create the ultimate masterpiece. The masterpiece has a name—Osvaldo Calixto Amador—and he is the medium, the creator, and the created. Within me lie all yesteryears and all that shall forever be.

Beyond personal history lies the universal, and it is from this unshakable sphere of the universal soul that all springs forth. All the foundational, raw elements of everything and nothing are within our spirit. Where there is love, inevitably there is art, and where there is love, there is God. Indeed, Picasso, the hidden harmony is better than the obvious. I remain with an open heart.

> *"It is good to love many things, for therein lies strength, and whosoever loves much performs much, and can accomplish much, and what is done with love is well done."*
>
> —Vincent van Gogh

CHAPTER 10

> *Have I not a free will? The roach, as beautiful as a butterfly, perspective changed. Beauty is everywhere I choose, let this be so, everything is beautiful, including the roach.*
>
> —Osvaldo Calixto Amador

How I came to this title, *To Kill a Cockroach*, deserves its proper immersion. I suppose I could go way back to my love of animals and my sensitivity to God's creatures. I could go back to *Black Beauty*, the book that empowered my passion for literature and horses. Here again, the hidden seed is more absorbing than the obvious.

I have related that my understanding of killing contradicts my conscience, God's conscience. Killing myself was an easy thought; killing any part of God's creation is another thing entirely. I had to learn that I was part of the same sacredness in all of creation, and this is what this writing is all about: a journey of self-love that started with the thought of having to kill a roach. Cutting a tree, ripping roots, killing rats in my attic, all of it is a conscientious trial.

I remember the moment it became clear that killing a roach was no different than killing a rat, a cow, and so on. I try to forget desperately that, in some parts of the world, dogs are bred to eat. I try to forget that eating a fish with eyes is not that much different. I knew I was getting into a rehabilitation project when I bought Campina. I did not realize how Campina's rehabilitation would coincide with my own.

Campina's attic was full of rats, and I could hear them parading through the walls. I had the unfortunate experience of coming eye to eye with a couple of them inside my living space. To kill or not to kill was only part of the question; how to kill was just as meaningful. Suffice it to say that this twisted Shakespearean question—whether to kill or not to kill—became hours, days, and weeks of profound meditation for this writer.

Although we share about 99 percent of our DNA with chimpanzees, making them our closest living animal relatives, rats and mice are not too far behind. Can someone say torture? Yes, it was torture to make this decision, but I made it. I am glad for the spiritual teaching of the *Gita* when Krishna revealed to Arjuna that killing in this realm was not to be taken lightly but also not to be obsessed about like Ozzie obsessed about killing rats and roaches. Campina came with its challenges, and rats and cockroaches were among the most meaningful challenges since it required the extermination of God's creatures.

The first time watching *To Kill a Mockingbird*, I was stuck and remained stuck after Atticus (Gregory Peck's character in the film) tells the kids, "Shoot all the blue jays you want, if you can hit 'em, but remember it's a sin To Kill a Mockingbird." For a man like me who loves blue jays, I remained stuck on why Ms. Lee, whose book is full of radical empathy, would choose such a statement. I knew that Ms.

Lee's heart was in the right place, yet I love blue jays. It has taken me a lifetime to appreciate the invaluable hidden facades of the seemingly obvious, to persist when pulled in by the spirit of eternal wisdom. I gained myself when I learned to trust in that knowing, that intuition that I no longer ignore. I knew when I first read *To Kill a Mockingbird* that its fruits were exponential and that I would return to grasp them when I had ripened.

When I decided to have a voice on a page, the title slowly became evident. Killing and hatred have always been the biggest human conundrums to me. I also realize that I am not immune to any human virtue or failings; I have it all. The constellation of my life once led me to feel like a roach, and I began to pity the creature that gave me such unmitigated spontaneous goose bumps at the mere sight of it. I felt empathy for the roach, and I knew—I know in my heart—that it is a living creature with intricacies of which I can only vaguely perceive.

Lee's words in *To Kill a Mockingbird* instantly metamorphosed into *To Kill a Cockroach*. I wanted to reason it all out in my hard head, to discern the contradictions in Lee's words as in my world. *Black Beauty* is a part of my world, as is *To Kill a Mockingbird*, and the gifts in their brilliant light have been a guiding star. I can't do it; I can never reconcile the incongruities. At best, I decided to write about my questions, my quest, my own frailties and hopes, and the roach. That Florida roach on my porch—so unaware of itself, so fragile, enjoying the same elements, the same air, with such *nonmaleficence*, exposed to my will to kill it—brought literal tears to my eyes. I knew more dice had been thrown, and this time, I had the awareness, which made it all particularly haunting.

The pearls of wisdom learned from reading *To Kill a Mockingbird* came back, tempting me to explore further the interconnections between my life, the roach, and the dynamism of Ms. Lee's semi-autobiographical story. The author's subtle and not-so-subtle victorious attempts to reconcile evil versus good are but one of the many parts of her genius. The characters are filled with the contradictions inherent in our humanity, the same incongruities I have struggled to understand in my life.

In her use of symbols, I found many elements that paralleled my own human journey. She wrote a masterpiece of universal archetypes. This does not surprise me; *To Kill a Mockingbird* is a classic Pulitzer Prize–winner that transcends its historical birth and the individual story. Part of its genius lies in uniting the individual with that universal soul in which we all converge and become one. Aside from the storyline of a young girl coming of age in a difficult time in the history of the United States, where prejudice and hatred were commonplace, and people were expected to look and behave a certain way, there is injustice and the exploitation of the innocent. Sadly, there is the killing, the killing of the innocent.

The more I read the story, the more I saw myself in every one of her Maycomb citizens. The characters are archetypes, depicting people like my parents and friends who have come and gone. The lineage of barbarity is all there in black ink on white paper. My very own thoughts are splattered on each page as if the author knew my world intimately. Scout, the writer's semi-autobiographical younger self, struggles to fit into a world she finds hypocritical and obstinate. Not unlike Scout, Osvaldito tries to fit in while being called a maricon. Atticus, her father, is always the wisdom behind the conundrums facing her moral compass; he is my mother and my father, always reminding me of an ancient wisdom that comes in all vestments.

This piece of historical fiction is one of the deepest revelations into Harper Lee's inner world. Her seemingly natural public conviviality hid her extremely private persona. I related to her own sense of privacy and her journey to find answers where there are possibly none. It is evident when Atticus answers the children's questions about the evils of killing by saying that they did it—and they will do it again—that Ms. Lee understood the tragedy of repeated history.

One of the characters in her book, whose nickname is Boo (Arthur Radley), is a hermit who attracts the town's gossipmongers because he shows very little interest in the outside world. At one point in the story, Scout comprehends that Boo stays in a shell because the world can be frightening and unjust. He is not a grinch at all—as the unprovoked slanderers spread this delusion—he is just a scared little boy, very much like Osvaldito. In the end, he saves the kids' lives, both Scout's and Jem's, and in doing this, he becomes one of the greatest heroes in this story.

There is Dill, a young boy who lives next door to Scout during the summers. Dill is a character purported to represent Truman Capote, one of Lee's best friends and the author of *In Cold Blood* and *Breakfast at Tiffany's*. He is the little boy with the most active imagination. He develops this imagination as a survival skill, for he is neglected and abandoned by his kin. He is Osvaldito at the Grand Union, feeling neglected, making up stories as he walks through the aisles, creating his own adventure that leads to the treasure of *Black Beauty*. He is the child who sees a river and, in his mind, makes a raft, a magic carpet ride, an odyssey beyond the grasp of the embittered adult world he inhabits.

The scapegoat in the novel is the innocent Black man Tom Robinson, falsely accused of raping a white woman simply because he is the easiest target for the deposit of hatred and evil. A Black man, a Jewish man, a faggot, a maricon, all the preferred repositories of prejudice and hatred. The predators know their prey, and they prey because they know they can. They know they live in a society that too often looks the other way when the people getting hurt do not resemble the image in the mirror. This is evil hidden in the actions and expressions of ordinariness, endorsed by a society enshrouded in a false religion, in a false God, in good academia, accolades, and middle-class attire with upper-class aspirations. Hatred is sanctioned by those who blatantly contribute—as well as those who do nothing.

Harper Lee's radical empathy makes clear two things for this writer: Vulnerable populations are easy targets for hate and the most unimaginable crimes; and a society, a belief system, and an entirely zealous obstinate radical mind comprise the most excruciating threat to all creatures and the universe itself as we understand it. Atticus, the embodiment of wisdom and a gentleman, refuses to use a gun because he understands that his sure shot gives him an unfair advantage over God's creatures. Stomping a roach gave me a sure shot, and without questioning it, who would I be?

The themes in *To Kill a Mockingbird* are a chain wholly intertwined with the unscrupulous, extreme world of the twenty-first century. Hate crimes are not a thing of the past, and neither is prejudice. In part, this is why *To Kill a Mockingbird* remains a classic, and I predict it will be read by many generations to come. A writer of the caliber of Harper Lee dives deep into the well of the unconscious and subconscious mind, bringing the tough questions to the forefront.

I was introduced to the work of Carl Gustav Jung early in my life, and I became familiar with his ideas on the collective psyche. In one of his brilliant theories is the thought that we all share a universal mind, a collective psyche that is separate from the individual psyche. This collective psyche is perceived in all art without the need for evidence. We perceive Mozart's symphonies not merely by hearing, but by feeling the universal mathematics of the silence between the notes. Similarly, we perceive beauty in Monet's water lilies not just by looking but by the spirit shrouded within the works. In Lee's work, we can see ourselves as plainly as black and white. We can see the collective mind of society working to cosign an evil; if we pay close attention, we can see ourselves.

This spirit is, for a writer, the truth. It's the fictional or nonfictional narration of the writer's imaginary or perceived reality that transcends our mundane veils and captures our imagination and our inner world. It transports our whole being in a flight of hidden truths known to that universal soul of which Jung so eloquently wrote about. True artists stand at a precipice, wide open and ready to free-fall. They are propelled by the spirit of all ages. That spirit gives rise to creation, the yearning for expression, for the incorporation of the individual into the whole and the return home. Harper Lee's valor lies in her truth as she saw it, and she took that plunge, risking what every artist fears: alienation rather than integration. Truth can be a scary thing, especially for she who discovers and reveals it.

Beyond a shadow of a doubt, I have a passion for all of the arts. Equivalently, I have an inborn passion for all of nature. It was this constitutional nature that led me to contemplate the cruel fate of the cockroaches. I had heard *To Kill a Mockingbird* before ever reading Ms. Lee's words. Here, I can see Jung's ideas at work in myself, in my own laboratory of life. I did not set out to write about a roach. I did not realize when the ominous feeling arose within me, that beautiful Florida breezy evening in my porch, that I would be writing about it one day. Like the most important things in my life, the true nature of things emerges spontaneously. It is then followed by that knowing, and without a doubt, the expansion of my consciousness bursts, and an opening occurs that widens my conscience and my heart.

We imagine, create, and dare to believe in a power some of us call God. Then we lash out at creation itself. Often, we play God, and often, we mock God. Some don't even believe in any form of a higher power other than randomness. Yet, we kill, we hate, we point, and we love all in the name of God. If a man's heart is pure, no further God is needed. If a man's heart is soiled by hate, I can't imagine needing a God more. If a man has neither, he has already met his creator. No matter how I slice it, love is God for this man, intelligibly uncomplex.

True wisdom is a combination of which humility is essential, but without the heart, that organ that beats to its own rhythm, and without which we cease to exist, no real discernment could ever take place. Unquestionably, I feel that without the rationale, the inquest of all our attainable human faculties, we fail in our most important mission of this incarnation: to learn the deepest meaning of love.

From all our ancestors, be it the cavemen, or from the mythological tales told by those first storytellers, we learn that reliance on a power greater than ourselves has been supplied by our manufacturer since the beginning of the history of humanity. Perhaps the need for, or the need to deny, a higher power is encoded in our DNA. From the Sumerians to the Lascaux cave artists, man has been expressing himself and pushing creation, creating a complex system of his understanding of his world through his own eyes as well as the eyes beyond this realm. It takes a lifetime to believe and a lifetime to deny the existence of something that can't be proven by our mere senses and/or intellect. Either way, this is not for the faint of heart, the cowards; this is for the spiritual warriors whose calling is beyond their dominion.

Lee gathers her characters and the societal circumstances in a seemingly ordinary scene in the make-believe town of Maycomb, Alabama, in the 1930s. Part of the brilliance in the novel is the human element, the depth of the characters, and the stellar wisdom applied to the mundane, everyday lives of the white Southern churchgoers whose hatred and prejudices are prevalent in every crevice of this community. Lee applies the golden formula of our human journey, that funny thing called conscience. It is that conscience that draws the reader to become Scout, Atticus, Jem, and/or Dill. Maycomb becomes the micro for the macro. It is *The Scream*, the painting by Edvard Munch, that can appall the onlooker, but it cannot be ignored.

CHAPTER 10

The roach is that creature I detested, I abhorred, which brought the pendulum of my conscience to a standstill. Is it a sin to kill? Is it a sin to kill a blue jay but not a mockingbird? Where are these distinctions made? Are we better for making the distinctions? Are Krishna's words a mild inebriation, the opium for the masses? Atticus finds himself killing the rabid dog, Maycomb's mascot, for the good of the townspeople. The wise man who defends the innocent "Negro" because it is the right thing to do finds himself killing a beloved image, man's best friend, the dog. He must kill this dog for the good of all, and he does it pronto, with one shot, so as to avoid any lingering pain to man's best friend. The pendulum can swing rapidly, and every man must decide for his own salvation.

Every man is a world, and every man answers to a higher authority, whether he is aware of it or not. The remnants of a life are not buried in a tomb; the remnants of a life are stuck in our souls, confined within the walls of our consciences, in our minds, in our sleepless nights, and in the dark hours of our lonely abyss. Hell is our own conscience or lack of it. Even an atheist may admit that we would do well with a good moral compass. We can't point to it, we can't anatomically study it, and we can't do away with it; it is a blessing and a curse. Every man must wrestle with his demons aboveground as a wise investment for his journey underground. I have wrestled with mine: the good, the bad, and the ugly.

Maycomb was Miami, and it was Hialeah. Not unlike Tom Robinson, the innocent Black man found guilty and killed for a crime he never committed based on prejudice and hatred alone, Osvaldito was the mockingbird. It is a sin to kill the innocent. It is a sin to corrupt the mind and soul of a child whose only culpability was to have been born. There are many ways of killing; there is the usual killing that destroys the body, and then there is the attempt at the extermination of the spirit of another human being.

Having been born a maricon made me a target for religious zealots, and perhaps this was the starting point to question everything. In the name of religion, kill that "Negro" to save the reputation of a white woman. In the name of God, exorcise that child's faggotry out of him. It never ceases to amaze me how class hierarchies based on color, gender, religion, and/or economics can make devils out of otherwise good men. If you follow Darwin's theory of the survival of the fittest, these hierarchies may very well be the form to separate and advance our individual as well as communal interests. I am not a fan; it seems to me that Darwin missed an important variable. It would be of utmost importance to incorporate conscience, goodwill, and love into Darwin's revelations, and perhaps they have been, for I am no expert in Darwinism. There are certain variables that science will never be able to explain, and love is one of them. Here, I concur with Einstein and prefer his ultimate finding when he says that love is the greatest force in the universe. History can be a sad tale indeed if the evolution of our conscience is deprived of that light that only radical empathy can harvest.

Killing a roach is perhaps as inevitable as killing an ant under our very soles while walking obliviously in the world. For under our *chancletas* (flip-flops) lie microscopic lives with complex hierarchical patterns much like ours. I know how eccentric this all may seem, for to inquire about such lofty ideas, for which answers do not suffice or may even exist, may intimate a flagrant disrespect for time. Yet human questioning is as old as human stories themselves. I do not propose that there will be logic in any of this for anyone. I write here about a process I undertook to understand the man I have become. It is a tall order to consider such towering notions, and at times, it feels like moral arrogance, hypocritical, and a gigantic path toward moral failure.

I have considered these questions, but I had no choice. God has no morals; only human beings venture into the exploration of ethics and moral philosophy. God is all, God is love, and God needs no explanation or scientific exploration. God is. All creatures have their niche, none of which require a moral inquiry to justify their existence. A dog is as happy defecating in the woods as performing sexual acts in the light of day in a crowded plaza. There is no moral probe in his actions; just being a dog suffices. My awareness of right and wrong was revealed to the eyes of a little boy called Osvaldito. It was taught by a society and family that served as templates of what not to aspire to. It was given in vignettes by a mother who had to desperately hold on tight to a cliff for her own survival. My conscience and my thought processes were given to me by a benevolent spirit that is merciful to the Tom Robinsons of this world.

In the end, a few of Maycomb's characters find a change of heart. We learn that Scout and Jem find their own center, their own balanced pendulum. Scout finds reassurance that most people are good deep inside, while Jem concludes that there is injustice in the world and finds no consolation. I find myself in both Scout and Jem. I have lived the injustices, I have suffered the indignities, and I have looked into the eyes of the devil himself. I also believe there is good and evil in everyone. I have reconciled with such questions as to kill or not to kill a roach. If I have free will at all, then I must always choose right from wrong—and always consider my sure shot. God is not moralistic, but consciousness is, and like our hands, feet, and eyes, conscience is a tool, and its purpose is to guide our thoughts and actions.

We are given a conscience to exercise, and how we exercise it may very well create our own hell or heaven. In the end, ultimately, it does not matter whether you believe in a god; that is not the true question. The real question you should ask yourself is if goodness exists as well as evil, which side would you rather invest your small allowance of time in this existence? Love creates, and evil destroys, and if God is all of it, what aspects of it feel most righteous to your moral inquisition? This is the real question regardless of religion or your god. We don't need another god or another preacher; we need love, and we desperately need to make God synonymous with love.

We are toddlers whose first impression of the world is all unto itself. We learn the limits of boundaries and the effects of our actions as we enter a higher level of conscience and maturity. A healthy development entails a growth in limbs and a growth in awareness of thoughts, actions, and that proverbial world of consciousness. What good does humanity gain to believe Jesus is the only son of God, Muhammad its only prophet, Abraham the beginning, and Moses the only messenger of all good commandments when we slaughter our brothers and sisters in their names? Where our hearts are, that is where our God is. We live by the sword of our thoughts, words, and actions, and we will die by the same.

As for me, this struggle between prey, predator, ego, humility, shame, love, self-realization, and good versus evil has been a quest handed to me on a silver platter. The kind of dysfunction that came with my cradle is not one that you get over with an encouraging word, a few sessions in a therapist's office, or a kind friend who lends an ear. My life was traumatic. I suffered repeated traumas, but, like an alchemist, I turned rusted metal into gold. That existential feeling, those desolate feelings of loneliness and emptiness, has been filled with a unique knowledge that we are all one; even in a blade of grass, there is a life-form that is mystically intertwined with mine. The struggle is real; we are the uncelebrated champions in between the pages of our history books.

Bicycling along the boulevard named after the pilgrim who searched for the fountain of youth, Ponce de Leon, I came across a bookstore. It was a hidden treasure. I had missed the real discovery, for this bookstore was more powerful than my inspiration. Agartha Secret City was a fountain of words, and youth was shelved in the eternal poetry of the sages. I wanted to see what was inside, so I double-parked my orange bike from Zayre (the equivalent of today's Target, except truly affordable for working-class families), and in I went. I would have been around thirteen, give or take a few lifetimes.

There were books and more books about God's other houses! Who was this guy named Buddha? Who was Alan Watts? What was *The Tibetan Book of the Dead*? Oh, my heavenly Father, I felt like I had died and gone to heaven. I wanted to see it! I wanted to be shown! My eyes were being opened wide, and not to see had ceased to be a choice. The first book I read from Agartha Secret City was *The Tibetan Book of the Dead*. I hardly understood it, but not unlike with *Black Beauty*, I knew it had otherworldly black gold pumping through its pages. I read *Siddhartha* by Hermann Hesse, and it showed me what to see, how to see it, and why to see it. Siddhartha left the familiar to discover his own nature, and I was being catapulted into new terrains of spiral galaxies from uncharted territories.

It was Buddhism that taught me how to meditate. It gave me the tool that has allowed me to be present and aware of my inner and outer worlds. In my teens, I discovered the Eastern philosophies and was in awe of their pragmatism. This tool has taken on many forms throughout my life, but mediation has allowed me to be more conscious than I ever dreamed I could be. Agartha Secret City and the VHS video store had me cornered. All coins that passed through my inquisitive young hands went toward seeing the stars on the giant screen and toward learning all I could about the Tao, Zen, the Koran, Confucius, and all the colorful and picturesque Hindu gods. It was the Grand Union of God's houses!

How very rich is this God; he has houses in all the world destinations. He serves and has servants of all colors and races and shapes and forms. Her teachings are in all the world's languages, in palaces, mosques, cathedrals, tents, pyramids, huts, and underground meetings in villages where her devotee's risk everything to hear her gospel. Although I no longer look for answers in books like I did back then, I can lose my shirt in bookstores. There is such a thirst in me, such a curiosity about everything, that I need a few hundred lifetimes to learn it all. I very much concur with Socrates in that the more I know, the more I know that I know nothing at all.

I suppose I could say that *To Kill a Cockroach* began with awareness, but a little voice inside me tells me that *To Kill a Cockroach* chose me rather than I chose it. The chaos and the twisted journey had a purpose. I am a delicate balance from nature, weeding out the unnecessary, passionately caring for the living, creating and making fertilizer with the manure I received. I am happiest in simplicity. I am comfortable in contradictions. I am the king of my jungle. I am Madama Butterfly. I am brave. I am vulnerable. I am man. I am woman. I am child. I am ancient. I am hurried. I am timeless. I am wise. I am a fool. I am a roach. I am its exterminator. I am everything and nothing at all. I am human. I am God. I am consciousness aware of itself. I am the subjugator. I am that I am. I am love.

On February 27, 2016, *The Economist* published an obituary about the author of *To Kill a Mockingbird*: "She was a plain, chubby, chain-smoking southern girl, living in a cold-water flat in New York and working as an airline-reservation clerk." It has been written that Lee died peacefully and alone. She was a lover of love, a true artist who wanted neither fame nor gold. She wanted only love.

After reclaiming my double-parked orange bike on Ponce de Leon Boulevard outside Agartha Secret City, I pedaled slowly, letting the gentle breeze intersperse with my thoughts. With me now was a new adventure that fit inside a small plastic bag with the logo for Agartha Secret City. Inside this bag was my newfound talisman: *The Tibetan Book of the Dead*. Like my slow pedaling, I gently learned that the book was about the "bardo." The bardo is what our consciousness experiences after death. It is about the evolution of the spirit, the soul, that which is eternal in us. I trust my eternal conscience, for it has led to nothingness, which is everything. I can kill a roach. Spirit will never die.

I will forever be a lover of love; this is my ultimate purpose in this incarnation, my own private myth.

CHAPTER 11

Hope will never be silent.

—Harvey Milk

From the moment I got off the plane in San Francisco, I felt a freedom I had never witnessed before. It was palpable in the smooth lightness of the breeze. Even the airport's filtered air drifted tenderly, embracing the sojourners passing through. San Francisco is a welcoming fest for all. San Franciscans walk openly with fluid movements, offering tokens of kindness with their glances and infusing smiles. The relaxed appearance, the sun's glow, and the whistling of its magical freedom were felt in the city's soul. Everywhere you walk in San Francisco, you will surely find random acts of kindness. If acceptance had a city, this would have been it.

It was 1981, and the world was my tambourine. I was sixteen years old, cute, and in love with my twenty-three-year-old boyfriend, who could afford us the very best. Even before arriving in San Francisco,

CHAPTER 11

I had been treated like royalty in Eastern Airlines' first-class La-Z-Boy-style bulky leather recliner seat. Back then, first-class seats looked more like love seats than anything else. We had drunk champagne aboard the luxury liner that carried its human baggage to the freedom destination. This was the first time I had traveled in first class, and for a boy from the Cuban hood, it felt like a downpour of opulence had drenched me with fairy dust. Ignatius showed me first-class living. I had an inclination from films, but Ignatius blew the roof off my ideas of royalty.

Ignatius came from old money and had been brought up right. Money did not affect him with the typical grandiose self-entitlement I found later in the nouveaux riches with the highest ambitions. He was not into class hierarchies and would fit in, blend in, and be accepted in any social environment. In other words, he was a true gentleman at twenty-three. I have learned throughout my years that real class, in the sense of social graces, cannot be taught or bought. Being well-bred is a natural condition belonging to what I call "the Godly Aristocracy."

The Godly Aristocracy is that nobility, that God-given simplicity, arrived at by pure grace and authentic humility. There is a luminous spirit in a man who begrudges the inequity in classifying God's creatures, especially his own species. God's nobility is an essential, constitutionally ingrained character trait belonging to the well-born regardless of societal titles, education, or economics. Unlike the self-proclaimed elite who struggle to imitate earthly princes and kings with their display of unwarranted airs—resulting in vulgarity rather than appeal—the nobles of the Godly Aristocracy require no accolades and repel all pretenses of titles and supremacy. Instead, they consent to a higher principality, which few in the material world can possess.

I have been blessed with the experience of diverse environments.

Osvaldito learned poverty well as a child seeing his mother struggle to provide the very basics, a roof over our heads and bread on our table. This scarcity will always be part of the man. Without a doubt, poverty made me a better human being. A man's education, title, and position in society say little, if anything, of his heart and conscience. Ignatius was one of those men who, from an early age, was rooted in divine grace, and that light shone for everyone who came into his sphere. I do not believe authentic humility can be learned, but a man who forgets where he comes from has lost part—if not all—of his soul.

No matter where life has taken me, I give thanks for the blessing that Atticus taught Scout: Walk in another's skin and get to know them. Mami was loved by all who knew her, but it was not because she gave the best parties, had any title, or had any economic wealth. She was loved because she belonged to the Godly Aristocracy. My mother's nobility was not of this world, and those who witnessed her essence tasted the honey that poured freely from her soul. For the few who detect God's light in his children, these are privy to a nectar seldom tasted on earth. I am always eyes, mind, and heart open to all of God's creatures regardless of their labels, for I know that the well of richness comes from the most unexpected places. I am a rich man in a poor material world that often loses its sense of the good inherent in all of creation.

In San Francisco, unlike in Miami, I was treated like royalty. Ignatius's warmth, loving, and highly passionate dogma treated me to a full life like none other I had known. I was often uncomfortable with the new luxuries bestowed upon me, for it was all very new. The feeling of being undeserving had taken root at the core of my being, and it would take a lifetime to tear it from my umbilical cord. Material possessions have never been a destination; they have often been distractions on the way home. I have learned to accept the nectar from the gods in whatever package it may arrive, but my solidarity is with the human spirit rather than the fleeting fleshly desires.

But Ignatius would never have had it any other way. I was to be pampered, and pampered I was. Upon arrival, we had a convertible Mercedes-Benz waiting for us at the airport. We drove topless in a beautiful machine that I later saw Richard Gere driving in *American Gigolo*. Somehow, Richard Gere looked much more comfortable riding these wheels than Ozzie did at sixteen. We went to the historical Fairmont Hotel with breathtaking luxuries waiting in our suite. At our hotel, we blended with the array of international patrons. San Francisco was heaven, and the beautiful smiles of the San Franciscans themselves adorned us with a welcoming warmth that could raise the dead.

Our trip coincided with the San Francisco Pride parade on Castro Street. In a matter of minutes, the scenery from the Fairmont Hotel to Castro Street changed as drastically as a tropical rainforest compared to a barren desert. We arrived on Castro Street, looking somewhat preppy in our polo shirts and khaki pants, and we stood out like sore thumbs. Ignatius and I were clueless about what to expect; it was our first time in any gay pride parade. It was back to the Fairmont for an appropriate wardrobe rearrangement. We looked around, got a glimpse of the trend, and went back to our room to make things right. We entered the Fairmont Hotel, looking respectable, and what happened next did not shock the staff, but it stunned me.

I had painted my hair pink and purple and created a homespun mohawk sprayed with an entire bottle of the best Paul Mitchell hair cement money could buy. Punk was the fashion, and a mohawk was it for me, even if a bad temporary one. We borrowed the hotel's scissors and cut off the sleeves of our expensive plaid polo shirts. I wore tight Levi's, and Ignatius wore shorts—or was it Bermuda shorts? It was one of those; he had great legs and could get away with either one. What we both wanted was to fit in. Initially, we'd looked like a Cuban version of a Ralph Lauren commercial. Now we were punk rocker wannabes, although anyone without a dozen beers in their belly could tell we were only playing severely poorly cast roles.

I would have never guessed it but seeing men walking hand in hand together felt intoxicatingly perplexing. Of course, it was more than just men walking hand in hand; these were oversized, Marlboro Man, Heineken cowboy, butt-flashing, leather-clad, strapping Adonis gods who were totally comfortable in their own skins. It took time for my brain and eyes to get used to the heterogeneity parading by on pink neon floats like those in the Macy's parade, except these floats were drenched in steroids.

The Human League's "Don't You Want Me" was blaring on one float, and the then obscure music of that divine three-hundred-pound drag queen who John Waters had cast in his films was playing on the next one. As the next float came along, Blondie's voice blasted out of the ten-foot-tall speakers growing out of the glittering purple float. The half-naked, rock-hard, beautiful young men danced to all the rhythms without missing a beat from float to float. How they could twirl a baton or snap open and shut their colossal Chinese fans while rhythmically moving every inch of their oiled bodies to the intoxicating rhythms without missing a beat will never cease to amaze me. Cirque du Soleil had nothing on the acrobatics of these gay men on Castro Street.

It was more than culture shock; it was a new beat in my heart that I could not discern. It was a concoction of excitement, lust, fear, or simply a new drug whose name was freedom. The energy was fearless; I had never witnessed such magnanimous, raw, sensual, free stamina. After all, I had just left Miami, where everyone looked the same, and those who didn't wouldn't dare parade with such boldness down one of Miami's main roads. Castro Street that day was a welcome initiation that spoke to me much like Woodstock spoke to the counter-culture hippies of the sixties. I was learning that Miami had its gay enclave, but it was nothing like this; this was sovereignty material. Ignatius wanted to hold hands, and it was the first time I held hands in public with another man with whom I was romantically involved. Thinking back, as I write this, it strikes me as overly dear that we did this, and I am glad for this memory.

When you get two Cuban studs together, aged sixteen and twenty-three, one of the certainties is inexhaustible energy. The party went on for decades, but the reality was that it was only days. I loved San Francisco, but I could never live there—even if I wanted to. The driving alone would kill me. You see, I am terribly afraid of heights. That thing that Hitchcock made a film about—*Vertigo*—yes, I have that. I was lucky that Ignatius did all the driving in the rented Benz because I would have never been able to press the pedal on any vehicle facing a steep downward hill like those in San Francisco. Although I was not driving, every time we came to one of those corners stop signs, I would look down and think, *What the funk?* Just writing about it, and I feel nauseous. Other than the steep hills and the brick walls that are often the view of any living quarters, I really loved San Francisco.

In many ways, I did leave my heart there. I was sixteen, in love, and the world was my rainbow. San Francisco was an essential ceremony to have experienced as a sixteen-year-old gay man. I experienced freedom, the power of pride in oneself, and a thriving community that was empowered and not ashamed of its members. I experienced being able to love my boyfriend freely and hold hands without fearing being killed. I, like the animated caricatures surrounding me, experienced joy despite the hatred we certainly had all experienced in our lives. For to be gay is to have experienced prejudice and hatred in one way or another at one point or another: This is a sad fact.

These men and women danced, laughed, and created for themselves incredible symbols of pride and freedom in their own unique and colorful ways. Arriving back in Miami felt unnatural. Once a man experiences a certain freedom, it is hard to cage his nature. Part of our history has been lived and fought in stiletto heels, three-foot beehives, and long, sequined thrift store dresses. We come in all sizes, colors, and shapes and from all ethnic, religious, social, and economic backgrounds. Not unlike Cubans, we are Black, white, blonde, Chinese, Jewish, short, fat, skinny, Catholics, Protestants, *brujeros*, and mystics alike.

When gay pride is mentioned, I can't help but think of the boldness of these men and women on Castro Street. This boldness is not disrespect as many would have me think; rather, it is venting the hatred in the haters' faces with glowing sequins. I would rather have sequined, butt-flashing homosexuals venting their pride than white supremacist zealots venting theirs with violence and their abominable Confederate flags and semiautomatic weapons.

The Stonewall Inn is a gay bar in Greenwich Village, New York City, where a battle was fought with high heels, leather pants, skirts, and formerly preppy Catholic altar boys. The word "Stonewall" was coined as a nickname for Confederate General Thomas J. Jackson, who was described as "standing like a stone wall" as the enemy approached. On July 3, 1969, when Osvaldito was barely four years old, some fearless drag queens with their gay brothers and sisters formed a "stone wall" against the oppressive police force that regularly raided the bar for no reason other than harassment for harassment's sake. The Stonewall raid and its aftermath marked a significant change in the attitudes of the gay community toward the police. Rage overcame fear. It was bold and courageous, and the unarmed infantry fought it with only determination and courage as their armor.

Once we were back in Miami, San Francisco began to feel so far away—and I do not mean logistically. Miami had a gay community. In fact, the gay community was my friends and had become my chosen family. In those days, if you were gay in Miami, everyone knew you or knew about you. It was impossible not to know about those like us in what was, back then, a small enclave of a gay populace. My group was the in-between group. There was the in group (the group with the hottest and most fabulous), the low group (the not-so-great-looking but usually the funniest and loudest and the real trendsetters), and my group, the group everyone knew because we could intersperse with either one of the other gangs if there were a genuine desire to cross the unspoken lines that vaguely divided the unspoken truth.

Regardless, my friends belonged to all tiers and were between sixteen (myself being one of the youngest) and the older generation, the thirtysomethings. Not to mention there were the divas, the survivors, Miami's own Quentin Crisps. These were the wisecracking, cigarette-smoking mature gay men who had the most exquisite apartments in town put together by a meticulous thrift store collection. They knew all the designers by name, called everyone "my dear," and had moved to Miami from LA or New York. These divas let us young ones know we had much to learn about gay etiquette and how to be truly fabulous in the gay world. They spoke about Judy Garland and gave us lessons that would last a lifetime.

In those days in Miami, everyone went to the same places on the same days. There were actual dates back then, and your friends and their friends would be the third, fourth, and fifth wheels. The theaters would show the new films on Thursday nights, so we knew where the gang would be. We had the Miracle Theatre in Miracle Mile, the Plitt Gables, the Riviera Theatre, and the Falls. For foreign films, we had the Arcadia and Cinematheque, but only the real movie lovers knew and went to those. I learned early on to go to those cinemas alone because no one could handle the kind of films I enjoyed.

It was in those theaters that I first saw Reinaldo Arenas being interviewed in *Conducta Impropia* (*Improper Conduct*). The film documented the Cuban Communist government's treatment of homosexuals under the Castro regime, and it was a horror to watch. Luckily, it was also in these theaters that I saw *La Traviata* and films by Almodóvar for the first time. They played the Ingmar Bergman and Fellini films that necessitated a genuine love of film. Then Friday and Saturday nights were Cheers, Fire & Ice, the Copa (in Lauderdale), Salvation (I only went to the Salvation in downtown Miami in the old Salvation building), San Francisco (the first gay bar I went to in the Grove), Thirteen Buttons, and On the Waterfront. On Sunday, it was the 21st Street Beach on Collins to soak in the rays and then an early tea dance at the Seagull adjoining the beach. It was tea dance Sunday nights at Uncle Charlie's and sporadic visits to Sappho's and Hattie's in the Grove.

Everyone worked and/or went to school. Some worked for their parents, and others had wealthy parents and did not work. We all dressed accordingly from the best store in town called Burdines (now Macy's). There were hardly any new faces in the crowd; even if we did not know each other by name, we knew each other by glances. It was Miami in the eighties, and drugs were everywhere. If there was a party, there were usually cocaine rooms where you entered to snort the white powder provided gratuitously by the fabulous host, followed by bowls of Mary and Juana. If you were at the disco (no boys' or girls' restrooms; we all went into the same one), you stood in line to glance at your beautiful youth reflected back at you from the overcrowded mirror. You waited in long queues even if one of the restrooms was empty because the longer the line, the more vital it was to partake in this social ritual. It did not matter; the lines were part of the crème de la crème, and you never knew what gossip you could overhear while the people in front snorted their coke and swallowed their Quaaludes.

I was in a long-term relationship for most of my life and was single very few times for very short times. In the gay community in those days, it was considered long term if you had a relationship for more than six months. Suppose you had a long-term relationship for a year or more? In that case, that was the equivalent of having moved to the suburbs with a white picket fence, with two kids going to private schools while your partner worked at IBM, and you became a department supervisor at the fabulous Burdines.

In many ways, having a monogamous long-term relationship sheltered me. The message I received from the priest when I was at my lowest remained loud and clear in that funny thing called consciousness. If you are with someone, be it a woman or a man, make sure it is always for love and nothing else. I was fortunate enough to discern the difference between lust and love, so that my hormones did not take the best of me. I adored Ignatius with all my heart and soul, and he loved me as much. He spoiled me with affection and luxuries, and in my sixteen-year-old mind, we would be together forever. Love has always been the answer for me; it's not that lust hasn't won many times over, but that's another topic.

After San Francisco, Ignatius and I took a short weekend trip to Disney World, and our friend Joey came with us. He had just broken up with his boyfriend and was staying in the room next to us. He had gone out to begin the day without us because he was an early riser, and we, indeed, were not. Ignatius and I had that passion that sixteen- and twenty-three-year-olds have, and mornings were a great time to disperse of some of that raw sexual energy. I knew when to let my hormones take over; I have been blessed that way.

In any case, we were having breakfast served in the room after having scattered our youthful energy as *Good Morning America* played in the background at low volume. I heard the words "gay cancer," which got my attention. I turned the volume up to listen to the rest. My life would never be the same, and the change started in a wonderland like Disney World. The news spoke about a few dozen men in New York who had come down with some rare form of a disease they could not identify, but at that point, it had been observed only in gay men in New York. Some men died rapidly after being diagnosed with the "gay cancer." There was nothing more to know or do, for the news spoke of its rarity and confinement to the gay community.

We went on with our day as planned. Despite the life-sized Mickey Mouse, the glittering lights, and the wonder of Cinderella Castle, the fantasy of Disney's lively crowds couldn't break the spell that had encapsulated my very being that morning. Etched in my mind were two words: "gay cancer." Dante's hell flashed in and out of my mind's eye, along with Pluto and Donald Duck. Life has often felt more surreal than any Dali painting, and the ghosts of shame and guilt accompanied me to the Haunted Mansion. The chills inside this Disney ride were real and eerie for me. The ghost staring back from the cobweb mirrors was too close for comfort.

We barely spoke about it, and neither Ignatius nor Joey seemed to have taken the news as harshly as I had. I was upset that I could not toss it aside or obliterate it entirely as they seemed to have done. That night, back in our hotel room, after making love and allowing our ecstasy to ooze its very last drip out of our young bodies, lying in bed, I asked Ignatius why he was not more upset about the news we had heard in the morning.

He replied, "*Eso no tiene nada que ver con nosotro, bebe.*" He used to call me "baby," and he told me that what we'd heard had nothing to do with us. I wanted to believe him, so I did. The reality is that it had everything to do with every human being on the planet.

The next day, it was our drive back to Miami from Orlando. Once again, while packing to head home, we heard the news in the background, and once again, the "gay cancer" echoed in the wonderland hotel room. This time, I heard that the doctors thought the "gay cancer" was sexually transmitted. Sexually transmitted? I had just spent an eternity having sex-slash-making-love with Ignatius. Was this it? Was I dying now at sixteen? Did I let my hormones out just once too many? Was sex a punishment? Round and round went my head with the old familiar friends: shame, guilt, and darkness.

In Miami, the noise of the gay cancer was getting louder by the day. The numbers from New York were increasing, and if it were not the poppers (amyl nitrite inhalers some gay men use to achieve a momentary high), it was sure to be sexually transmitted. No one knew how it was sexually transmitted. The news was as varied as the thoughts of the causes. Loud voices began pleading to stop all sexual activity in the gay community. Some Christian zealots asserted that this was God's punishment. They said the gay community was no better than Sodom and Gomorrah, and we were to be extinct. The gay cancer was being proclaimed across all pulpits as evidence of biblical prophecy. Since 1977, Anita Bryant had been on a rampage to convert gays to convey God's message of indignation and hatred toward the unnatural act of homosexuality, and the AIDS crisis gave her an excuse to amplify her hatred.

In San Francisco, I had witnessed acceptance and love like nothing I had experienced before. My coming out of the closet was on an upward movement with the feelings of empowerment I had brought from the city of Franciscan angels. I felt sexually alive, deserving of a full life for the first time. I had the looks, the hormones, the money, and the man to go along with the love I had been searching for since the beginning of time. Now, there was a huge cloud hovering over me. Suddenly, the rain on my parade was pouring torrentially, and this tsunami could melt all my future dreams and hopes into oblivion. I started to use my brain to think, and this turned my world topsy-turvy because I couldn't think my way out of this. Should I ever have sex again? Should I stop the hormones from wanting to play? In Tina Turner's famous song, she asks about love. "What's love got to do with it?" I loved Ignatius, but was he to be the cause of my death? Could I even touch him and not feel aroused?

***

His name was Carlos, and he was a beautiful blond Cuban with the brightest smile, the most cheerful demeanor, and a body like Michelangelo's *David*. He used to call me Osito, meaning "little bear." Carlos lived in Miami and did bartending at night while he finished his law degree at the University of Miami. He had left North Florida, where his family had disowned him for being gay. I thought Carlos should have been modeling, for he had a perfect face and body. Going out with Carlos was being invisible; men, women, cats, and dogs all threw themselves at him. He had a magnetism that exuded sexuality from every pore of his young, beautiful skin. But more than that, Carlos was a noble heart, a good man, a sensitive soul with the best smile after a young Tom Cruise.

Carlos called me one night to tell me he was not feeling well, and, as usual, our conversation lasted for hours. He and I talked about everything and nothing at all. Our friendship had developed naturally and easily. There was mutual trust and mutual interest since he also loved books and films. I loved Carlos, and talking to him was like talking to a big brother who I admired and respected.

He interrupted our natural trivialities and said, "Osito, I am scared. I hope this is not the gay cancer."

Carlos was barely twenty-three years old and was as strong as a horse, but I immediately understood his fear. Carlos could always have the very pick of the best-looking men in all places; oftentimes, even supposedly straight men gave themselves freely. I knew about his sex life because I was one of his best friends, and I also knew that Carlos was limited in sexual partners because he had law school and work to contend with. But none of this mattered; it just took one time, one person, one wrong person, and you were it.

"Of course not, Carlito! You must have the flu or something. Are you crazy?" I did the best I could with my clenched stomach. I, too, feared every cough and every sneeze, and his fear was not meant to be dismissed. However, I had nothing better to offer than being as ordinary as we had always been.

Carlito died less than six months after that conversation. He was so full of life, of dreams, that even days before his death, he cried while whispering his desire to go on even in a dilapidating body.

While Carlito was dying at Mercy Hospital, Diego and Raul were getting sick; they were both in their early twenties. Then came Elan, Carlos, Jose, and Joey, our Disney companion. Rudy was one of the funniest friends I have ever had, and he went as fast as a blink of an eye. Angel, Jose, Joel, Luis, and Roberto all died consecutively, one after the other.

These funerals were sad events, full of young men who barely looked like they had left high school. The dying were handsome, intelligent, funny, and kindhearted young men with dreams and goals. Some even had supportive families. Some killed themselves, like my good friend Andre. Andre and Coco, his beautiful fluffy white Maltese he loved so much, died together in his apartment alone from an overdose of pills. I attended two suicide farewell parties, as they were called, of two dear friends disintegrating in front of our eyes. My brave friends wanted to die their way, saying goodbye in a small gathering of true friends and then taking their own lives afterward. This was the most surreal time in my life. With each death went my smile, my laughter, my joy. I was slowly and rapidly falling into a deep depression that brought me to my therapist, my Marlo Thomas Jewish mom, Angelina.

My anxiety was tangible, my fear was unyielding, and my mood was somber and debilitating. All my hopes for a bright future turned dismal. I lost twenty-three friends in a few years. These losses were men who shared my history, they were my chosen family, and I loved them all. Having to say goodbye to each one—in the most dreadful and mean environment created by prejudice—was disheartening and hell itself. It was not enough that these men were dying isolated, left abandoned by their loved ones, but then the world kicked the dying, screaming hatred and repulsion. After all, it was only the maricones who were dying; it had nothing to do with real people. The world went on hating, and few cared to lend a helping hand. These young men knew Osvaldito, Ozzie, Osvaldo, and Calixto, perhaps better than he did. The gay cancer became AIDS (acquired immunodeficiency syndrome), differentiated into HIV (human immunodeficiency virus) by the difference in the number of T-cells. But no matter what you call a killer, I had lost my community of friends, my family.

My anger at AIDS and HIV was intense. My emotions vacillated between exasperation, depression, and hatred because my gang that used to call me to know what I was wearing on a given Saturday night to go to the disco could reach out no more. The gang that got together on Thursday nights to see the new movie at the Miracle Theatre now got together at the funeral home. I had no one to call, and I was afraid of who would be next. I had lost a community like no other I had ever had. I had survivor's guilt and a carousel of anxieties. The United States government, especially the radicals in the Republican Party with their hero, Ronald Reagan, as president, did little to nothing to stop the gay holocaust this nation and the world experienced.

Silence was the consent that spoke loudly about the deaths of these depraved individuals (the faggots, the maricones), affirming AIDS as godsent. Some of the same proud, zealous, right-wing Republicans were losing and would lose their sons and daughters as the years went on, proving that a virus is not prejudiced—only people are. I am making a grand generalization here, and I do not like it when I do, but it was and has always been in my lifetime the radical Christian zealots who have caused so much misery in a community whose only fault is who we love.

The only way out of this virus was to fight and fight with all our might. The gay community mobilized, starting in New York City with one of the bravest and most outspoken voices of the AIDS era, Larry Kramer. Larry Kramer hit the pavement with his ACT UP (AIDS Coalition to Unleash Power) grassroots political group. He was angry, as was I. This might be bygone times when unspoken evil was sanctioned and accepted by some of our most sacred and trusted institutions and politicians, but I remember much too well. I will never forget, and we shouldn't, because in Atticus's words, they will do it again.

Family members abandoned their gay sons, leaving them dying on their deathbeds alone without the comfort of a loving embrace. People stayed away from the hospital AIDS ward, and some nurses and hospital workers, not excluding some doctors, refused to help AIDS patients. This was a massive genocide empowered by ingrained homophobia. The dying and suffering were "maricones," the roaches, the reprehensible, the morally corrupt, the Boo Radleys of Lee's mind-blowing book, the repository of prejudice, injustice, and hatred. The God-forgotten children did not have to die, and AIDS could have had a different course had it affected a different populace like, unfortunately, it did later.

Let there be no doubt: I am a Christian, but not one of the ones who make the noise, the well-indoctrinated churchgoers; the loud preachers with the vehement damnation; the white-gloved Southern gossipers of Maycomb, Alabama; the obsessively prejudiced stained with hypocritical corruption; the pious ones like Scout's teacher. No, not I. I belong to the stray vermin repudiated for my sins. I love and understand the teaching of Jesus, and his love is in my heart.

I can only respect those who understand that our humanity binds us—not our gods. For what good is a God that separates and condemns? Christ never wrote a word in his life, but what is ever so clear is his teachings on love and the love of thy neighbor. My Lord was a revolutionary, for he fought against the establishment, including the religion of his time. He was unorthodox only because his mission was love and not institutions. The rabbis, Pharisees, and ruling Romans thought him a threat because he practiced what he preached. Some of today's Christians preach but rarely practice what Jesus taught.

I have absolutely no doubt that Jesus himself would have been marching with Larry Kramer and the gay activists to help alleviate the pain of the suffering. He was in every man and woman I saw, giving time, food, shelter, money, and, most importantly, loving arms to the dying. Quentin Crisp wrote an exceptionally profound statement: "Health consists of having the same diseases as one's neighbors." Quentin's message mirrors Harper Lee's radical empathy.

The effort to volunteer was painful for me, but I gathered the strength to go forward in a crusade to feed and help the dying. The exhausting part was that these were my friends; if I did not know them by name, I knew them through their eyes. My community was quickly becoming a hollow shell of itself. A formerly robust, muscular, tall, Rock Hudson–type man with AIDS soon became a crippled, sunken image resembling that excruciatingly heart-wrenching sculpture of Christ being carried by Mary in *La Pietà* by Michelangelo. I was emotionally, physically, and spiritually bankrupt. The inundation of AIDS in the gay world was a war zone. No matter where you looked in the gay community, the casualties were everywhere.

The grassroots organization I volunteered with became the Health

Crisis Network. We made slow but forward movements. When it became public that Rock Hudson had AIDS, it was one of those times that the White House, and Ronald Reagan specifically, made a sincere sound of compassion. This virus soon began to get the world's attention—but not until too many were infected and too many had died. Communities were devastated; the African American community was followed by the Latino community, and soon it hit Middle America. A wild forest fire spreads, and this was a combustion like no other.

In 1994, Pedro Zamora died of AIDS complications at the age of twenty-two. He was a beautiful Cuban American boy from the hood. I met him briefly through my best friend, Jorgito. For the brief moment I knew Pedro, he offered such joy and a zeal for life that anyone in his presence could feel his love light. Pedro battled HIV with a badge of courage like few could. Perhaps it was his youth or perhaps it was love, the love inside him. He made it his mission to empower the younger generation to protect themselves against HIV by using condoms. Whenever I become too tired, too weary, or overwhelmed with the inevitable trials in life, I remember these heroes who gave me many lessons through their life and through their death.

I was working on my degree, I was working, I was volunteering, and I was witnessing the burial of everyone I knew. But I held up. I cried. I was mad at God and angry at the world, but I stood. I was a soldier of love fighting hatred and prejudice. Then came the news that put the lid on my emotional coffin. Jorgito was my soulmate in unexplainable ways. We knew each other when our acne was in full hormone overdose. He was, at the very least, my best friend. There was nothing Jorgito did not know about me and nothing I did not know about him. He was my confidant, brother, and family, and he was dying. Jorgito had no family, for they abhorred the thought of who he was. When Jorgito told me he was HIV-positive, I froze, literally. My blood went cold, as did my whole body.

I had dropped by his house as I had done so many times before to chat, eat, relax, and catch up on our domesticities. There was nothing out of the ordinary about that late afternoon except his mood was solemn, which was a rarity. He asked me to sit with him in his outdoor courtyard as the orange-red Florida sunset started to mellow on the horizon. We drank wine spritzers together under a royal poinciana tree that was shedding its cardinal red foliage.

Sitting face to face with Jorgito and hearing the news that he had just received his second test result that confirmed he was HIV-positive made the redness of the horizon feel like the apocalypse had sounded its horns. When I could speak, I remember the exact words I told him, and they were so ironic and asinine that I am embarrassed to this day: "Please tell me this is a bad joke." Those were the only unfiltered words of a hopeful friend. I have gotten in much trouble in my life for lack of filters, so I now have them on a scheduled ongoing delivery from Amazon. As I have painstakingly learned, I cannot afford to immediately speak what comes to mind; a pause is necessary, a filter. A civilized world requires a little white filter sometimes, and I can't miss the Amazon delivery truck.

With an angelic renunciation, he grinned slightly and looked down. Barely audible, I heard him say, "I wish I could, but it is not."

I regained my composure and declared emphatically, "We will beat this!"

There was nothing more to do for either of us: We both knew the reality.

I cried for weeks alone, with Angelina, and with God. Jorgito left us rather quickly; he died at Mercy Hospital while I embraced him, whispering stories of our now faraway youth. I helped bury Jorgito with the spiritual guidance of the Catholic father who once spoke to me about love.

Watching Jorgito's coffin lower into the ground was like watching the last semblance of my life end. Surrounded by maple trees that created a natural dome, the Franciscan father hugged me tight. I felt the love of Jesus in his embrace. I thanked him for all he had given me. He was still handsome, graying, but the love in his aura made him forever beautiful. These are the unsung heroes, especially of the Catholic Church. I drove away from the cemetery that day proud that I had been able to keep it all together for my best friend. A few miles onto the highway, my strength gave in—as did my malnourished stomach. I had to park the car by the curbside and let the torrent of tears rush through me as I vomited out the car's door. I had been strong long enough; I couldn't be anymore.

I had come out in San Francisco with a celebration that soon became a funeral procession. The eighties were a cruel time to be a young gay man. My younger years were spent fighting the demons, the legacy of the Cuban Revolution, the brutality of family dysfunction, and the oppressors in the schoolroom. Now I had buried everyone who had given me my first sense of belonging. In Anna Sewell's *Black Beauty*, the author's intention was to promote the humane treatment of horses by humans. Harper Lee intended to bring to light the injustices and prejudices in America. Larry Kramer gave a voice to AIDS, and Jesus of Nazareth, a teacher and prophet born in Bethlehem, gave his life for God, whom he made synonymous with love.

Conscience can create demons and angels in all of us. I am forever grateful for those who came before whose consciousness created a mirror for me to see myself and reflect on my real purpose in this world. I died a slow, painful spiritual death from which no human power could have saved me. By the time I was thirty years old, I knew more than I ever wanted to know. I was a war veteran from an unspoken, unheralded bloodshed, and Atticus's words were forever echoing in every cell of my being: "And they will do it again." This is how I ended, and Campina began.

My paintings, my writings, my endearing mutts, the blue jays, and the beginning of my restoration were conceived from the ashes. From losing everything, I began again. It was a slow and painful journey, but in Harvey Milk's words: "Hope is never silent." Even when we can't hear it, it is forever carrying us through. Man, lives on hope, and a fool is he who believes otherwise. Marta gave birth to a boy enveloped in hope. It is the hope of my ancestors, the dreams of my father, and the blood of my brothers and sisters that sustain the man I have become.

It does not matter how many times we fall off, for you can be sure that we will fall off many times over. What matters is to know hope, to know that we will rise again; if not here, we will rise there, in that mystical land on the other side of our mortal grounds. The nobility of the human being is in his warrior spirit. In this brief existence, we must leave footprints of hope for those who come behind us, as those who have come before us have done for us. We must do this valiantly, as our brothers and sisters have always done. In every act of kindness, we obliterate its opposite. In every creation from love, we inspire hope. Voice your loving-kindness in your own unique creation, for the world will be a better place because of it. If silence is your choice, harm none, and that shall suffice.

"What does love look like? It has the hands to help others. It has the feet to hasten to the poor and needy. It has eyes to see misery and want. It has the ears to hear the sighs and sorrows of men. That is what love looks like."

—St. Augustine, *Confessions*

CHAPTER 12

I have now lived in this happy place a whole year.
Joe is the best and kindest groom [...]
I feel my strength and spirit all coming
back again [...]
I shall never be sold, and so I have nothing to fear.
And here my story ends. My troubles are over,
and I am at home; and often before I awake,
I fancy I am still in the orchard at Birtwick,
standing with my old friends under the apple tree.

—Anna Sewell, *Black Beauty*

If I have learned anything at all about life, it is that the only certainty is change. It takes courage to die, and it takes much courage to live conscientiously. God's children should all have a resting place, a home, a family, and not the least, a loving and caring community. Even in the cockroach world, disturbances in kinship groups result in observable developmental disorders.

Harper Lee and Anna Sewell each published only one book while alive. *Black Beauty* and *To Kill a Mockingbird* are considered classics for all the ages. Notwithstanding both books' literary genius in style, these stories touch readers' hearts by reflecting our own struggles. In Osvaldito's world, the battle was real. My incessant need to create stems directly from this childhood. My conscience has been the autocrat hastening the need to understand the injustices, the cruelty inflicted against the innocent, and the hypocritical institutions that masquerade as the saviors of the multitudes. It has taken some deep diving into some very dark and lonely places to uncover my own prejudices and biases. In the end, the clay has only been smoothed, never fully restored to its unblemished state. I know my spiritual work will continue to my very last breath. If I have any regrets at all, it is the loss of the right to my innocence. I had a right, like every child, to be a child.

There are more of us who love than those who hate. Hate may have its place and time, and often, it may feel like the victor, but how can it be when we look at the eyes of the innocent? Osvaldito was a small boy who felt he had no one, but he grew up to become a man that he would have respected, admired, and—most importantly—loved. He was called by many names, but none were truly his. Osvaldito grew up to be a proud man who loves another man. Most importantly, he did not become a monster while becoming. The struggle is real, but love is the greatest power of all—and you are it incarnate.

The Cuban Revolution tore my family apart, and alcoholism and family dysfunction broke the sanctity of my God-given right to a secure and joyful childhood. Child sexual molestation and neglect planted shame and terror in a child whose only guilt was vulnerability. AIDS took the lives of those who accepted me and helped me form a new family for myself. I should have been dead a long time ago. I am a "maricon" to many, a "spic" to some, and nothing better than a roach to others. I found a better world, a better place inside myself, and it was by choosing to love rather than hate.

It is a fad these days to say that we are the masters of our fates, as we may sometimes be, and internally we certainly are. For no one can have access to our soul and our conscience unless we allow them. I can't help but wonder: For each Osvaldito who makes it, how many others do not? It is blasphemous to say that hard work and the choices we make in life make us successes or failures. The only truth is that some choices can be made *by* us, and others are made *for* us.

I was gifted nuggets of gold to cherish, and for this, I am eternally grateful. My mother's words resembled so much of Atticus's wisdom: She gave me a moral compass, her true legacy. My grandmother's hard work and discipline taught me about perseverance and that there is good even in the worst of us. Undoubtedly, there was my father's resilience and his heroic, unselfish act of giving me freedom at the cost of his own life. And if that was not enough, the beasts that tore me apart in words and flesh were my greatest teachers of all.

Man's ego is a baffling and cunning faculty that led Narcissus to fall in love with his own image. I am not made in the image of God; I am made in the image of the human species. Like Narcissus, I have fallen in love with men, but not a man's image, rather his universal soul. The only godliness in me is his gift of my ability to love, my ability to have radical empathy, my ability to sculpt my conscience, and my ability to forgive.

I am not God, and I thank God for that. I am a speck of a ray from the sun, and only when I give warmth can I imitate it best. I am godly only when I can show others the love God has shown me. I can feel God's mercy only when I can give it. I can have God's compassion only when I feel it for all sentient beings.

Life is beautiful, and it is love that makes it so. Every creature known to humanity responds to love and kindness—just like every creature responds to fear and cruelty. Love is that universal sensibility that transcends all species and understanding, and yes, oh yes, including the roach. Knowing love is to know pain, to be conscious of the other, and to awaken to that universal mystery that others are me as I am them. Those people, those creatures, those are me. Ms. Lee gave us a mirror, and if we are courageous, we will look directly into it. It has often occurred to me that it would be easier not to look; not being aware can seem blissful. But to look the other way is to turn my back on that love that I feel I am called to serve. I have been blessed with the wisdom to know the essentials: to listen to all birds and to have my own voice, my own song, my own symphony. I will not be sold again; like the land, I do not belong to anyone. I am nature itself.

Walking through my garden, I see a tiny flowering weed rising from the crack of an old cobblestone pathway. These teardrops of life indicate the complexity of an ecosystem whose true wisdom is beyond my human grasp. Sometimes, in the distance, I hear the swaying language of the dense bamboo stalks whispering in harmony, brushing against each other like a lover's gentle embrace. With each palm frond that falls, I glimpse the natural rising of a new one pushing through to its birth, sending quiet salutations to the bright Florida sunshine.

Perched up on the oak tree is my wise old friend the owl, delectable to glimpse, its barklike feathers blending with the majestic oak trees that were already part of Campina for ages before my arrival. Walking underneath the canopy is a little white ball of fur, Little Man. I remember the nights he walked alongside me with his usual unquestionable courage. Walking like a lion, smoothly, without hurry, he was the king of this garden. The other six furry kids sailed on the whims of the wind, each taking their own direction and scenting their own interest, coming back together deliberately with an unmistakable sibling curiosity. Their disengagement came as quickly as their inquisitive flocking, always secure in the love surrounding our sphere.

CHAPTER 12

Little Man was a Maltese, my little boy from Winn-Dixie. He entered my life on the most ordinary of days. His story comes with a little girl whose mother left her at the supermarket to sell her puppy. She was untidy, dripping with sweat, barely able to carry him in her small, frail, muddy hands. "*Senor, por favor, comprar mi perrito.*" Her faint voice tried to reach each passerby who neglected to see or hear her. She pleaded to all who entered the overcrowded, bustling market. "Please buy my puppy."

I wanted to walk away from this, for I had six furry kids waiting at home. I didn't—I couldn't—walk away. The desperation on Little Man's face, coupled with the little girl's discomfort, gripped my heartstrings and twisted them to shreds. All I did was ask the little girl, "Hola, what's your name?" And I was in labor. The seconds and minutes felt like hours. My labor contractions became closer and closer as I asked Julia questions. I will spare you the gory details, but Julia's mom then appeared with an exact price for Little Man: two hundred dollars. His little body and big soul were sold for two hundred dollars. Little Man came home with me that day and slept curled under my armpit, as he did every night for nine years until his very last breath. He would never be sold again.

He was small and as cute as a button, but that was not what made Little Man irresistible; his grandiose personality made him distinctly sublime. He was hugely loving and protective of his pack. Oh, yes, he certainly was the alpha male. I had two male kids: Lusito, a peanut-colored Chihuahua, and Little Man. Lusito was an old soul; he was quiet, shy, and had no interest in being any alpha. Although Lusito was bulkier and certainly sturdier than the five-pound fur ball, you wouldn't know it by Little Man's demeanor. He walked like Simba in *The Lion King*, chest out and head held high with assurance.

Watching my kids on my makeshift farm was and is the joy of my life: each one with their own story, each one so profoundly unique, and each one such an immense gift from my creator. I particularly enjoyed watching and sensing their irrefutable love for one another. Blackie was the big girl of the family. Driving on my way to curate an exhibit of mine, I suddenly saw this long-haired black cocker spaniel look-alike dog walking desperately near an extremely busy intersection. I knew this dog was on the verge of being run over by a good old Floridian speeding driver. I can't gather the words so that the reader can visualize the stunt I pulled in rush-hour traffic to save this dog's life. Suffice it to say that Evel Knievel had nothing on me.

Blackie was the biggest of all my furry kids at the time, weighing more than twenty-five pounds. Teresita, Cujo, Raggedy Ann, Lusito, Kika, and Little Man were minuscule next to her. Bringing Blackie home did not come without potential danger. The plan was to foster her and keep my little ones safe in the meantime. When Blackie walked into Campina for the very first time, I was in deep prayer that she would not attack one of the gang. One bite from Blackie to any of my other furry kids, and they could have been a goner. I was cautious in the introduction, had a plan, and was ready to jump into action if the occasion called for it.

Teresita, my wired, caramel-colored terrier mix, was the alpha female and the first one Blackie met. They stood face to face. Teresita was on top of an ottoman, allowing her to be at eye level with Blackie. I was tenser than I care to admit. The others stood on the couch behind Teresita, intensely watching the exchange taking place between their leader and the potential foe. They were a united front observing the diplomacy of the canine summit. This could have been *Clash of the Titans*. Instead, Blackie gently turned around and went on to explore what would be her home for over ten years. She yielded all the power that could have been hers with a simple slight growl. This was but one of the majesties in Blackie. She had the ability to overpower and crush all the pack; instead, she chose peace with a simple, genuine humility that represented strength rather than weakness. Blackie lived happily ever after at Campina, never lost and certainly never sold!

Looking into Blackie's eyes was like looking into God's eyes. Blackie was one of the gentlest souls I have ever met. She was plainly love itself—if you can call love plain. She galloped in her happiness, much like Black Beauty galloped in her youth in the fields with her mother. Blackie had the whitest teeth, which she would proudly expose with the gift of a smile. I never knew a dog could intentionally smile, but Blackie did, and she knew well the effects of her smile on her daddy. She was black, and Little Man was white. Little Man was fierce and critical of any new acquaintances. Blackie was a lamb and welcomed the whole of creation without hesitation. She had the gift of a trusting nature. She was clumsy and cuddly and would sense my sadness before I did. She lived like a queen, and she died like one too. In her older years, she fell off the bed and broke her back. She suffered minimal pain and passed away with the help of a loving home euthanasia.

From the time I stopped traffic to invite her into my station wagon filled with canvases and paint, Blackie was loved. Teresita and Blackie were a team and never questioned each other's authority. Teddy was wise, smart, and an amazing leader. She was approximately twelve pounds, give or take a few, with the cutest wiry blonde hair on any dog alive in the world. I admit my bias, and so be it. She took Cujo, her cute little shih tzu sister, under her wing immediately upon Cujo's arrival. This was not unique to Cujo alone; Teresita did the same for Raggedy Ann, who was the runt of her litter. Teresita was a natural caretaker; it was in her genes. She was a mother, an older sister, a confidante, and a reliable source of wisdom, courage, humility, and strength. When Toto died, Teresita and I had some alone time to bond, and boy did we bond. She was my rescuer. Her tiny little body came with one big, joyful, caring heart. She was a maintenance-free dog who understood her daddy with just one look.

She worshipped me and demanded little of me or her pack. Her respect was earned easily without effort or force because she was a natural-born leader, the type of leader with a heart. She was the type of leader everyone wants to follow because of the natural kindness exuding from every pore. She was unselfish, giving freely of all her worldly possessions, which amounted to her favorite stuffy toys, bones, and food. There was never any form of greed emanating from her. The world leaders could learn a thing or two from the likes of a mutt like Teresita. Nature is the grand maestro of all that we ever need to learn, and dogs are the best of the natural teachers.

So much time was spent in our family farm/garden that Teddy became the best land surveyor of our mini wonderland. She and I were able to see the fruit of our labor. I planted, and she fertilized. There were only a couple of times that I saw Teresita lose her temper, and both times had to do with Raggedy Ann. More about Raggedy later but suffice it to say that Raggedy Ann was the most liberal, hippie, bohemian flower child on this side of San Francisco. She would have been the leader at Woodstock, Snoopy in *Peanuts*, and the goth punk rock child that every parent endeavors to understand. I do not know what was going on the day I had to call Teresita out for going at Raggedy Ann. I am not a betting man, but if I was, I would certainly place my money on Teresita because I know that Raggedy Ann could be rebellious, possessed of a mischievous inclination that would melt my heart. She knew how to pull rank, and she did.

Teresita was the first to pass. She lived a long, joyful life with many siblings. She died from a cancerous tumor that grew until her little body couldn't support it anymore. I was with her when they gently helped her pass to doggy heaven. I held her and spoke to her while looking straight into her eyes, letting her know Daddy was right there with her. She was a trouper to the end, never a whimper, never a complaint. She was grace personified—or, better written, "doggy-fied." Her loss was a loss for all of us, and the whole gang felt her absence. From the time she arrived at Campina, her spirit never left; she was home. My pain gave way to my responsibility, trying hard to masquerade the anguish of losing our little leader with the big heart. I miss her so very much, my little blonde girl with scrawny little legs. I love her with all my heart and soul: love does remain.

With Teresita gone, it seemed only natural that Blackie would take on the role of the leader of the pack, but this was not always clear because of one tiny, almost minuscule matter called Kika. Kika is a skinny junkyard dog who happens to be a Chihuahua. She came to me with mange and a bad case of neglect and malnourishment. Her neglect was so bad that her ribs and mange were the most visible part of her entire physique. She has tiny, perfect, pointy ears like those of Dobermans whose barbarous owners have given them ear-cropping surgery for the vanity of it—and, might I add, the vanity of the owners, not the dogs.

Kika has big, black, watery eyes that in her youth could spot a squirrel under a ton of vegetation from a million miles away. She earned the nickname Artemis the Huntress because, in her imagination, she was a big, robust huntress with an unyielding power to be reckoned with. Interestingly enough, in Greek mythology, Artemis is gender neutral, and Kika never learned to squat to pee like all her sisters. Instead, Kika lifts her leg like her two brothers. She is a playful little girl, transforming herself at a whim into a boxer dog, a Muhammad Ali type, at the drop of a bone. She is a petite, feminine, gentle flower one minute and an ominous huntress boxing champ the next. Her menacing powers almost drove all the lizards up the trees, but the lizards caught on that she was all bark and no action.

It took time for Kika's mange to cure, and she needed a lot of attention. Of all the dogs I have loved—and I have loved them with my entire heart and soul, not one receiving extra attention but each one receiving special attention according to its needs—Kika needed the most love. It was not just a gut feeling; she had a history of severe abuse. She was found in an abandoned garage in a warehouse district in Hialeah. My niece, who found her, told the story that Kika had been abandoned to fend for herself. She was barely a year old when she was found covered with oil, wandering the empty garage. At first, Kika was very skittish; she trembled and did not trust me or anyone. To this day, she is fearful when she eats. It is as if someone did some horrible deed while she ate. Fortunately, she was a tomboy at heart and hit it off immediately with Lusito, my peanut-butter-colored Chihuahua.

Lusito was a year older than Kika and took her under his wing. Kika lived out loud as a tomboy. She was Scout in *To Kill a Mockingbird.* She loved to follow her new buddy/brother around. And in between their scavenging in the deep woods, she would wrestle Lusito like a pro. She had this little butt bump that she used to distract Lusito in the middle of their match. The butt bump was her trademark. She used her whole butt to push him and tackle him down until she could pin him. It was Mark Twain's Huckleberry Finn and Tom Sawyer in the Chihuahua world. Artemis, the huntress, scavenged for lizards but only to show her might because she never actually had any malice. Meanwhile, Lusito, the wise, serious brother who let his hair down only with Kika, followed her in her escapades as her protector. Lusito was her knight in shining armor.

Lusito and Kika were Huck and Tom, Laurel and Hardy, Lady and the Tramp, and no pair of Chihuahuas could have sung a better mariachi tune than these two imitations of Hansel and Gretel. I gave Kika all the space she needed to warm up to me. I understood that humans were not her most trusted creature. She and I had this in common. I knew she was observing me from afar in her leisure time, and I knew that she felt the love in the gang. However, she was not ready until she was ready, and I knew well that trust has to be earned, and it is a very treasured commodity that does not come easily for some of us.

Lusito was a pet shop boy from suburbia. Until recently, he was the only child from a breeder. All the others had arrived miscellaneously, from empty garages to middle-of-the-road traffic jam rescues, but Lusito was bought and paid for with a good old-fashioned American credit card, but that stopped—he would never be sold again.

I have never been able to go into a pet shop where they sell puppies, but this was a special occasion. Lusito was meant to be for my best friend, Hector; his Chihuahua had just died, and I saw the sadness in him. His parents and I devised a plan to surprise him with a new dog, which meant going to the pet shop where they sold puppies. This is true friendship and love; Hector knew this well. If it had been for myself, I would not have done it. Hector's dad, also named Hector, and I went into a small pet shop where Lusito was being reprimanded by the owner even before we walked in. The reprimand consisted of putting him in a cage alone because he had been too rowdy. Hector's dad was to purchase the surprise puppy, but he gave me the gift of choosing the dog. Hector's dad was as surprised as Hector was because when we walked in, I immediately chose Lusito.

As soon as we left the pet shop and got Lusito into my car, he felt more like a parrot than a puppy. He immediately perched himself confidently on my shoulders as if he had done this with me for many lifetimes. Lusito and Hector Jr. were a hit. They were buddies, one made for the other, and Lusito became a road traveler from puppyhood on. Hector Jr. would bring Lusito to my animal farm upon leaving for work and then retrieve him on his way back home. I was his babysitter, and he loved the daycare center to which he was entrusted. Eventually, Blackie came into the picture, and Hector and Blackie bonded. There were times Blackie went home with Hector and Lusito stayed with me. Soon they all just became one, and no one left for more than a couple of hours—or an eternity for a loving dad.

Lusito was a serious, pensive, wise little boy who did his own manicures. Indeed, it was frightening to see, but Lusito cut his own nails to perfection. This is not the imagination of a creative writer: He did his nails and never, and I mean never, did he bleed or did they look uneven. The parrot-perching habit remained for the rest of his life. He liked to be as high as possible, as a shepherd looking over his sheep, and he was the most sensitive little boy who knew way too much. Sometimes I could look at him, and he would look at me, and I could literally read his thoughts. I am certain he could read Daddy's love and feel it too. How ridiculed those of us who can understand our furry kids can often feel by those who, for their misfortune, have never felt this bond.

He died of fluid in his body that would not go away. He lived a full life, and of all my children, he was the one who shared the part of my personality of being extremely shy, cautious, introverted, and a loner. He did not need much or require much, and he was extremely accepting. Aside from the normal puppy extravaganzas of ripping up his toys—OK, dismembering them is more like it—I never had to discipline him. Even on his deathbed, he was kind to me. Somehow, I felt his acceptance of his fate. I heard him spiritually whispering, "*Don't cry for me, for you have been the best father a doggy could have.*" I felt his peace. Osvaldito felt Teresita's presence upon Lusito's entrance into doggy heaven, and he whispered it to Daddy. I love my inner child's wisdom and how it shows up at precisely the most needed times.

When it rains, it pours, and when it pours, it thunders. Teresita's death was followed rather quickly by Cujo's stroke. As I wrote earlier, every child has its special needs, and Cujo was an exceptional genius of a dog. Her genius came at a price, as does most genius, for she was extremely aware, often very scared. I lovingly diagnosed her with obsessive-compulsive disorder. Cujo was aesthetically extremely beautiful. Her face was perfection with her wet button nose, as was her hair, which unfortunately gave us both a lot of maintenance hardships. When I got her, she literally fit in the palm of my hand. The irresponsible creature who had allowed Cujo's and Raggedy Ann's litters without thinking of the puppies' futures demanded I take her before I felt it was appropriate. I hand-fed Cujo every couple of hours with baby food for weeks. Even at this stage in Cujo's life, she was extremely contemplative. She was playful in the way all puppies are, but Cujo would sit and watch me with an intensity that did not feel age appropriate.

When Raggedy joined the pack, Cujo and Raggedy became instant playmates. Cujo followed Raggedy Ann's lead. I believe that Cujo was never truly aware of her uniqueness, her beauty, or her genius. Unlike her sister Raggedy Ann, who could not care less what anyone thought of her, Cujo cared too much. These two were opposites. Cujo was needy, required a lot of attention, and always felt left out. I, in turn, gave Cujo a lot of attention, but I always felt I could have done more. Raggedy Ann did not want much attention. In fact, she felt she was above us all. She was not snobbish in any way. She was just extremely comfortable in her own fur. Talk about an artist archetype—she was it. Raggedy's fur was as white as snow, her skin was light pink, and her eyes would change colors according to the light and her mood. Cujo had a blend of white and blonde fur that neither Paul Mitchell nor Sassoon could ever duplicate in its highlights.

Cujo would lick the walls when she was bored, and Raggedy would hide far from us, sitting strategically in a position where she could analyze the pack but be apart from it. Cujo barked for attention or just because. Raggedy hardly barked, but she sang at her caprice. If I ever sang, which I often did around the farm, when I hit that high note channeling Barbra Streisand, Raggedy would sit and join in with her little lips perfectly shaped round in a blowing-a-whistle position and sing. Raggedy's sensual call to the gang to whistle would be immediately followed by a chorus of six perfectly tuned vocalists. She was undoubtedly irresistible and a provocateur. She would have been a casting agent's dream. She had many faces with her many moods, and like a true artist, she could transform herself at leisure. Depending on the music, the hymn resonated with a doggy gospel choir or a jazz ensemble. It was a scene to be savored to watch these seven unique furry kids creating a spontaneous hood orchestra at Raggedy's whims. She wore the crown proudly as the leader, the crazy-looking conductor in front of the orchestra.

Needless to say, I adored Cujo, and I can understand when parents feel guilty for not doing the right thing, doing the wrong thing, not doing enough, and even doing too much. I always felt that Cujo needed more; no matter what, I was not enough. I know in my heart I did my very best, and I could not have loved her more. Cujo was so special, and ironically, her genius was her adversity. I watched her grow from a handful of fur to a beautiful shih tzu whose behavior went far beyond her species' ordinary intelligence. She could solve pathways, used her paws in extraordinary ways, and had a sensitive relationship with her environment like no other. There was not an ounce of meanness in her. Never in the eleven years that I was fortunate enough to be her daddy did I hear her growl. This is remarkable. She was a lamb, a sweet innocent genius of a lamb. She was Boo in *To Kill a Mockingbird*. Cujo and Boo shared what, in my mind, is that special innocence, that genius of sensitivity that is so often misunderstood.

I woke up one early morning to find Cujo whimpering. Having had a stroke, her hind legs were paralyzed, and she could not move. I knew inside that Cujo was aware of her circumstances. She might not have been able to verbally bark it, but knowing her as well as I did, I knew her intelligence would not be betrayed by a mere stroke. It was sad to say goodbye to Cujo because, even to this day, I feel I should have, could have, and needed to do more for her. It was too early to depart from Cujo. She was, is, my precious little girl who I adore, and Daddy would have wanted to be certain that she knew how much she was always loved. I know she did, but it was never enough for me.

In Mark Twain's autobiography, I read a passage that broke my heart and made the rest of the book inconsequential. I came to a passage where he writes about his son's death. They had been riding in a carriage in the cold weather, and Twain underestimated the importance of a blanket to cover his son's legs. Shortly after this carriage drive, his son died of diphtheria. In his autobiography, I, as the reader, was stunned at his openness with his true feelings. He confessed that writing the words was the first time he had admitted this to himself. This was humbling for me, for I felt he had allowed me into a sacred space. I am writing about that space we humans hold inside ourselves, held shut with an uncompromising lock for fear of releasing it. If that sacred place is opened, we fear the release of all the agony, shame, and guilt may bury us alive.

I loved each one of my furry kids without favorites, each one taking my heart on an unbelievable magical journey. They all transitioned one after the other, and this was to be expected given their relatively close proximity in age. Teresita, Cujo, and Raggedy Ann were a year apart, give or take a few months. Raggedy Ann was the last to go of the sisters. She left doing what she loved best: eating. It was time to make that decision that is never easy: the humane euthanasia call. This is tough, and I hate it. But I had always understood that when I was entrusted with these precious gifts, I had to always do the right thing for them and not for me. Keeping a furry kid around, sick, crippled from old age, and in pain, for my sake? I just can't. I knew that the quality of Raggedy Ann's life had deteriorated to the point that she was not enjoying life anymore; worse, she was in dire pain. She was blind and deaf and had lost all her teeth. She rarely wanted to go outside, for she had grown tired. There were many days that I carried her to most places, and not the least, she missed her sisters.

I prayed for weeks, meditated, and asked God to remove me from having to make this decision. Somehow, he always gives me the answer and the courage to follow through. Raggedy was not reacting to any kind of stimulus, not waking up but for a few minutes of baby food because she could not chew or digest much. The time came, and she went home like most of my other fur babies. I have been lucky enough to find a vet who comes to my house and does the euthanasia in the comfort of my furry animal's loving home.

Before Raggedy departed, I prepared some of her favorite treat: cheese. I usually ground the provolone to the smoothness of little specks resembling sand. I wetted the tiny, nanometer pieces of cheese so Raggedy could eat them from my hands. She did this up to the moment that the vet gave her the injection that would put her to sleep. Raggedy lived her life on her own terms. She was adored by her brothers and sisters. Her daddy gave her everything beautiful from inside himself. Frank Sinatra's "My Way" was written for Raggedy Ann Amador. She was a scruffy, independent, would-be queen who abdicated her throne willingly for her freedom. She was playful and standoffish because she had to be. She was an introvert and an extrovert at random. She was a contradiction, and she knew it and liked it. She was a sweetheart with a need for detachment. Raggedy was a diva—and certainly not because she made any effort to be one. She was born that way, and the diva was engraved in her genes.

Losing the three sisters came as I was losing my mother. My babies started departing this world when my mother was getting ready to transition. My mother was my best friend, and she and I spoke three, four, and often five times a day. During the loss of my babies, I did not want to burden her with my grief. She was getting dementia, and it was difficult to hold a normal conversation. The funny thing is that I always did understand my mother; even during her worst episode of dementia, I felt her rather than heard her. I did feel it was hard for her, for a part of her knew; not unlike Cujo, she knew.

The day Little Man died, I wanted more than anything to share my grief with my best friend, but it was not to be. My mother loved Little Man. She would always want to know how Little Man was doing. My mother and I had no conversation where she did not, with her heavy Spanish accent, ask me, "*Como esta Leetle Meen?*" It was there, a bond between Little Man and my mother. Mami was diplomatic and would ask me for the rest of my kids, but I could tell that there was something special going on with Little Man, as there had been with her and Toto.

Little Man's passing was not expected in any way, shape, or form. He was relatively young, very healthy, and as active as a beehive in springtime. He died of COPD (chronic obstructive pulmonary disease). We were in our paradise, otherwise called the garden, and it had rained earlier in the day. There was nothing unusual about Little Man lying on the semi-wet bricks in my yard, but I remember looking at him and thinking, *I do not want him lying on the semi-wet pavement.* The sun was out, and he was happy lying there, taking in the sun's rays and feeling snug. I was torn between interrupting his moment of bliss and allowing him to savor our sacred spiritual ritual. I allowed him, for this was not uncommon. There is no evidence that this was what brought on the COPD; it is me opening up my sacred place of guilt. Much like Mark Twain, I have always felt guilty for this, even if this is purely speculative.

A few days after this, Little Man started with a sneeze for which the vet prescribed medication that I gave religiously. The sneezing would stop, and difficult asthmatic breathing would erupt. He was taking all sorts of medication before I heard the word "COPD." Finally, I thought, a true diagnosis after all the meds and the veterinarian's trials and errors. It was a horrible diagnosis because in order for his breathing to be normal, he would have had to live like John Travolta's character in *The Boy in the Plastic Bubble*. Little Man would have had to live inside a chamber that would provide him with the oxygen he needed to breathe normally, twenty-four hours a day and seven days a week. The inhalers the veterinarians were prescribing were not working, and his breathing became more and more labored as the days passed. I was speaking to several vets simultaneously, and they all were taking away any remaining hope. Watching Little Man in a corner, bundled up with labored breathing, was too much pain to bear. I felt this was a big cosmic mistake.

When Little Man was gone, as soon as the veterinarian left with his little lifeless body, I crawled into bed in a fetal position. I pushed my face into a pillow and yelled; I cried with an agonizing bellow that tore my organs apart. It never ceases to amaze me how much stronger we are than we believe ourselves to be. Little Man's departure, my mother's illness, and the loss of any community and family cemented a total mental discombobulation. I had to put into practice what all my otherworldly mentors, the books on my shelves, and the spiritual beings that had gone before me had taught me. There was no other option. I had no one to rely on. It was as if everything I had ever learned from *Black Beauty* onward was a spiritual lesson that had brought me to this exact time of detaching from everything I loved and cared for.

As I sit and write this, Kika, my mangy little girl, is mangy no longer. She is lying behind my bureau as I write our family's history. In her bed, our bed, she lies cozy, wrapped in an old-fashioned quilt I bought more than twenty years ago in a thrift store for a couple of dollars. She has no teeth, has glaucoma, and, like her dad, is hard of hearing. Her pointy ears are still pointing straight up. She is aware that this is Daddy's time to write. The lights are dimmed, a candle is glowing with the scent of pine, and Daddy is covered with a similar blanket, older and more worn than hers. Like Linus van Pelt, we both love the sense of security we find in our granny's quilt. Every now and then, I glance at her from my desk, and she glances back; we are happy to have grown old together. She is my endless baby, for her personality is as jovial today as the day she learned she could trust me. No matter how old she and I get, there is a little Kika in her that is still alive and well—just as there is a little Osvaldito in me who is happy to tell the secrets we have learned.

Like her dad, she is a survivor. After Lusito died, she felt lost; her best friend was not physically around to bump butts with her. She survived one of the biggest losses in her little life up to that point. At times, I thought she would go right after, but Blackie, her big sister, stepped into Lusito's huge shoes. Now she has lost Blackie, and for a while, it was touch and go, for she did not want to eat and was apathetic, withdrawn, and without her usual occasional spring. In her old age, she has become fragile, has lost much of her muscle tone, and her shiny, round black eyes have become hollower. But she is still my baby, my little girl, the apple of Daddy's eyes. I am comforted knowing that she is wrapped up in her blankie, that she remains, and that she knows without a shadow of a doubt that my heart belongs to her and that she will never be sold in any way, shape, or form. We are home.

"The greatness of a nation and its moral progress can be judged by the way its animals are treated."

—Mahatma Gandhi

EPILOGUE

It is good people who make good places.

—Anna Sewell, *Black Beauty*

I have arrived at another end, another goodbye. I have felt the spirit of my father and the spirit of my mother with me throughout the journey of writing this tale. It has all been a magical flowing from the everlasting. What I have written emerges from the gift of silence. My heart has remained open, dented here and there like the Velveteen Rabbit, but only because it has loved much.

I have heard the whispers of my ancestors' courage, enabling me to synthesize the darkness with the light. I have been redeemed with a glimpse of the empyrean, that formless heaven in which all is love. I have learned that the virtues I admire most in a human being were in my mother, my father, my furry babies, my birds, my friends long gone, my garden, and my very own untapped nature. I have learned the lessons that my grandmother's God had started at the Grand Union.

Osvaldito learned to love what Osvaldo, the man, couldn't love in himself. And it all started with *Black Beauty* and learning how to read.

Toto's patience and unconditional love were a lesson much absorbed into every cell of my being. Blackie's humility, coupled with Teresita's temperance, taught Osvaldo lessons that Osvaldito incorporated into the man I would become. These lessons could not have come from more superior beings than the four-legged orphans God placed strategically in my life. Little Man's courage is within me. My father's courage is within me—as it always was.

Kika's resilience, her adamant inner child, taught us all that pain can be transmuted into joy with the playfulness of a child, just like my mother's jovial spirit resounded, wherever her six-inch heels clicked. Lusito's acceptance, his calm, angelic soul, shall forever remind me that the river flows with a knowing, its destiny, its merging, into that big body of water called acceptance. The Okeechobee Waterway was not a dream; it was a life raft drifting me to further lands of make-believe that saved my life. What was once thought of as vileness became an imaginary world that gifted me the love of art. The river, like God, echoed its secrets to my soul and taught me to acquiesce to life's inevitable cycles.

Surrendering to the almighty currents that keep the firmaments in place was at the core of Lusito's essence. He will always remind me that peanut-colored, four-legged Chihuahuas can be birds perched on Daddy's shoulders if the two accept that nothing is as it seems.

Cujo was my genius, and true genius can never recognize itself, for it goes against its own nature. Some truths are reflections, and others are projections, but all are a lesson on the journey home. The value of any wisdom is the quality of life it brings us; other than that, it is all vanity.

Raggedy Ann, the universal symbol of independence, with her bohemian soul, taught Osvaldito that what others think of him is not as important as what he thinks of himself. She taught me that there is no cause worthwhile in which a good growl or two is not justified. Unequivocally, she showed me how to sing to the rhythm of my own beat. An important ingredient in anyone's life is to live it our own way as Raggedy Ann lived: without regrets or shame.

Another awakening with that familiar feeling that Mami is not gone—and neither are any of my furry kids. My young years remain inside of me, as vivid as the ray of sun from the Florida morning. Their love is in me; their souls are in me. Sometimes I close my eyes, and I see them all. We are together in a paradise known to children and the Boos of this world. Osvaldo understands that Oz had nothing to give him. If I could see, hear, and experience the blessings of my life in the countryside, it's because it was already within me.

Campina was never about a place or a time; home is in the internal beating of my very essence. The love we share is home; it is not an edifice of concrete bricks. No one we have ever truly loved dies. Love is the radar, the interceptor between this world and the one beyond. We are interconnected through a web like Charlotte's. Nature is home; it's your home, and it's the home to all life-forms. Naturally, we are never alone.

If you have not understood a word I've written, know that I've written about the love I have been blessed to feel. In the end, I write to you of a dream, a world so much different than the one I would have consciously chosen. Some dice were thrown, and I lived to tell the tale of the effects of the game. This story belongs to a brave and wise little boy who hid in a closet with a flashlight, in fear, but who was courageous enough to explore the unknown, to learn that he was a unique expression of God's love. If I can leave any footprints, they are the remnants of paws, furs, beaks, colors, and the unconditional love that nature has so prodigiously sheltered me with. I am a man who loves a man, without shame or guilt, proud and honored to have the blessing to feel any love at all.

I remember Jorgito's eyes, Carlito's smile, and my weekend rendezvous with the old gang; it's all here in a blink of an eye. Memories serve as the lighthouse guiding us through the storm. We hear our loved ones' voices, their laughs, every teardrop that ever fell, and we feel every embrace, for as long as love remains, all remains.

Osvaldito is here, safe, and joyful; he sings Whitman—he sings! Some days, he dances, accompanied by Raggedy's symphony. He brings new light to my world every day. I smile to him, proudly introducing the man he has become. We are Jem, Dill, and Scout running around and learning everything for the first time. I, we, all of us together have not laughed and had this much fun in years. Maycomb, Alabama, is just a fictional place where reality met the imagination of a little girl who grew into a writer. Campina is just a geographical space where my outer world reconciled with my inner sanctum.

Something shrivels inside me when I forget to be a child, when I allow my imagination to wither and die. Dreams are meant to be had forever. This is the story Osvaldito wanted to share, and this is Ozzie's fairy tale. There is no single story that could contain my worlds, no single place, no single time. One life is many universes unto itself. This is my magic: planting trees, splashing paint, writing words, and finally having a voice. My truth is an unbounded frontier created from the magical world of my beautiful inner child.

I beseech you to look closely within your heart at the seemingly ordinary world we have been briefly gifted. Use the broken pieces to mend your pain. Sensitive souls are gifted like no others. We can see in the deepest darkness where light resides. We know we don't belong to ourselves; we belong to love. We must use all our might to save the innocence in others and in ourselves. Speak of love as if your life depended on it because it does. There is no other goal worth a life other than love, and no story is worth writing without it.

TO KILL A COCKROACH

I will never look at a roach the same way again, for it too has its beauty, even if hidden, as Picasso reminds us. I do not need to understand or even like them, but we are aligned with invisible forces that caught my conscience. There are no secrets; we are guarded until we are ready. Give kindness to the square peg, for it may very well be yourself who you are saving. New friends are old ones in different attires. The most courageous and loving action we can take is in recognizing the value of the other, regardless of its semblance. Our humanity unites our species, and our hearts unite our souls. You will return home; we all do. Leave traces of your love for those who come after, for it is those who came before who paved the road with love, sweat, and blood.

Whenever you feel the warm embrace of love, you are united. We are in perfect harmony; we are God's eternal creation. Tell your truth, tell your story with courage and faith. Put your lips together and blow a tune of your own. Raggedy awaits, wand in paw, ready for your very own symphony. Splash your paint and build your sandcastles. The love of your intentions will echo for millennia to come.

"To be admitted to Nature's hearth costs nothing. None is excluded but excludes himself. You have only to push aside the curtain."

—Henry David Thoreau

Made in United States
Orlando, FL
20 September 2024

51713796R00168